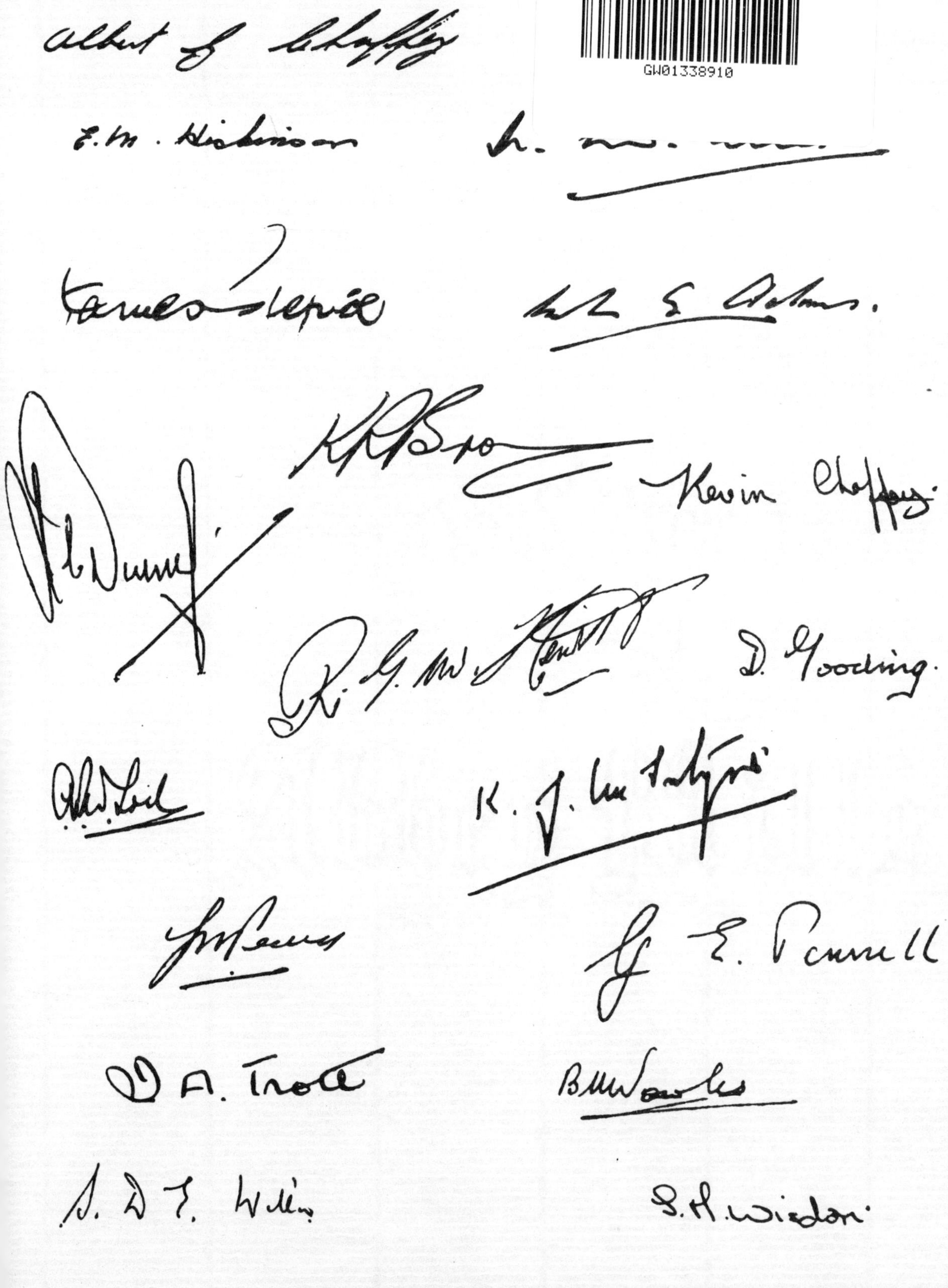
Kevin Chaffey
D. Gooding

The Pride of Poole
1688-1851

by Derek Beamish John Dockerill
John Hillier

A FACSIMILE REPRINT
FIRST PUBLISHED BY THE BOROUGH & COUNTY
OF THE TOWN OF POOLE, March, 1974

POOLE HISTORICAL TRUST, 1988

Copyright © DB, JD, J H 1974

ISBN 0 9504914 7 0

Designed by Graham Smith, Poole Museum Service

Printed and bound in Great Britain by
Biddles Ltd, Guildford and King's Lynn

Foreword

This volume is the product of original research from documents and photographic material mainly within the archive collection of Poole Corporation. It is not intended that it be a full and complete account of the history of Poole from 1688–1851, but merely a brief account of some aspects of corporate life in the Town leading up to, and encompassing, the first major reform of Local Government. When the complete and annotated history of Poole is finally written, this volume will have served its purpose in illustrating the rich vitality of Poole by sketching one short episode in its recent Past.

DB, JD, JH   March 1974

Preface

"The introduction of the new municipal system has produced in the Borough of Poole a state of party hostility, unparallelled in its rancour by any acerbity of conflicting feeling which the previous history of the town has developed. It would be a melancholy task to dwell upon the evils necessarily resulting from such a state of things. Whether the new system of municipal administration contain any essential advantages which may practically prove an adequate compensation for such evils; and whether such extreme of party rancour be the mere temporary effervescence of popular feeling, consequent on the acquirement of a novel franchise, are questions to which time will give the most satisfactory solution".

'The History of Poole' by John Sydenham
(Published by Sydenham, 105 High Street, Poole, 1839)

It has often been claimed that the success in achieving a generally peaceful government in England lay in the English genius for compromise; the ability of parties in dispute to agree on a middle course. The parties to the disputes in Poole from 1835 onwards exemplified the complete opposite. They compromised nothing. They pursued every cause to the very last — they used the law to the last appeal; they considered the end justified any means. In the process they reduced the once proud and wealthy Corporation of Poole to a bankrupt nonentity of a Council. Its extensive properties were sold or in the hands of receivers, and even its silver-gilt maces, once proudly carried at the head of its processions, had been sold at auction by its creditors. The Corporation could only inspect their own documents and such title deeds as they had by paying their deposed town clerk (who had seized them as a lien for the payment of his debts) two guineas a time. The new Council within a few years of its existence had not even enough money or credit to feed the prisoners in its gaol.

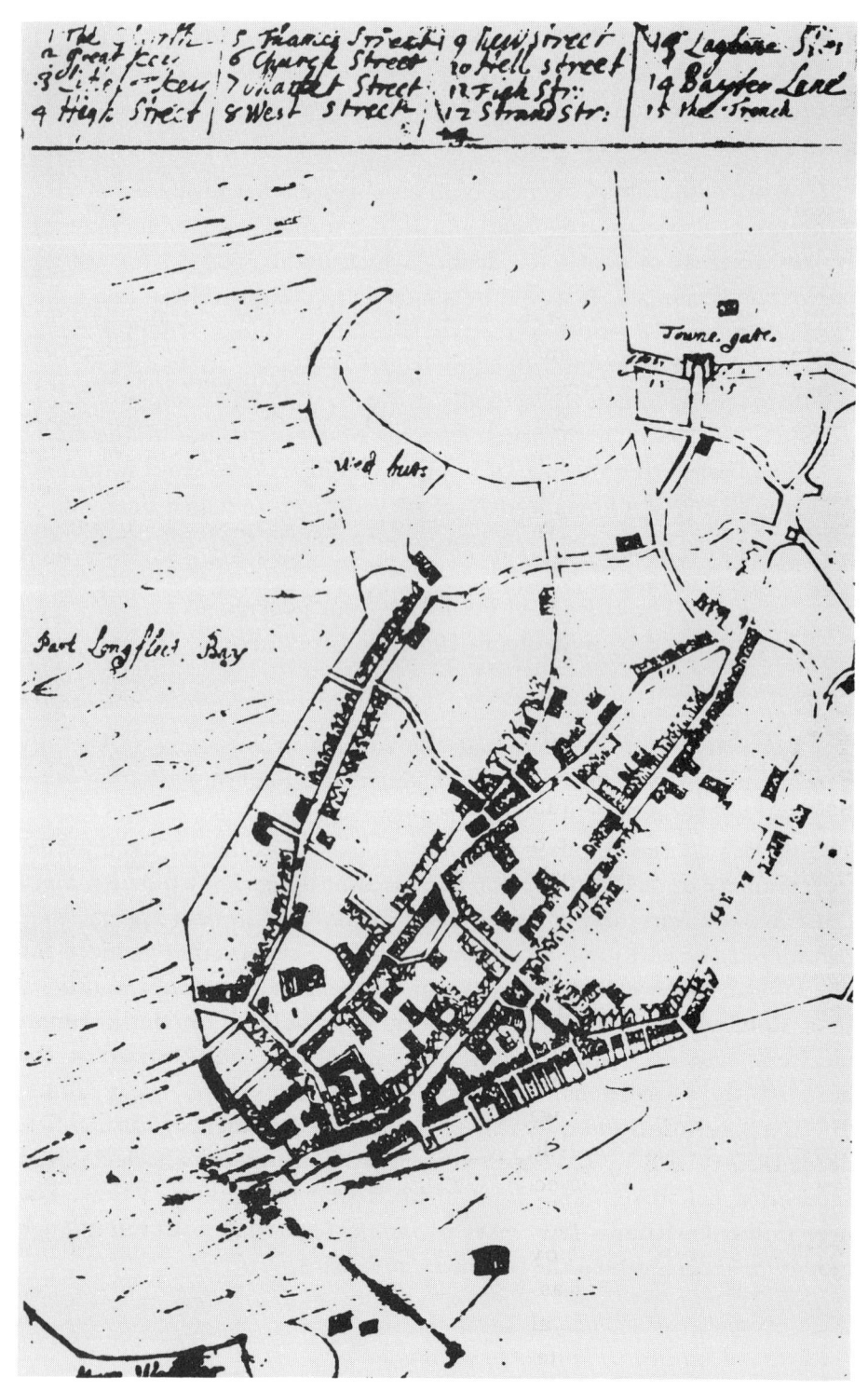

Plan of Poole 1634
Found with the correspondence of Charles I at Pythouse

The possibility of the present borough of Poole having its origins in a Saxon or Viking raiding rather than trading settlement which would be quite in keeping with the later medieval character of the town is still to be finally proven. What is certain however, is that from this period there did exist a maritime community of considerable size, and that by the Norman Conquest Poole was already a port with substantial continental trading interests.

In the high medieval period (12th, 13th and 14th centuries) Poole expanded and became an extremely prosperous town with interests almost exclusively centred on the harbour and maritime commerce. Indeed, in this period Poole experienced a boom in wealth and population only paralleled by its later connection with the Newfoundland Trade. The wealth provided by its trading concerns enabled the merchants to purchase many immunities, liberties and rights from the neighbouring Lord of the Manor at Canford, and from the Crown, which formed the basis for corporate life till the reforms of the early 19th century.

By the 15th century Poole was one of the largest towns on the south coast, defended from the land by a large tidal ditch with guarded crossings, and from the sea by its sturdy and numerous population. This is illustrated by the fact that a surprise military raid on the town in 1405 by the Spanish and French was eventually beaten off by the rallying of the inhabitants.

Many substantial courtyard houses built of local stone have been discovered, several still standing, presumably the merchant residences, and the material discovered from this period suggests that Poole had considerable contacts with all of the major trading ports of the Continent, the Baltic, and the Mediterranean. It is very evident that Poole, surrounded as it was by sparsely populated areas containing no substantial markets, had little in common with the county and hinterland either politically or economically.

This is amply shown by the attitude taken by Poole in the Civil War, when the town was regarded as a 'fortress for Parliament' in a predominantly Royalist area. With the more organised national governments both in Britain and on the Continent in the 16th and 17th centuries, the extensive and wealth producing activities of the so-called 'free ports' of Europe had been severely curtailed, and Poole had suffered in this recession. However it still retained enough wealth and strength in the Civil War to be a serious threat to Royalist activities in the area, and to be a prize worth having.

With the advent of the trade in the North Atlantic in fish and associated products in the late 17th century Poole began its second period of boom, and in a similar fashion to the earlier medieval period, the wealth from this trade occasioned extensive building in the town in the 18th century, the architecture of which still dominates sections of the Old Town today.

With the rise in this trade from 1688 (the Glorious Revolution) and with the Borough regaining its ancient liberties and rights, new families and merchants rose to prominence. The active life and character of the town in the 17th and 18th centuries and the personalities produced by it form the essential background to the strife and intrigue that occurred in the early 19th century.

A resident of Poole today who found himself transported back to the Poole of 1688 would naturally be amazed at the state and the size of the Town and County of the Borough of Poole. If he approached by road he would pass through dreary heath land and might well encounter a highway man. He would have to journey far down the peninsular until he reached a narrow neck of land some thirty or fifty yards wide at high water in the harbour. There he would see the remains of the town gates where the Towngate Bridge now carries 20th century traffic over the railway, and pass down the High Street to Fish Street, Old Orchard and the Quays, the centre of the old town. To his eye the town would have an unfinished appearance. The Quays would stretch over a comparatively short distance from approximately where Hamworthy Bridge now stands to a point near the Old Town Cellars. Past them he would see small landing stages and warehouses built by individual merchants. Beyond, his eye would travel over mudlands to Baiter, where only the town gallows would break the horizon, backed perhaps by smoke arising from the salterns on the mudlands on the harbour shore. Across the water in Hamworthy the Corporation's new ballast quay and some small shipyards would be the main landmarks, together with the Passage House, a public house which was the terminus of the ferry boat, the only link between Poole and Hamworthy.

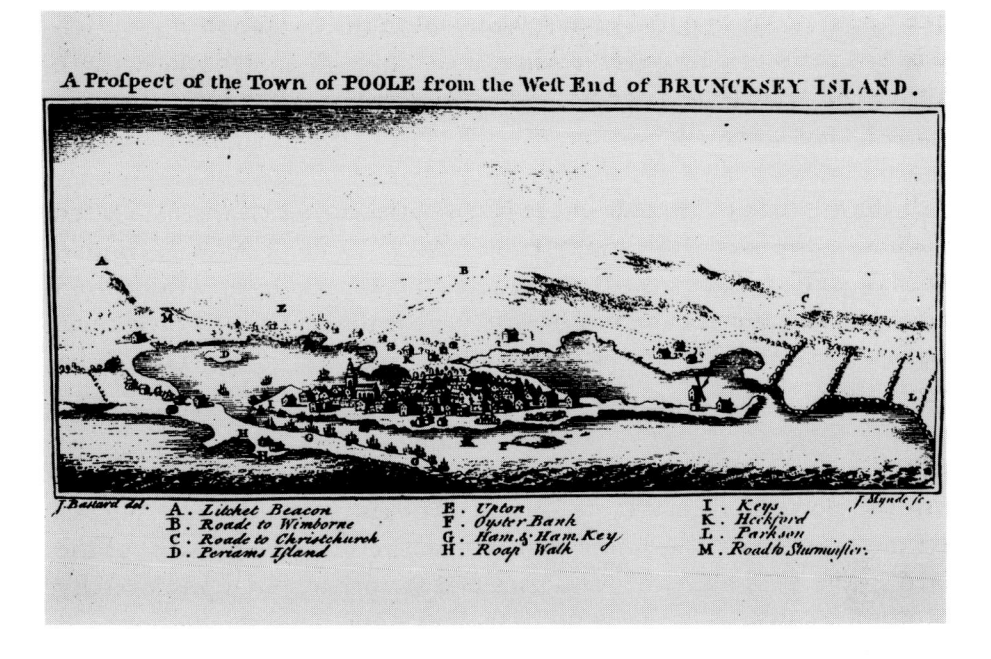

View of the town of Poole from the west end
of Brownsea Island showing
salient features

If he could speak to any of the busy merchants he would see on the Quays he would probably find them disgruntled; they would tell him forcibly that the liberties of the Borough were in great danger. Not long before, in 1683, Charles II had forced the Borough to surrender all its prized privileges which rested on charters granted by the Earl Longspee in 1248, William Montacute in 1371, Henry VI in 1433 and 1453, Queen Elizabeth I in 1568 and Charles II himself in 1667. By 1683 King Charles had grown alarmed by the radical attitude which Poole and other parliamentary boroughs were demonstrating. He was convinced by the country gentry of Dorset, who were jealous of Poole's rights to self-government and fearful of its religious and political radicalism that, as they put it, "the inhabitants are so universally corrupted that it will be impossible to find loyal men to support a corporation therein". Deprived of their extensive liberties, the inhabitants of Poole now feared that the wealthy Lord of the Manor of Canford, Sir John Webb, would be able to resume effective control over the town, a fate rendered more odious to many of the inhabitants who were Protestant Dissenters by the fact that the Webbs were staunch Roman Catholics. The accession of the Catholic King James II in 1685 and the favours he showed to his Catholic subjects intensified the dismay of many Poole people and they welcomed the news in the summer of 1688 that William of Orange was willing to invade England and overthrow King James. Indeed, some of them played an active part in the Revolution of 1688, and throughout the 18th century the Hyde family enjoyed a pension of £50 per annum for the services they had rendered to William of Orange by carrying messages for him at the time of his invasion. To give such assistance to William against the lawful ruler of the country was a very risky business, as many West Country people had found to their cost when Monmouth's unsuccessful rebellion three years earlier had resulted

William III 1650–1702 (William of Orange)   William Hyde

in many being hung, drawn and quartered or sent off to near slavery in the West Indies or America by the notorious Judge Jeffreys in the "Bloody Assizes". The Hyde's courage apparently extended to the ladies of the family, because Mrs. Elizabeth Hyde helped her husband Thomas, reputedly carrying some of the messages tucked into her skirts. It was fitting that Thomas Hyde should become Mayor in 1696 and that his descendants should not only enjoy their annual pension but also play a leading role in Poole affairs in the 18th century. His son George Hyde was elected Mayor in 1757 and his grandson, Thomas, was Mayor in 1764.

James II had in fact some thoughts of using Poole harbour as a safe anchorage for his fleet while it waited to drive off William's expeditionary force. The harbour was not however as safe as it had appeared to one of his advisers, because Poole men were able to capture the only ship of his navy that ventured into the port at the time of the Glorious Revolution. This was the "Speedwell", a fire ship commanded by Captain Edward Poulson. In December 1688 he reported despairingly that "on the morning of the 11th instant he was inveigled into the Antelope tavern at Poole and there seized as a prisoner; at the same time his ship was seized for the Prince of Orange,

19th century print of the Antelope Tavern

one Robinson taking command of her. His cabin had been rifled and all his money taken. Robinson had offered the command back to him if he would carry the ship to the Prince's fleet at Plymouth". Captain Poulson rejected this offer and was later able to escape from Poole to Hurst Castle, from where he sent his doleful report to the Admiralty. Another Admiralty report of the incident shows that most of the Speedwell's crew had deserted the ship when it put into Poole, aided no doubt by the inhabitants of the town who so cunningly took the ship from her Captain.

The Revolution brought the restoration of Poole's cherished liberties and through the 18th and early 19th century the Corporation enjoyed control over the borough, which was to grow significantly and to prosper, especially after the 1720's when the Newfoundland trade recovered at length from the depression caused by wars against France, and Poole merchants were able to open up a new and profitable trade with South Carolina.

As one would expect there was a strong nautical flavour about the members of the Corporation at this time. The leading merchant families, like the Phippards, the Jolliffes and the Westons at the beginning of 18th century and the Lesters, the Garlands and the Jefferys a century or so later, were well represented amongst the burgesses.

Three Phippards and three Westons were members of the Corporation in the early 1700's and they found room for another Weston and two more Jolliffes when a fresh batch of members were created in 1747. If we consult a list of the Corporation in 1812 we may find no few than eleven members of the Garland family and four Jefferys.

They were joined at the monthly Corporation meetings by people of lower rank in Poole society, men like John Brinklow, a mariner, and William Wise, a shipwright, elected in 1715, or Samuel Bird, a woolcomber, and Edward Allen, a gunsmith who were granted the freedom in 1747. Naturally, as long as the Corporation themselves chose the new members of the body, they selected their own relatives, friends and dependants.

It is no wonder that George Garland should serve twice as Mayor, as well as M.P. for Poole, that his brother-in-law should be elected Mayor eight times between 1789 and 1801, and that four of George Garland's sons should each have a turn as Mayor between 1815 and 1830. The leading families in the town of course expected their friends and dependants who were on the Corporation to support them in general and they were not often disappointed. The mariners, shipwrights, gunsmiths and other "lesser" men who were called on to vote for the great merchants and their relatives accepted them as the natural leaders of the town, and by and large, these merchant princes of the day were responsible men who did their best for Poole, freely spending both time and money on its affairs. The old Corporation which disappeared in 1835 was most certainly not truly representative of all who lived in Poole. Nevertheless, its members were a reasonable cross section of Poole society who were united in their great pride in the borough and its privileges, and in their dependance on the good fortune of its trading ventures.

The names of some of the burgesses stand out from the yellowing pages of the Corporation records as particularly distinguished men. Peter Jolliff, born 1659, won national fame, when on May 20th 1694, as Captain of a small ship, the "Sea Adventure", he rescued a Weymouth fishing smack from a French privateer three times the size of his own craft. Undeterred by this, he so pressed home his attack that the French ship was driven ashore and wrecked near Lulworth. Ten days later, another Poole seafarer, William Thompson, out fishing with just one man and a boy, attacked a Cherbourg privateer with a crew of sixteen. So daring was his onslaught on the enemy that after a two hour battle, the privateer surrendered and Thompson brought her triumphantly into Poole Harbour. When the King saw the Admiralty's report on these actions, appropriately endorsed "Poole Heroes", he rewarded them with gold chains and medals. In addition, Captain Jolliff received a commiss-

Peter Jolliff Medal, obverse inscription
His Ma[ties] Gift as a Reward to Peter Jollif of Poole for his good Service agt the Enemy in retaking a Ketch at Weymouth from a French Privateer and chaceing the said Privateer on Shoar near Lulworth in ye Isle of Purbeck where Shee was broken in peeces 1694

ion and William Thompson was awarded the prize he had so gallantly taken. Captain Jolliff's family became one of the first families of Poole in the 18th and early 19th centuries; his descendants served as Mayor on seven occasions and his great grandson, the Reverend Peter William Jolliff, was Rector of Poole for the record period of nearly seventy years from 1791 to 1861. After a period away from the town the Jolliff medal was presented to the Corporation and is now one of the most prized items in the municipal regalia.

Schooner 'Mountainer' of Poole — John Tilsed master

In later wars other Poole sea captains gave a good account of themselves in brushes with enemy ships. Captain Bowden, commanding his own ship, the "Bowden", was approaching Lisbon Harbour in 1740 with a cargo of cod fish from Newfoundland when a Spanish privateer approached. One broadside from the Bowden's guns put the enemy vessel to flight, with the groans and cries of its injured crew echoing across the water. In 1759 Captain Best of the "Friendship" of Poole, also showed that the spirit of Peter Jolliff and William Thompson was still very much alive. His ship had been taken by a French privateer but Captain Best, with the help of his mate and the cook, "a boy and a foreigner" as the newspaper report put it, fought the eight man prize crew and beat them to retake his ship.

Nor should it be thought that Poole men were only successful in the arts of war. 18th century Poole produced a poet, a noted composer of hymns and an antiquary of some fame.

Henry Price, the only man whose occupation has ever been entered in the Poole burial registers as "poet", was the son of a Poole brewer and innkeeper, who kept "The George" in the medieval building now known as Scaplen's Court, and maintained as a museum of local history by Poole Corporation. Educated at Oxford, he served in the Royal Navy and afterwards in 1733 became a Landwaiter in the Customs Service. Possibly because he found it difficult to follow his craft as a poet while carrying out his duties in the Customs, or possibly because he drank, as his biographer, Mr. F. Putnam, suggests, he left the Customs in 1741 and next appears in 1750 shortly before his death, as a teacher at the Free School. From 1739 until his death, he bombarded the borough and the neighbouring counties with his poems, none of which were of a very high quality. In fact, he acted more or less as Poole's Poet Laureate and produced verses to commemorate various notable events in the borough. When Frederick the Prince of Wales visited Poole in 1741, Price responded with a poem beginning:

"Surpris'd, O FREDERICK, I stood,
When first thy manly Form I view'd:"

Evidently Poole's poet was exhausted by his efforts to commemorate royal visits and the exploits of Poole merchants in trade and war, because his last recorded verses which appeared in 1749 were addressed to his butcher about his bill. Perhaps like many poets he was hard up and hoped that Will Gosse, the butcher, would take the poem in payment of his bill!

Henry Price collaborated on occasions with his contemporary, William Knapp, the hymnist, whose reputation in the arts stands on much surer ground. Knapp had property in the High Street and Strand Street and was the Parish Clerk. He is remembered for his very real contribution to the progress of Church music. He published two books of music, the best known, his "Church Melody" being produced in 1753. In 1968, on the 200th anniversary of his death, the roof of St. James Parish Church rang again with such famous tunes as Wimborne, Canford and Wareham, in a William Knapp festival organised by the Society of Poole Men. His version of Psalm 107, sung to the Poole New Tune, opening:

"They that in ships with courage bold
O'er swelling waves their trade pursue
Do God's amazing works behold
And in the deep His wonders view"

sums up the spirit of the Poole he knew. A Wareham man, who moved to Poole with his family, Knapp probably started life as a glover. Some of his descendants, who live in Lytchett Minster, attended the 1968 celebration.

Poole's contribution to antiquarian studies in this century was made by Sir Peter Thompson, a descendant of the famous William Thompson and one of three Poole men to be honoured with a knighthood in the 18th and early 19th centuries. His early career was similar to that of many Poole men. As a youth he had gone to Newfoundland and subsequently returned to London as a prosperous merchant. Unlike many Poole men who made their fortunes in the Newfoundland trade, Sir Peter had ambitions to improve his education, as well as his social and political standing. His interest in antiquarian matters won him the fellowship of the Society of Antiquaries in 1743 and later the fellowship of the Royal Society. He also gained an introduction to Whig politics through a fellow antiquary, James West, for long the right hand man of the Duke of Newcastle. As high Sheriff of Surrey he was knighted in 1745 and subsequently served as M.P. for St. Albans. Although his career had taken him away from Poole he had the interests of his native town very much at heart. In the 1740's he built for himself a magnificent house in Market Street, fortunately spared to this day, and from there he played a leading role in Poole politics and municipal affairs. In a century when the rights of town corporations were frequently disputed, his knowledge of Poole's history and ancient liberties, gained from his vast collection of books and archives was invaluable to the rulers of the borough. He was also a very useful intermediary with the national government when the borough wished to gain favours for the town and its trade. A correspondent of

Entrance doorway of Sir Peter Thompson's House in
Market Close

many learned men of his day, he collaborated with the Reverend John Hutchins, the author of the celebrated History of Dorset, supplying him with the material on Poole's history. When he died in 1770 at the age of 72, his obituary in a local newspaper commented on him as "a gentleman of benevolent and social disposition. In his public station and commercial engagements he acted with the strictest integrity, and an uncommon love of literature made him an agreeable and valuable companion to men of taste and learning". Few of his fellow townsmen may have shared his learned interests but they had good cause to appreciate his very real contribution to the town's progress.

18th century print of Brownsea Castle, Brownsea Island

The Corporation which Price, Knapp and Sir Peter Thompson adorned had a wide variety of responsibilities. Chief among them in this period of frequent wars was the duty of providing for the physical defence of the town. The principal threat was of raids or invasions from the sea which could ruin the port and its shipping and destroy the town's prosperity. In times of war the leaders of the town were quick to look to the defence of the harbour by mounting batteries of guns at Studland and on Brownsea Island which could command the harbour entrances. Frequent appeals were made to the Government to provide convoy protection for the annual Newfoundland

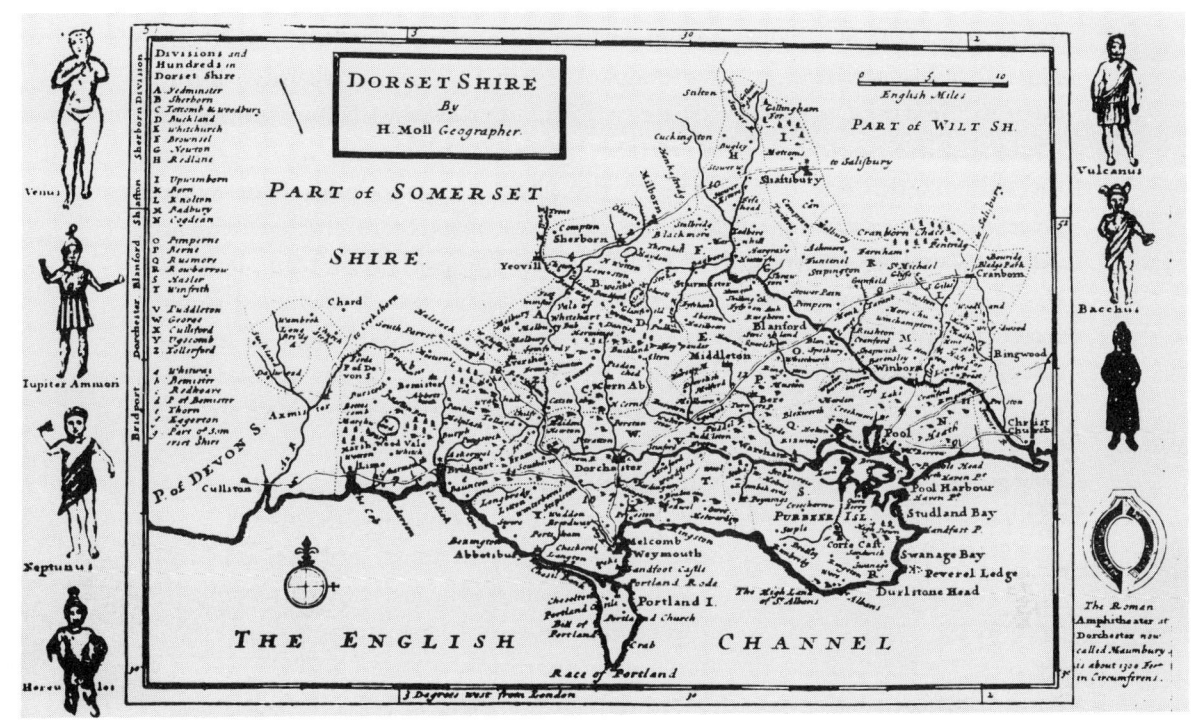

Map of Dorset 1724 showing pre-eminence of Poole as the largest urban bloc

fleet against enemy privateers. Sometimes these privateers lurked just outside the harbour waiting for their prey as in 1757 when a French ship captured Poole's largest sloop near the Harbour bar. On this occasion it was alleged that French prisoners of war released from captivity in Poole "after mild treatment" had given information on the weakness of the defences on their return to France. During the Napoleonic Wars the Corporation co-operated closely with the Government in making preparations against the threatened invasion of Bonaparte. The survey of resources available in 1803 reveals that the Poole volunteer infantry force numbered nearly 500 men, while the bakers of Poole were capable of producing 2030 loaves from their 16 ovens in a twenty four hour period. Even Poole's animal population of 23 cows, one calf, 3 sheep, 199 pigs and 115 horses were also standing by to play their part in the emergency. The following years estimate of the Borough's resources listed a force of "Sea Fencibles", a number of Pioneers and a total of 1333 persons who, in an invasion, would be "incapable of removing themselves by reason of age, infancy or infirmity".

When it came to supplying men for the army and the navy in wartime Poole's attitude was not so straightforward. The town's Justices willingly committed undeserving beggars and other ne'er-do-wells to serve in the forces. In 1706 Samual Rogers and Henry Wherwell of "Abbey Milton" were forcibly enlisted by the magistrates in Colonel Churchill's Regiment of Marines, and two country folk, who may well have come to Poole seeking employment, were thus taken off to an unknown fate. On the other hand, the operations of the press gang were regarded with great suspicion and resentment by Poole people, from the wealthiest merchants to the common folk of the town. The press gang took, if they could, able-bodied seamen whose loss the town could ill afford if its economic life was to continue. When the press gang was near at hand, the Mayor and Magistrates frequently used delaying tactics so that the word could be spread and men could get into hiding, sometimes in the heathland outside Poole. One stratagem that was employed by the Mayor was to put off signing the Impressment Certificate authorizing the press gang's activities for any possible reason — because it was Sunday or because of more urgent municipal business. Another way of cheating the press was for the Mayor to issue a long list of "protections" exempting men who were allegedly pilots, from being impressed. Despite these efforts, the press gang naturally carried off numerous Poole people in many a "hot press" as the local newspaper put it. In February 1762 one young man was actually carried off to a man-of-war

Impressment Licence

Portrait of Benjamin Lester

from the door of St. James Church where he had gone to be married. Pressing also took place out at sea and Poole ships returning with passengers from Newfoundland were naturally fair game for the Royal Navy. When the "Joseph and Mary", which had been given up for lost, limped into Poole in 1741, her master reported that 15 of her hands had been taken off by a naval vessel. He was perhaps luckier than the captain of the "Two Brothers" in 1770 who lost 50 men to impressment and had his ship damaged into the bargain by the man-of-war which stopped him in the Atlantic.

The most notorious episode in the activities of the press gang in Poole came in 1794 when Benjamin Lester's brig "Maria", commanded by Captain Randall was hailed by the press gang's tender as she was about to enter Poole Harbour. On board were some fifty fishermen returning from Newfoundland and it appears that they refused to allow the ship to stop at the press gang's command. At this, the press gang opened fire on the "Maria", killing the pilot and two others, and wounding five other men. A mob quickly gathered on the Quay and were only prevented from lynching the officers of the press gang by the Magistrates backed up by some of the troops stationed in the town. The two lieutenants and midshipman of the press gang were arrested and the Coroner's juries found cases of wilful murder against them. It was intended that they should be tried in the town but in view of the great ferment their deed had aroused in Poole, the Admiralty intervened and undertook to discipline the three men.

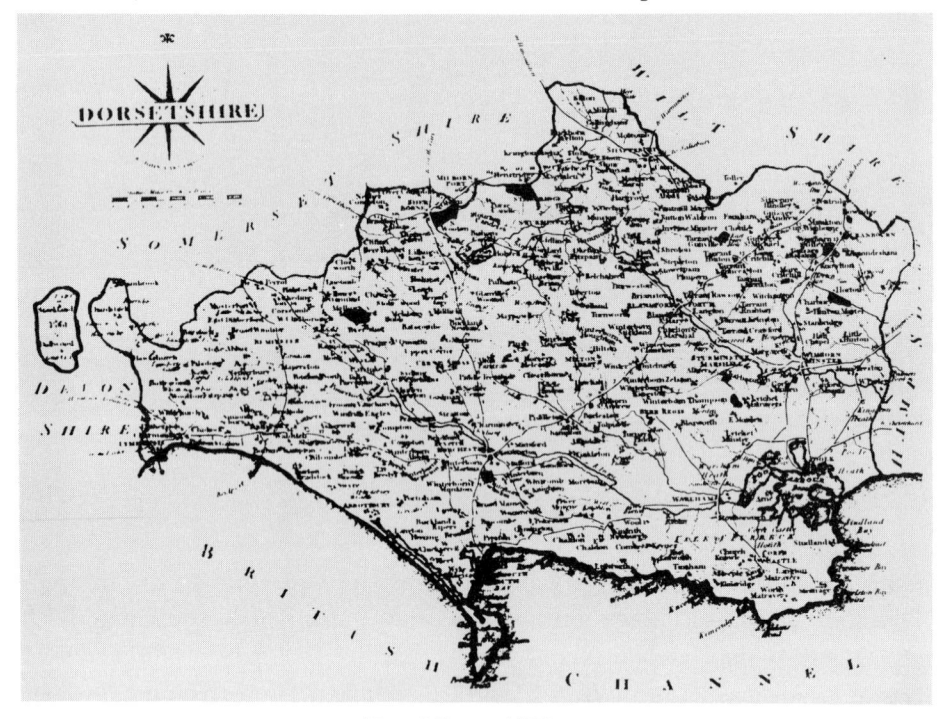

Map of Dorset 1787

A method of defence which naturally appealed more to the inhabitants of Poole was privateering. Here it was possible to strike blows at the enemy and realise fat profits from the ships and cargoes taken as lawful prizes. On occasions the enthusiasm for privateering was so great that even privateers from other ports were feted. The Captain of the Bristol privateer "Southwell" was given the freedom of the Borough after he had brought in a French privateer in 1744. (He also received the possibly less welcome honour of having one of Henry Price's odes dedicated to his exploit). Poole herself appears to have equipped three privateers during the Seven Year's War against France and Spain. One of them, the "Fox", distinguished herself by taking a prize of cargo worth £20,000. The "Fox" was armed with "eight carriage guns and fourteen swivels" and carried a crew of seventy men. Her sister ships were the "Speaker" and the "Dorset".

Tho France and Spain invited, join their Arms

And rouze the nations with unjust alarms,

Tho' Prussia's monarch, wavering still remains

And Belgia still her promis'd fleet detains,

Yet, blest with Health, if you vouchsafe your Aid

Poole may now flourish, and bring back her trade.

Wealth buys or builds the warlike ship with ease,

Wealth rules the land and triumphs o'er the seas,

Sails, yards, masts, muskets, cannon, powder, ball

Are Yours at Will: for money conquers all".

Henry Price poem

Written on the occasion of Captain John Wingfield of the Bristol Privateer "Southwell" capturing and bringing into Poole Harbour the Cherbourg Privateer "Le Bon Laron" and for this being made a burgess of the Corporation of Poole.

In both the American and Napoleonic Wars, Poole privateers were again active. In 1778 the "Tyger" cutter was fitted out as a privateer by a group of sponsors which included William Spurrier, a leading merchant and later Mayor of the Borough. She was soon preying successfully on Dutch shipping, bringing in two captures in the year she was commissioned. Three more privateers, including the "Active" and the "Union" were sent out in 1779. They were armed with as many as twenty carriage guns besides swivel mounted weapons. In this way both the leading merchants and the common "mariners" of the town were able to take revenge for the losses of Poole ships to the enemy, do their patriotic duty and share the prize money.

Salisbury prison Sarum Street: used as overnight lock-up and occasionally as an alternative to Town Gaol

Through war and peace the town's rulers also had to concern themselves with law and order. It fell to the Sheriff and four Constables to assist the Borough Magistrates in the upkeep of the peace and the punishment of wrongdoers. Beggars and petty thieves might receive public floggings, sometimes at the tail of a cart. Others might find themselves in the stocks or, if they were women convicted as "common scolds", suffer the ducking stool, which was a fixture on the Quay. Two prisons were available; one, under the old

Guildhall in Fish Street, was by the mid 1700's a loathsome and crumbling building which was no match for a prisoner determined to escape, who might dig his way out as some did; the other, "the Salisbury", still adjoins the Town Cellars, and because of its small size was suitable only as a temporary lock-up. One of the improvements made in the town in the later 18th century was the replacement of the Fish Street prison by a new gaol in King Street, which offered much more secure and wholesome accommodation, and was later thoughtfully equipped with a treadmill. Occasionally men or women convicted of more serious crimes might be transported. Constance Savage was dispatched to Savannah, Georgia, in 1764, on the Poole ship "Indian Queen" to serve her sentence of seven years' transportation for a felony.

Although the death penalty was prescribed for a wide variety of offences up until the reform of the criminal law in the early 19th century, comparatively few death sentences were handed down by Assize judges in Poole in the 18th century.

Those who were sentenced to death for stealing appear to have had their sentences commuted to imprisonment, as happened in the case of William Tucker, a sheep stealer in 1794. It seems that only two Poole men were actually executed, for murder, in this period. The first case, in 1740, created a great stir in the neighbourhood because of its ghastly details. A young Witchampton woman was found dead on the heath at Parkstone, "her head almost off". "She was big with child" and beside her lay not only the murder weapon, a knife, but also a quantity of children's bed linen. Her murderer, Henry Smith, the owner of a saltworks at Parkstone, escaped in a fishing boat and hid at Bishop's Waltham, where he was given away by a lady he knew. Tried at Dorchester, he was sentenced "to be hanged in chains at the spot where the murder had been committed". Twelve years later, Anthony Colpis was tried in Poole with his wife for the murder of a woman "Widow Buckler", who had been thrown from a window three stories high. Mrs. Colpis was acquitted but her husband was executed at Windmill Point at Baiter. The Sheriff was in charge of the proceedings, and, as was customary, allowed the condemned man to say his prayers and address the crowd who had come to see his execution. Indeed, the local newspaper commented on the humanity of the Sheriff who "indulged him in his own time, which was near two hours".

Other Poole men who were responsible for the deaths of others were luckier than Colpis. Thomas Gleed was convicted of manslaughter in 1765, after a child he had struck on the head, died. He was sentenced to be "burnt in the hand", and was apparently the first man in Poole to suffer this punishment for a very long time. The same sentence was carried out under the Sheriff's supervision in 1781. A sailor, one John Thresher (or Thrasher), had been so angered by his wife's efforts to get him to come home from a public house that he had beaten her to death in his drunken fury. For this manslaughter he was "burnt in the hand" and given twelve months' imprisonment.

The Sheriff also acted as the inspector of weights and measures for the Borough and in September each year, just before his term of office expired, would hold the "Sheriff's Tourn". At 8 a.m. he and a jury would begin a tour of the shops of the town to examine the weights and measures. A small number of deficiencies were usually discovered by the end of the tour at about 6 p.m. The offending shopkeepers normally forfeited the defective scales etc. and paid a fine of 5/-. Bakers seem to have been particularly prone to using incorrect scales because it was seldom that a "Tourn" ended without the prosecution of at least one baker. It was customary for the Sheriff to regale the jury and his friends "with an elegant supper", often at the Antelope "after the fatigues of the day".

Effective law and order also meant that inns, ale-houses and other places of entertainment had to be licensed and supervised as today by the local authorities. There were indeed few places where Poole's inhabitants could relax other than inns and ale-houses.

The New Inn tavern Thames Street

As one might expect in a sea-faring town, public houses and inns were numerous, totalling at least thirty by 1826. By that date many familiar names had appeared — the Shipwright's Arms, the Jolly Sailor, the Dolphin, the Portmahon Castle, the Royal Oak, the Globe, the New Inn, the Swan and the Poole Arms amongst others. A more modern touch came with the Air Balloon.

Apart from ensuring that these hostelries were licenced the Constables had to supervise their good conduct, for example, preventing them from opening their doors during the hours of Divine Services. In 1827, three publicans were fined for allowing tippling during those hours. By the

New Ballad
Herring
Fishery

1820's too, the Magistrates were insisting on earlier closing hours in the evening and decided that 10 p.m. was a reasonable hour. The problem of control was complicated by the existence of many smaller establishments, which did not aspire to signboards, but freely dispensed ale and strong liquors. Judging by the records, widows frequently kept such alehouses and quite often fell foul of the law, like the good lady in 1738 who was prosecuted "for selling Geneva and other spirituous liquors in her house without a license". It was probably establishments of this nature which could easily become the resorts of those seeking rather more scandalous pleasures than liquid refreshment. The Widow Simmons was accused in 1736 of keeping "a disorderly house, being the generall rendezvous for alle Travellers and Vaggabonds". A little later the Magistrates had to deal with a more ingenious proprietor, Stephen Frampton, who entertained vagrants in his "scandalous and disorderly house..... which he procures to his house telling them that he is a Constable and can give them protection". Even the Fish Street gaol was not beyond suspicion. In 1777 the Keeper of the gaol was dismissed "for suffering it to be used as a common bawdy house". It was a problem which continued into the later 18th and early 19th century, doubtless made worse by the large numbers of troops in the town during the Revolutionary and Napoleonic Wars, and Mrs. John Easter, prosecuted in 1793 for keeping "a house of ill fame and a resort for disorderly and idle persons of both sexes", was but one of a long line of such entrepreneurs in Poole.

There were occasionally other forms of entertainment for the general populace, some of which created problems for the Magistrates, the Sheriff and their assistants. Poole's annual fairs were a mixed blessing. In 1832, it was noted that "vagabonds were there in great abundance. One gentleman was hustled and robbed of a gold watch worth 20 guineas".

The coming of the theatre to Poole in the later 18th century brought considerable opposition from sections of the populace but this was overruled by the Magistrates who presumably saw no evil in a programme like that for December 1771 which began with "a new Pantomime Entertainment, Mother Shipton or Harlequin in Masquerade" and continued with Hamlet and "a Tragedy called Charles I with entertainment of the Honest Yorkshireman".

There were dangers of disorder too in the horse races staged in Poole in the 1700's, as in 1776 when the racegoers were surprized "by the appearance of a methodistical gentleman who got into the stand and harangued them very much against such evil acts of dissipation".

In contrast, such diversions as Poole Regatta, which can be dated as early as 1775, and the display of a camel imported from "Grand Cairo" in 1761, appear to have posed no great problems for the rulers of the town.

Poole people naturally looked to the municipal authority to deal with the wide variety of public nuisances that could beset a community crowded together in a comparatively small area. Chief amongst their complaints was the state of the roads, where, before the introduction of Tar Macadam in the early 19th century, "pitching" with stones was the best method of securing a reasonable surface. In the early 1700's frequent requests were made for the "pitching" of such principal roads as the High Street and Strand Street. Later in this 18th century when more and more land was being reclaimed from mudlands and the northern part of the town was also

The Quay end of the High Street during the late 19th century

developing, complaints were often made about the state of roads and paths left by the builders and developers. In 1765, the Mayor was reminded of the need to repair Market Street "near the new erected Market House". Not long afterwards, Samual White was accused of making holes in Lagland Street and not filling them up and of leaving bricks and mortar all over the place.

Obstructions on the roads, and the Quays, were in fact another very common complaint. Carts, barrows, pigs, timber, guns, stones of all descriptions, hogsheads and barrels of rice, pitch and old iron and many other solid objects were reported in this period as obstructing the ways.

In 1752, Messrs. Bowden and Turner were accused of "leaving empty pitch casks and staves behind ye Towne Cellars and obstructing Salisbury Street". At the same time a complaint was made about "a large flat stone that has remained on the Quay near three years, it belonging to James Keats of Corfe Castle". Richard Fabian of Wimborne was responsible for allowing "four hogsheads of bones to continue on the Great Quay a year or more". In 1769, one William Hillier was accused of "keeping piggs in the High Street" and some person unknown had left a large mill stone in Thames Street. The 19th century brought no relief from these hazards to those using the roads. James Manlawes, it was reported in 1822, had left "a number of cannons which carry an accumulation of dirt and filth at the entrance to Durnford's Lane" leading off the Quay. A year later Widow Wharton, who may have been a female chimney sweep, was reported "for putting soot near the road in Hill Street, for loading the same in the street and suffering her boys to beat out their soot bags against the walls". Frequent complaints too were made about generally more yielding and yet more insidious obstructions to the passer-by — dung, dirt and rubbish. In 1744 it was reported that one Frampton and others had deposited so much dung and rubbish at the upper end of the High Street that "carriages are obliged to break into the footway with great inconvenience in wet time to passengers (sic) on the road walking that way". Even worthies like Sir Peter Thompson were sometimes accused of like offences, as in 1761 when Sir Peter and others were reported for throwing wood and other rubbish into the road at the end of Nightingale Lane.

Possibly more direct dangers to public health and decency are revealed when Thomas Strickland was ordered to repair the wall of his privy in Town Gate Lane to "prevent the escape of any noisome smell through that wall" or Widow Culley to mend her hog sty because "the drainings of the sty come through the wall of the said house into the lower rooms" of her unfortunate neighbours.

Robert Randall's "necessary house" on the Great Quay was a problem for the Corporation for some six years after 1738 when it was first reported as "dangerous to severall gentlemen". Over a year later a warrant was issued for Randall's arrest but the repairs or improvements to this convenience were evidently not satisfactory because in 1744 he was prosecuted again, having allowed it to become "both incommodious and dangerous".

Since sanitary arrangements were so crude and inadequate we may have some sympathy for the town's schoolmaster and his charges who were reported to the Magistrates in 1770 in the following manner: "Mr. Willis the Schoolmaster for suffering his Scholars to do their necessary occasion against the Old Town Hall being very great nuisances, and we desire it may not be done for the future".

The Guildhall in Market Street circa 1836

The new Guildhall in Market Street (often then known as the Market House) also suffered the same indignity as may be seen from a complaint made in 1798 against "a most abominable nuisance, the filth commonly in the Market House, the shameful practise of people frequenting the nitches there causing such indecencies and rendering the place so unwholesome". The Magistrates ordered that "the same be immediately surveyed" but we unfortunately have no record of their reaction to what was found there. The aroma of the old town was hardly improved too by those inhabitants who used slightly more advanced sanitary methods like one John Churchill, who was brought before the Magistrates in 1754 "for emptying chamber pots in Towngate Lane". The records show that he found it hard to break himself of the habit because six months later he was in front of the Bench again for the same offence.

Again such hazards to public health continued to worry the town authorities into the early 1800's. In 1820, Deborah Knowles was accused of "emptying night soil in Paddick's Lane". As late as 1827, Maria Wiffin of Hill Street had a dung heap extending over the pavement, and a year later, one Fisher was reported for "an accumulation of

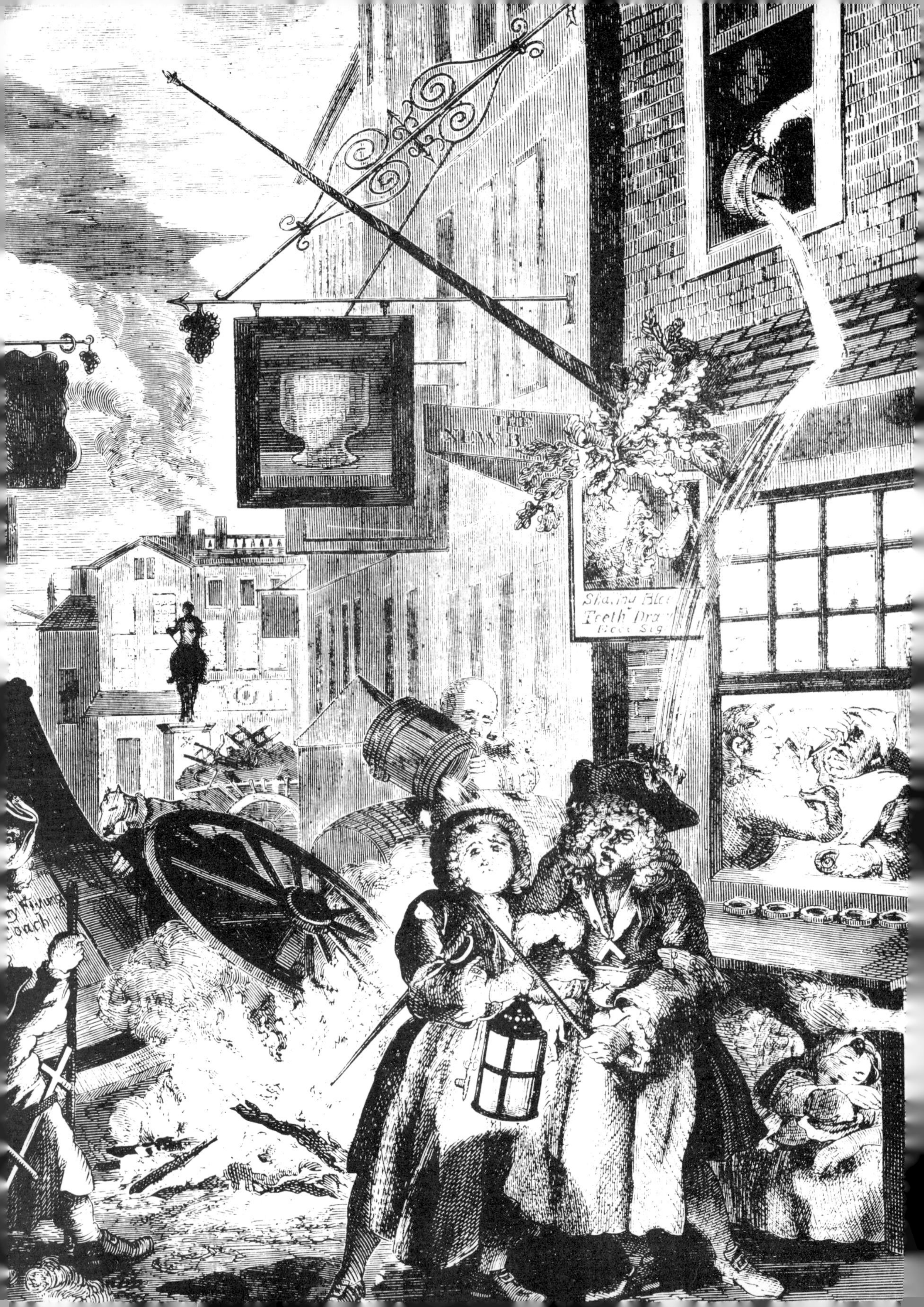
Teeth Dra

dirt, dung and filth producing offensive and pernicious smells at his premises in Thames Street, being injurious to the health of His Majesties subjects". It was appropriate enough in the era of municipal reform that the Magistrates should have been requested in 1833 to rebuke the Corporation "for not providing a convenient privy or privies for the use of seafaring persons and fishermen of the Port, for want of which nuisances are frequently committed on the Quays and particularly near the Fish Shambles".

The state of other public facilities and buildings was naturally also the responsibility of the Corporation. Sometimes the responsibility was fixed directly on the Mayor, as in 1767, when information was laid against him for allowing "the well of the Town Pump in Thames Street to remain open and uncovered, it being very dangerous for children to fall therein, being a great nuisance". The "Passage Boat" which linked Poole with Hamworthy was another favourite subject for complaint. On occasions the boatman was missing and the boat adrift; at other times the boat itself was in a decayed state. In 1770 the man who kept the Passage House at Hamworthy and was responsible for the ferry service, one John Osmond, was reported to the

Plaque on North
East Wall of Guildhall

Joseph Gulstone

The old Fish Shambles, Poole

Magistrates — "notwithstanding he has frequently been presented for not appointing a proper person for plying the Passage Boat, many complaints have been made of his pursuting (sic) in his neglect and this day the said Boat was adrift and several people waiting to go over, being a great nuisance". By 1784 the boat was described as being "in a leaky condition and not fit for passengers to go over in her", while in 1792 its state was such that "some passengers have complained they have nearly lost their lives in crossing the water".

Numerous buildings, including the Old Guildhall, the Fish Shambles and the Salisbury Prison were from time to time reported as being in such ruinous condition that they were likely to fall down.

The experience of disastrous fire in other Dorset towns such as Wareham and Blandford meant that Poole people were very much alive to the danger of fire in a crowded town where a number of industries involving the use of furnaces were followed. Dinah Sims, the Magistrates were informed in 1749, frequently kept a large quantity of heath faggots in the Fish Shambles "to the great hazard of setting the town on fire". In 1782 Mrs. Ursula Skinner's "fowels" were declared to be in danger of catching fire because her "fowel house" was situated against a bake-house chimney. The worst fire risk was however to gunpowder brought in by ships and when it was known in 1775 that the schooner "Industry" lying in the harbour had no less than six tons of gunpowder aboard, "the whole town being in danger of being demolished, and a very great nuisance", the "Industry" was promptly sent down to the lower harbour. A month later the town was alarmed again when fire broke out in John Hooper's wash-house, adjacent to a warehouse containing half a ton of gunpowder. Strong comments were made about how disgraceful it was that the Corporation had not erected a proper storage place long before, because they had obtained authority to do so nearly twenty years previously and the grave danger to the town was self-evident. Shortly afterwards the Corporation at last built the Powder house out at Baiter for the more secure storage of gunpowder. The foundations of this building may be seen to this day on the shore at Baiter.

After numerous delays the Corporation responded to many of these complaints about the state of the town and its services. The first major improvements were naturally enough made to the Quays and the harb-

View of the Quay 1833

The old Public Library

our for they were of prime concern to the merchants and their associates who ruled over Poole. A visitor returning to Poole at the beginning of the 1800's would have marvelled at the long extensions made to the old Quays both towards Baiter and Holes Bay. He would have seen evidence too of road to the Quays being widened and improved. Although many of the leading families were by now moving out of the town into country houses outside the borough, they retained sufficient pride in their place of birth and business to help embellish it. George Garland owned three country houses, at Stanley Green, Stone (Wimborne) and Leeson House (Langton Matravers) but remembered the poor in Poole and provided a range of alms houses at Hunger Hill in 1814. His son, Benjamin Lester-Lester, helped provide the first public library in Poole in a building opposite Scaplen's Court in 1830. Not long before, the Corporation had subscribed handsomely to the complete rebuilding of St. James Church and had erected a new market for fruit, vegetables and butter.

The members of the Corporation were born politicians and much of their energy was directed into political quarrels, especially of course at election times. All this political activity was perfectly understandable. It was the burgesses of the Corporation who alone at this time chose the two Members of Parliament for Poole. It was by establishing good relations with the government of the day that the burgesses, and the town in general, might enjoy a good share of all the many favours government had to offer — jobs in government service, pensions, contracts and all manner of considerations for the town and its trade. Few of the quarrels were concerned with political principles for most of the 18th century period. They arose from the rivalry between leading figures in Poole, each anxious to prove that he stood nearest to the source of favours and that he enjoyed most power in the town. Even if personal rivalries within the borough flagged, as they sometimes did, then leading personages from outside would stir up controversy by taking an interest in Poole politics in the hopes of securing one or both of the parliamentary seats.

Doubtless on occasions the town's leaders were so concerned with their political disputes that the good government of the town suffered but it was not until the 19th century era of reform, treated later, that this happened in a very serious fashion.

The political storms of the 18th century were quite frequent but soon blew themselves out. One of the worst upheavals came in the mid century when John Masters tried to dominate Poole politics. Like Sir Peter Thompson, one of his chief opponents, Masters was a local man who had amassed great wealth by trade and wanted power to match his wealth. He aimed at capturing one of the parliamentary seats in Poole but before he could achieve this needed to make sure of his power over the Corporation. Because of the great influence which the Mayor and Sheriff enjoyed in parliamentary elections he had to have his supporters in these offices. Masters was able to make himself Mayor in 1748 and 1752 but in the process had stirred up great opposition so that in 1753 two candidates claimed to be the right ful Mayor and two candidates insisted that they had been lawfully elected as Sheriff, one each for Masters and his opponents. When October 12th came, both sides went to the Guildhall determined to see their candidates installed. Masters, not apparently a very polished man, called his opponents, "dirty and pitiful dogs", while his Irish friend, Michael Ballard, jumped onto a table and began laying about him with his fists. In the midst of this confusion, the two rival Mayors struggled to seat themselves in the Mayoral chair, with the Town Clerk trying to swear in one of them and an Alderman trying to swear in the other, while one of the two contendants also attempted to read the proclamation of a riot. Masters eventually won the legal battle which followed the fisti-cuffs but his death not long afterwards was greeted with sighs of relief and genuine attempts by the burgesses to bury their expensive differences.

"What can you expect when the Government controls the mass media!"

Needless to say these efforts did not last long and the parliamentary elections of the 1760's saw more bitter rivalries and disorders. As previously, another Poole merchant, who had prospered greatly, was a leading figure as one of the candidates. This was Joshua Mauger, who unsuccessfully stood for Poole in a by-election in 1765 during which one Poole burgess, Benjamin Jennings, was said to have been offered 800 guineas for his vote but was unfortunately too ill to go to the poll even for all that money.

As always, the mob had an enjoyable time in this election with free drinks and party coloured ribbons for their wives and female acquaintances. Mauger's supporters aroused themselves on this occasion against Sir Peter Thompson who had opposed Mauger. Sir Peter told in a letter, which Mr. H. F. V. Johnstone of Poole had kindly allowed me to study, how Mauger's friends carefully left a barrel of strong beer near his house in Market Street and then inflamed the mob with "plenty of wine in half pint tumblers besides strong beer". Fearing for the safety of his paralysed sister in the house, Sir Peter went to meet the mob near the Guildhall and found it was led by a former Mayor of the town. They attacked him, pulling at his wig, but fortunately some of his friends helped him to take refuge in a house, and from there they sent for the Mayor to come and quell the riot.

Further elections in 1768 and 1769 brought more disorders and many charges and counter-charges of bribery and corruption which the private papers of one of the candidates show us were based on truth. Two "unreliable" Poole voters were paid their expenses to stay outside the town during the election campaign for fear that the other side would make them change their minds by offering them bigger bribes. One of these two, John Butler, was described by a candidates agent as "a slippery gent. to be dealt with quite at the last moment". The other side were aware too of Butler's difficult attitude. They had plans to curry favour with him by buying timber from him and apprenticing his son to a shipwright free of charge. If all else failed, they intended to prevail on Mrs. Butler to get her husband out of town on the day of the election. It was arranged that one of the opposition voters should be arrested for debt on the morning of the election so that he should be prevented from voting. The individual concerned was Richard Gleed of West Street, the shipwright who was busy trying to deal with John Butler. The plot to prevent him casting his vote failed, possibly because Mauger stepped in and bought a ship from him, paying the high price of £7 per ton, thus giving him the means of staving off his creditors.

Money changed hands very freely — even William Knapp, the Parish Clerk, was said to have taken £40 for his vote and in the last stages of the 1769 election it was calculated that votes had reached the price of £700. It was little wonder that the daughter of the aged and blind Joseph Wadham who received £200 for his vote should comment that "Providence was very kind in such opportunities to provide for him".

The amount of bribery and corruption alleged in the 1768 election which had resulted in Mauger's return, was such that the House of

Commons investigated the whole matter, declared Mauger's return invalid and order a fresh election. Not a few Poole voters trembled while the Commons were deliberating their conduct. A leading figure on the Corporation wrote, half jokingly, that he hoped "the Mayor and Aldermen of Poole won't be obliged to quit their houses for an apartment in Newgate Gaol. The retirement there to me at present, would be a very disagreeable exchange". The Commons' decision did not prevent money and favours carrying the subsequent by-election of 1769 in Mauger's favour.

The later 1700's and early 1800's provide more evidence of how high political feelings could run in Poole and how profitable it was to be a member of the Corporation and have one's vote in municipal or parliamentary elections courted by those struggling for power.

In the 1807 General Election the principal contest was between the Garland family, represented by Joseph Garland, and John Jeffery, another merchant prince who had already served as M.P. for Poole. Part of the campaign took the form of a "war of paper" with the rivals and their supporters hurling insulting printed words at one another. An open letter to Jeffery directly accused him of lying deception of the Poole voters and corrupt dealings with the Government to ensure Garland's defeat. Meanwhile the elderly William Spurrier, another eminent Poole man, found himself at the Bar of the House of Commons to receive the Speaker's rebuke for attempting to gain an advantage in the election by concealing the parliamentary writ ordering the election.

Gifts received by voters might include parcels of fish and cranberries from Newfoundland.

Nor was it just the Corporation voters who profited from parliamentary elections. Election accounts for 1826 show us exactly how much was spent on the mob by one of the three candidates. He recruited 57 men to cheer him on and intimidate his rival's supporters. They each received 6/- for their services and, as one might expect, many had to make their mark when signing for their money. The beer account totalled over £77 and covered thirty public houses. Ribbons cost another £61, the bell-ringers three guineas, while Bandmaster Turtle and his musicians were paid £41-0-2, including 30/- expenses at the Crown and another 20/-

To JOHN JEFFERY Esq.

"O, Sir, we quarrel in print by the Book; as you have
"Books for good manners: I will name you the degrees.
"The first the Retort courteous; the second the Quip
"Modest; the third the Reply churlish; the fourth the
"Reproof valiant; the fifth the Countercheck quarrelsome;
"The sixth the Lie direct. All these you may avoid, but the
"Lie direct; and you may avoid that too with an If."

SHAKESPEAR.

SIR,

YOU will observe, Sir, that I have adopted for my Motto to this Letter, a quotation which appears to me to be very appropriate to the Business in hand, and altho' I know you are no great Reader, perhaps you will find it amongst the Works of Shakespeare now in your Library, the leaves of which I believe are not much soiled, or of any other author.

IT has been said, Sir, that Heralds can make these Arms they cannot find;—you know to what I allude, and if your Friend, and rural Amanuensis, had been aware of your versatility, he would have been the last Man in the world, in my opinion, to have searched for the Motto which he has thought proper to assign you—it is, as you might have heard, a Quotation from Horace, the first line of a third Ode; and if you will consult your learned Secretary for a Translation, he may tell you *perhaps* if he is sincere, that it does not apply to you *at this time of day*; presuming therefore that some amongst you may be able to construe it, to them therefore I beg leave to refer you.

I come now, Sir, to examine the Reply which you promised last Night should appear in a few Hours,—"*The Mountain "laboured, and brought forth a Mouse*"—not one Assertion have you had the Courage to contradict without a Quibble; and one in particular which charged you with the bold and impolitic Boast " of having the Sanction of Government for your Support," you have very prudently passed over in Silence.

YOU are not surprised you say that "the Authors of the late Address should be unwilling to revert to the first Cause of the present political Struggle," nor was it their Intention till you had thrown down the Gauntlet.

THE Authors of the late address were not as you suppose, "desirous to shrink from a fair, full, and manly Investigation" of that first cause, as the motives which led to it are no doubt, more plausable than any you can adduce; and altho I never was in the Secret, yet exclusive of the personal consideration which Mr. SPURRIER might plead, I think I may venture to assert that your late reluctant Supporters, had strong, cogent Reasons for breaking up that ill-framed and heterogeneous Coalition—and by the way, Sir, permit me to observe, that it reflects no great Credit on you, to be no longer of that Party, as I am warranted in asserting in the Face of Day, that you would have continued it if you could by fawning, bowing, and cringing— No, Sir, they broke it up because they suspected (and with reason too) your political Honesty; they found out, perhaps, that you were not independent either in Principle or Fortune,—in Principle we know you cannot be by comparing your Declaration at your first Election with your subsequent Conduct. You declared, Sir, on the Hustings, that you were truly independent—that the Interest of your Constituents was uppermost in your mind—that you would not accept of any Place, Pension, or Emolument, for yourself or your Family, which is just as consistent as your assertion of this Day that " whilst you have Existence your earnest and best Endeavours will be exerted for the benefit of the Town." Permit me to ask you what Individual in this Town is indebted to you for any Treasury Favour— and yet such is the strange infatuation of men, that many to this day are blind to their own Interest, tho your Eyes have been always open, and even now like those of the Eagle are soaring to the Sun—no further Explanation is necessary on this Head, as every man that runs may read.

YOU very rightly observe, that if the Peace and Tranquillity of the Town have been disturbed, it can be attributed to no other Cause than to that Coalition which I before referred to, but observe it is not in the way that you take it, but by the Ingratitude which you have evinced towards your late very good Friends, Mr. GARLAND and Mr. SPURRIER.

"Mr. C. SPURRIER's unpopularity, and the earnestness generally expressed to introduce a third Person", did not justify, you, Sir, in going to Town for a new Candidate, as you must have known that the honorable resignation of Mr. GARLAND, could not possibly have any other object in view than the Peace of the Town, and you may be assured that the generality of the Town do not approve of your Conduct.

YOUR Observation on the Assertion you made in London, "that you had the Borough in your Pocket," is too puerile to be noticed, your Friends cannot suppose that we meant that you had the Bricks and Mortar in your Pocket, it is merely a Figure of Speech, a Metaphor, such as some of your Parliamentary Friends may use, when they say, "the House is up." No, Sir, what was meant by that Expression, was the Poll that you produced from your Pocket, when you offered to bet a Thousand Guineas that you carried your Man, and you stipulated (if I am not misinformed) to bring him in for a certain Sum.

THE Conversation which the Committee had the authority of asserting as to what passed at Mr. GARLAND's House in London, is ready to be verified on Oath, by the Testimony of two very respectable Witnesses; namely, that you assured Mr. GARLAND you were extremely sorry to find the Steps you had taken were disagreeable to him, and that if you had known it you certainly would not have made the Attempt of introducing a third Person.

YOU observe, Sir, that you did go to Mr. GARLAND's House in London, the day you arrived, and dined with the Family without seeing Mr. GARLAND. That you was there at seven o'Clock in the Evening, I do not deny, but that you dined with the Family and did not see GARLAND, that I totally deny,—get rid of this by a Quibble if you can,—and I can tell you how to do it, say, that part of the Family was in the Room at the time you eat your Chop.

YOU have thought proper, Sir, to introduce the name of Mr. M. A. TAYLOR, it is true that his Name was mentioned at the Meeting you allude to, but your Informant is not perfectly correct in the Report he has thought proper to make to you. Mr. TAYLOR is still a Friend to the Town and has still its Interest at Heart; and if he were again to become a Candidate, depend upon it that as "the burnt Child dreads the fire," he would be very cautious to whom he entrusted his Agency; and it is astonishing to me that you could have the Temerity of introducing his Name; for you may be assured he has still his Recollections about him.

THE Signatures which you have obtained to a Declaration respecting the Pledge is not easily to be accounted for, unless these Gentlemen have drank deep of the Waters of Lethe, and nothing else can possibly excuse them, as we can prove on Oath and which can be corroborated by many respectable Witnesses that what was before asserted is a Fact.

ONE of the Gentlemen who has thought proper to sign it, was never supposed to be of the Party that made the Stipulation, and one I observe you have omitted, who is ready to verify on Oath the Truth of what was asserted; and which you yourself have repeatedly acknowledged to be true since your return from London, excusing yourself for not fulfilling your promise by being obliged, as you say to call at BURLINGTON HOUSE, THE ADMIRALTY, &c. &c. &c.

THE Honor which you have done me by implication in your Address of this day, as supposing me the Secretary of a Committee, demands my warmest acknowledgments, as it is a Credit which I did not expect. How many Committees was you on during the last Parliament? *None I believe.*

YOU have observed that the Extract of the Letter which was quoted, was to make known the Independence and honorable Feelings of the writer—it you had stopped there you would have been right, but that would not answer your purpose— there was a libellous Inuendo annexed, which I disclaim, and I defy you to prove—yes, Sir, I defy you to prove it, as I stand too high, not only in the Eyes of your Constituents but also in the County of Dorset, to be wounded by the poisoned Shafts of your malevolence, of which your Quiver seems to be full—————— Let it be known, Sir, to all the world that the humble Competency I possess, is the fruit of honest Industry; what I have obtained was the Fruit of no Bargain, the production of *no Intrigue*, the Result of no Compromise, the Effect of no Solicitation—the real Property that I am in possession of was acquired by fair and honorable means, without Treasury Favour or Ministerial Influence—I have never abused the Trust of a Family of Orphans, or taken any Advantage of the Laws Delay; I have never courted popularity at the Expence of my Fortune, nor ever attempted to soar on the Wings of Ambition, out of the Sight of my Family; I am not conscious of the Guilt of moral or political Turpitude—I have never been a Public Informer—you cannot charge me with driving two Gentlemen from Parliament and of Consequence to a new Election, for being Contractors, tho' you know it was in my power to drive ONE.

I SHALL conclude without passing any Comments on your bold Assertion "that your Conduct in this as in every "other Instance has been perfectly consistent" this Assertion I leave to your best Friends to support if they can.

The SECRETARY.

IT is not at all surprising that Mr. JEFFERY should have forgotten the Conversation he held with Mr. GARLAND the first day of his arrival in London, after declaring to Mr. SEAGER Junr. and others yesterday, that he did not even recollect calling on Mr. GARLAND at all on that day, and expressed himself very much obliged to Mr. SEAGER for reminding him of it; And it is still less extraordinary that this Gentleman should with so treacherous a Memory recollect only a part of the Conversation which took place on the subject of Sir RICHARD BICKERTON on that day. Mr. GARLAND however pledges himself to prove on Oath, if necessary, that Mr. JEFFERY did say and that in the most positive and direct Terms, in the presence of Mr. AUDRA, that *if he had known before that the Steps he had taken would have been disagreeable to Mr. GARLAND, he would not have made the Attempt of introducing a third Person,* this can also be supported by the Oath of Mr. AUDRA.

POOLE, May 13, 1807.

JOSEPH GARLAND.

Moore, Printer, Poole.

at the Antelope where they had evidently stopped to refresh themselves. Elections then were far from democratic but certainly much more lively and dangerous than those of today.

Of course it was not just during elections that members of the Corporation and other Poole people of lesser rank were able to enjoy themselves. National events such as the King's Birthday or Coronation, the anniversary of the Gunpowder Plot, and the news of great victories or the making of peace were celebrated vigorously. After the defeat of Bonnie Prince Charlie at Culloden in 1746 the Corporation led off the celebrations and "in the evening the whole town..... was finely illuminated and a select number of gentlemen assembled at the house of Mr. Dudley Diggs on the Quay, when the loyal toasts were frequently repeated in full bumpers of excellent arrack and two half hogsheads of strong beer given to the populace at the expense of Messrs. Christopher Jolliff and George Tito, merchants".

Sometimes political differences caused trouble during such rejoicings as in 1798 when the town celebrated Nelson's destruction of the French fleet in Egypt. Those who did not illuminate their

View of Poole from Parkstone

windows had them broken by the mob and the Mayor-elect, and M.P. for the town, John Jeffery, found himself summoned before the Magistrates for his part in the disorders.

Looking back on the state of the town in the early years of the 18th century, we can see that Poole was enjoying an Indian summer shortly to be ended by the bitter controversies aroused by parliamentary and municipal reform in the 1830's. Although the Newfoundland trade fell away with the coming of peace, there were high hopes that it would be supplemented by commerce with the West Indies and South America. In any case peace would provide a revival of Poole's important links with continental ports and her valuable coasting trade with other British ports.

The Corporation could take pride in the way in which it had defended and advanced the interests of the borough. Although its members had been often corrupt and self-seeking it had in the main looked to the benefit of the town as a whole, especially in fighting off the attacks on the borough's rights made by the Lord of the Manor of Canford throughout the 1700's. The Webb family

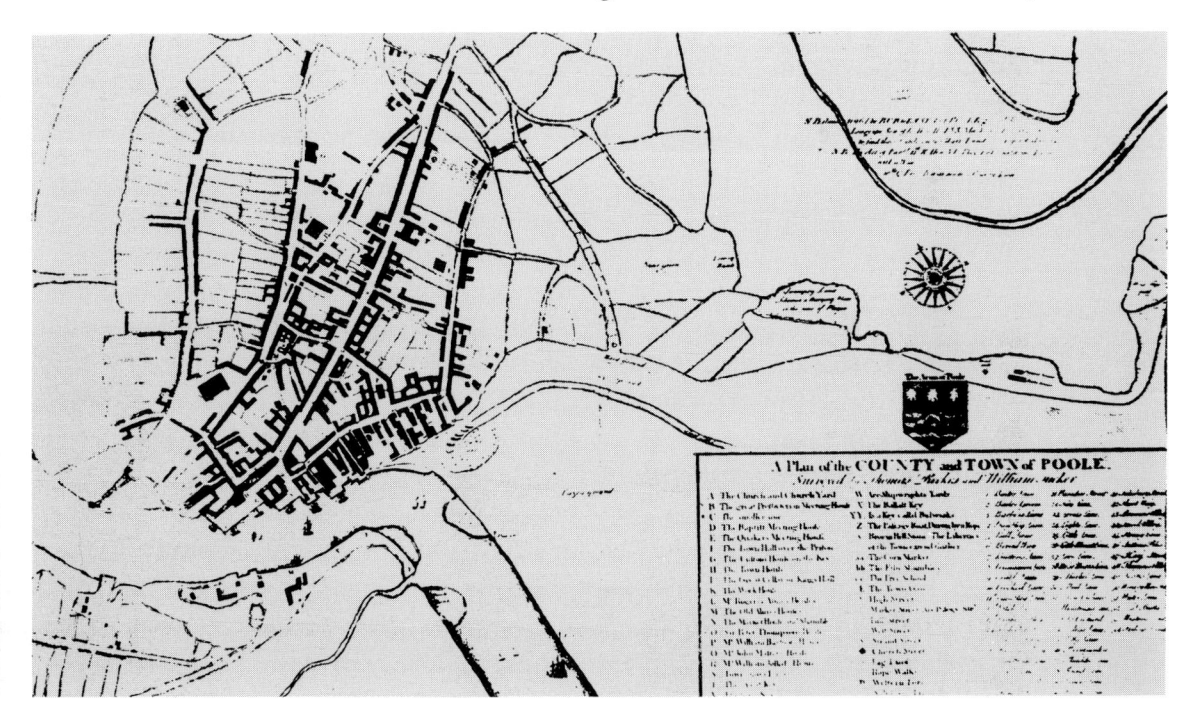

Map of Poole 1751

View of Parkstone and Poole Harbour from Constitution Hill

at Canford had tried by all means to claim authority over all of the heath and mudlands surrounding the town of Poole and if they had been successful the development of the borough would have been severely checked. Poole's leaders had responded manfully to the many challenges and had sometimes not been content with fighting expensive law suits. Physical force was used at times to overthrow the fences and other symbols of the Lord of Canford's claims to land which Poole men proudly insisted belonged to them. Now in the early 19th century those battles were over — the last of the Webbs had died without male heirs and by an Enclosure Act, adequate land around Poole had been provided for her continued growth. Moreover, by 1825, Canford had passed under the control of a new owner, William Ponsonby, who was anxious to be on good terms with Poole.

The improvements in the borough, in which the Corporation naturally played a part, made many Poole people confident that the new found peace would be prosperous. Road improvements opened up access from the High Street to the still lengthening quays. There were good prospects that a bridge would be built from Poole to Hamworthy which it was hoped would place Poole in a more advantageous position on a main route into the West of England. Already the importance of the town had been recognised by the extension in 1817 of the Royal Mail coach service into Poole and the turnpike roads to Wimborne and Longham were being improved by the lowering of Gravel Hill and other steep gradients. Just outside the old northern boundaries of the town a new and more fashionable area of housing was beginning to develop in Longfleet and was soon to be adorned with its own church, consecrated in 1833. Parkstone too was no longer "a rude hamlet" but was becoming another more fashionable area attracting wealthy residents from many parts of the country. Here also a church was consecrated in 1833.

Regrettably, the pride and confidence which Poole people felt in the promise of the early 19th century were soon to be shattered. Parliamentary and municipal reform proved to be too heady a mixture for the leaders of the town.

Scaplen's Court (The Old Town House)

In the period between 1790 and 1830, between the French Revolution and the accession of King William IV, the political institutions of Great Britain had remained frozen in a posture which every year became more archaic. In the last quarter of the 18th century the cause of parliamentary reform had been, if not universally accepted, at least respectable. It was supported not only by Fox, but by William Pitt, with all the enthusiasm that such a man of prudence was capable. Therefore it would have been a reasonable assumption, that by the end of the 18th century at least the worst of the current abuses would be cured.

With the storming of the Bastille, the cause of moderate reform was entirely discredited overnight, and as the terror rose, the fervour of the conservative element rose with it, until even to imply that the British Constitution was less than perfect had bloody connotations. Even the most stalwart supporter of reform, who had refused to be panicked by the early events, lost enthusiasm when the 'blissful dawn' of Wordsworth gave way to the sullen twilight of an authoritarian Empire

'Britons Strike Home', Peterloo 1819

Extract
FROM THE
SPEECH
OF
The Right Honourable WILLIAM PITT,
ON MOVING FOR
A REFORM
IN THE
Representation of the People in Parliament,
May 7, 1782.

"THE Representation of the Commons in Parliament was a matter so truly Interesting, that it had at all times excited the regard of men the most enlightened; and the defects which they had found in that Representation, had given them reason to apprehend the most alarming consequences to the Constitution."

"That the frame of our Constitution had undergone material alterations, by which the Commons' House of Parliament had received an improper and dangerous bias, and by which indeed, it had fallen so greatly from that direction and effect which it was intended, and ought to have in the Constitution, he believed it would be idle for him to attempt to prove. It was a fact so plain and palpable, that every man's reason, if not his experience, must point it out to him. He had only to examine the quality and nature of that branch of the Constitution as originally established. That beautiful frame of Government which had made us the envy and admiration of mankind, in which the people were entitled to hold such a distinguished share, was so far dwindled and departed from its original purity, as *that the Representatives ceased, in a great degree, to be connected with the people,*— It was the essence of the Constitution, that the people had a share in the Government by the means of Representation, and its excellence and permanency were calculated to consist in this Representation, having been designed to be equal, easy, practicable, and complete. When it ceased to be so; when the Representative ceased to be connected with the Constituent, and was either dependant on the Crown or the Aristocracy, there was a defect in the frame of Representation, and *it was not innovation, but recovery of Constitution to repair it.*"

"He believed that there was not a Gentleman in the House but who would acknowledge with him, that the Representation, as it now stood, was incomplete. *It was perfectly understood that there were some Boroughs absolutely Governed by the Treasury, and others totally possessed by them.* It required no experience to say that such Boroughs had no one quality of Representation in them; they had no share nor substance in the general interests of the Country; and they had, in fact, no stake for which to appoint their Guardians in the popular Assembly. The influence of the Treasury in some Boroughs was contested, not by the electors of these Boroughs, but by some one or other powerful man, who assumed, or pretended to, an hereditary property of what ought only to be the rights and privileges of the Electors. *The interests of the Treasury were considered, as well as the interests of the great man, the Lord or the Commoner, who had connection with the Borough;* BUT THE INTERESTS OF THE PEOPLE, THE RIGHTS OF THE ELECTORS, WERE THE ONLY THINGS THAT NEVER WERE ATTENDED TO, NOR TAKEN INTO THE ACCOUNT. Would any man say, that in this Case there was the most distant idea, or principle of Representation?"

AN Account of Expences
ATTENDING
A PUBLIC FESTIVAL,

Held at POOLE, on Tuesday, 26th July, 1814,

TO CELEBRATE

The Return of PEACE to EUROPE.

cwt. qrs. lbs.		£	s.	d.
35 1 2 Beef, at 74s. 8d. per cwt.		131	13	4
4 0 0 Suet, at 74s. 8d. per cwt.		14	18	8
4 Sacks Flour, at 55s. per Sack		11	0	0
710 Loaves, at 4½d. each		13	6	3
12 Sacks Potatoes, at 8s. 6d. per Sack		5	2	0
Salt		3	1	3
939 Eggs, at 1d. each		3	18	3
49 Gallons Milk, at 1s. 3d. per gallon		2	18	9
4 cwt. Raisins		18	1	0
Spices		1	9	6
Making 420 Puddings		1	16	0
1280 Gallons Strong Beer, at 1s. 6d. per gallon		96	0	0
11 Gross of Pipes, at 3s. per gross		1	13	0
12 Dozen Snuff Boxes, at 3d. each		1	16	0
16 Pounds Tobacco		4	8	0
8 Pounds Snuff		1	18	4
Earthenware		6	2	6
Baking		4	5	6
Pudding Cloths		4	6	11
Tea, &c. in the Field, during the display of Fire Works		12	17	0
Musicians		9	9	0
Labour erecting 70 Tables in the Market Place and adjoining Streets, at which about 5,000 persons dined, and fitting up a Booth in the Field, Materials lost, damaged, &c.		96	10	7
Printing, &c.		10	17	0
Balance paid the Treasurer of the Lancasterian Free School, for the use of that Institution		5	15	8
		£463	2	6
Amount of Subscriptions		£463	2	6

SAMUEL CLARK,
CHAIRMAN OF THE COMMITTEE FOR MANAGING
THE ABOVE PUBLIC FESTIVAL.

The inhabitants of Poole, throughout the wars of the French Revolution, were swept along with the patriotic fervour that united the nation, despite the adverse effect on their own commercial pursuits by the imposition of embargoes and blockades. In addition to the establishment of 'armed volunteer associations', public subscriptions were repeatedly made for various purposes connected with the defence of the country, and for the relief of the wounded soldiers and seamen and their families.

On one occasion, at a public meeting of the inhabitants, held at the Guildhall on 27th February 1798, books were opened for the reception of voluntary contributions towards the defence of the country, and no less than thirteen hundred pounds were immediately subscribed. On the previous day, the Corporation had voted a sum of five hundred pounds from their funds. Poole had also been designated as a general rendezvous for the militia regiments and thus had a garrison town appearance for a few years.

However, despite all the overt patriotism displayed by the inhabitants, several Poole vessels secretly broke the blockade of the Continent and made enormous profits on the discreet sale of 'unobtainable' goods such as French wine. Some of the more prominent merchant families made substantial additions to their wealth in this manner.

When the news of Napoleon's abdication was received in 1814 the celebrations of peace took a democratic shape in Poole, reminiscent of the street parties held to celebrate the end of the Second World War. A feast was arranged for 5,000 people, the Mayor alone sitting in a special place, "every other individual, gentle and simple promiscuously mixed". George Garland, one of the town's leading citizens, provided "one honest plum pudding of about a hundred weight" and the proceedings ended with a firework display.

After the final defeat of Napoleon, it might have been possible for moderate reform to be respectably resurrected, but the civil disorders in the England of 1815 and 1816 suggested to the establishment that any move in this direction might launch the country down the corpse-strewn path towards the tumbrels and the guillotine.

The Industrial Revolution was then raising great problems of unemployment and in the administration of the rising towns of the North. The Enclosure Acts had robbed thousands of the peasantry of the lands from which they had obtained their livlihood, and they had flocked into the towns looking for work. Radical groups had arisen inciting the malcontents and the out-of-work to rebellion, culminating in the Peterloo Massacre at Manchester, and the burning of the Guildhall at Bristol. The Government became fearful of the consequences and the quickly passed 'Six Acts' were designed to stop the agitation by force of law.

However, the crusade for reform continued and people began to believe that all their ills and all their tribulations would be cured if they could only reform Parliament.

The sort of feeling which was general then was satirised by Sydney Smith when he wrote "Ladies imagine they will be instantly married. Schoolboys believe that currant tarts must ultimately come down in price; corporal and sergeant are sure of double pay; bad poets will expect a demand for their epics; fools will be disappointed, as they always are".

Poole inhabitants like the Corporation at the time had felt that way for some time. Wm. Adey Esq., High Sheriff, called a public meeting of Poole's inhabitants and freeholders in the Guildhall on 23rd January 1821. "The very perilous and awful State of the Country claims the solemn attention of everyman", the proposed resolutions started. "We cannot hope for any change or improvement in our situation so long as the administration of public affairs is confided to the hands of any set of ministers who shall not prove to be really and practically responsible to Parliament". The Petition from the inhabitants of Poole to Parliament ended "your Petitioners ..... have been long fully impressed with a conviction that the only permanent security against a continuing mal-administration of the affairs of the nation is to be sought in an effectual Reform in the Representation of the People in Parliament".

Happily at this time Peel reduced the temperature a little by abolishing the death penalty for many crimes and Huskisson suppressed tariffs on the import of many raw materials and reduced some prices and, in

Schooner Sylph of Poole, David Pidding Master

1828, the Duke of Wellington abrogated the Test Act and Corporation Acts to allow dissenters to hold office in State and in the town Corporations.

Poole's trade, however, recovered greatly from the previous years' depressions in 1824 and Poole was relatively quiet until the end of the following year. At long last it seemed as if Poole would be linked by canal with the West Country. A Dorset and Somerset canal scheme had been projected back in 1793 and Poole merchants then took a keen interest in the possibility of a direct link with Bristol which might be made either by Wimborne or Wareham. The canal was a casualty of the war with France, but the revival of interest in a canal between Poole and Bridgewater in 1825 similarly produced no results. In fact it wasn't till March 1826, that the Dorset Chronicle reported of Poole, "The embarrassments which have been for some time past so severely felt in other parts of the Kingdom, at length affects this town

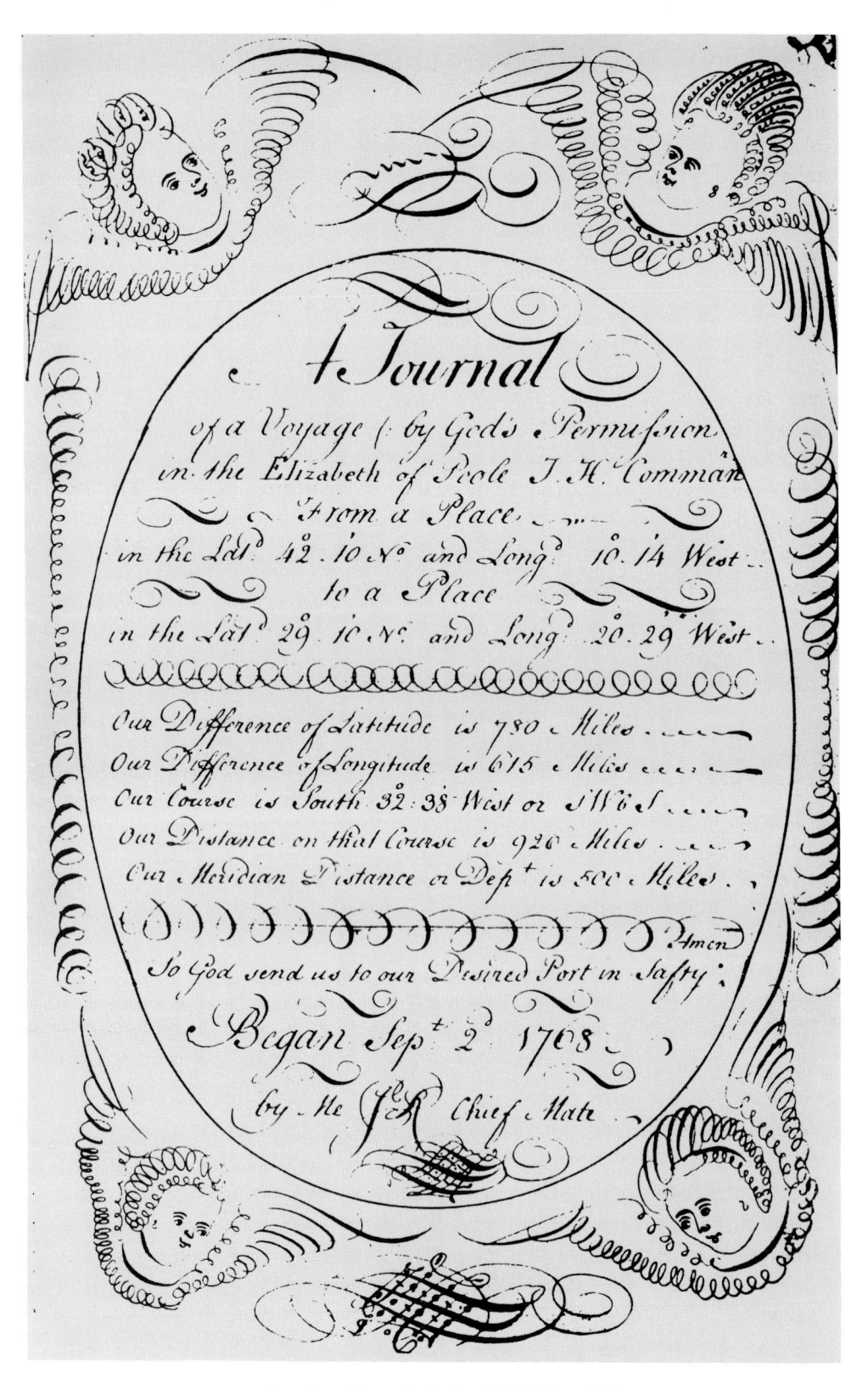

A Journal
of a Voyage (by God's Permission)
in the Elizabeth of Poole J. H. Comman.
From a Place
in the Lat.^{d} 42.10 N.^{o} and Long.^{d} 10.14 West
to a Place
in the Lat.^{d} 29.10 N.^{o} and Long.^{d} 20.29 West

Our Difference of Latitude is 780 Miles
Our Difference of Longitude is 615 Miles
Our Course is South 32.38 West or S W b S
Our Distance on that Course is 920 Miles
Our Meridian Distance or Dep.^{t} is 500 Miles

Amen
So God send us to our Desired Port in Safty:

Began Sep.^{t} 2 1768
by Me J^{c}R Chief Mate

Page from Journal of a local Chief Mate 1768

and neighbourhood. Business is at a standstill, and scarcely any money is in circulation: it is sincerely hoped that an amendment will shortly take place. Otherwise the evil effect which may issue will be great".

It was with this background that 1830 dawned in Poole — the year of revolutions against Kings and governments in Europe and which was brought home dramatically to Poole people. There were revolutions in Belgium, Spain and Italy and there was a new peasants' revolt in the South of England, with the rural labourers claiming a minimum wage of 14/-. They acted collectively and therefore their action was illegal and contrary to the Riot Act. There were incendiaries at work at Canford and in Parkstone and Lytchett threshing machines were destroyed: the Lord of the Manor of Canford and Poole enrolled over 200 special constables immediately afterwards but were happily not needed. Other areas were less fortunate and three men were hanged and no less than 400 sent to transportation.

But the revolution which had the most dramatic effect in Poole was that in France in 1830 and which led to Charles X of France sailing into Poole Harbour after the July rising against him in France.

It was said in Poole that the first substantial steamboat to come into Poole Harbour was the British Navy's "Meteor" which came in on 22nd August, 1830, to prepare for the arrival of Charles X and his family and huge entourage the following day. It was met by Joseph Gulston Garland, the Mayor, and D. O. Lander, the Collector of Customs, who took them to eat and discuss arrangements for the King's arrival to the Antelope Hotel.

The next day the Navy's "Comet" arrived with the King and his enormous entourage of Princesses, Dukes, Countesses, Physicians and others. Their ships landed on the Hamworthy side of the Quay and were met by the Mayor and Mr. Lander. The King and his immediate court went straight to Mr. Weld's Lulworth Castle in the carriages provided by Mr. Doughty of Upton House and Mr. George Welch Ledgard, a previous Mayor of Poole and the very respected Banker and Magistrate.

The rest of the King's entourage was somehow squeezed into the Ante-

WHEREAS

NOTICE has been given by the Visitor and Guardians of the Poor that "*a Public Meeting to consult the owners or occupiers of Lands, Tenements or Hereditaments assessed after the rate of five Pounds per Annum, about nominating for the approbation of the Magistrates, three proper persons to fill the office of Governor of the Poor House, pursuant to the Statute of the 22nd Year of GEO. the third, will be held in the Parish Church of St. James, Poole, at ten o'Clock in the forenoon, on Tuesday the 27th day of this present month December.*"

We, therefore, the undersigned, take this method of impressing on the minds of the Public, that, by the Statute before mentioned, the Meeting to be held as above, will have the power of nominating three persons for Governor of the Poor House, and that, *one* of the three must subsequently be *appointed* by the *Magistrates*. Also, that although the Magistrates have *unwarrantably been canvassed* for their support in behalf of *one Individual*, all persons desirous of the situation, are still at liberty to offer themselves as Candidates for the same, at the time and place above mentioned.

SAMUEL WESTON, Mayor.
SAMUEL CLARK, J. P.
JAMES SEAGER, J. P.
CHRIST. JOLLIFF, J. P.

Poole, Dec. 19th, 1814.

Controversy over appointment of 'Poor House' Governors

lope Hotel and London Tavern to await the unloading of the twelve state carriages which Charles had somehow managed to bring out of France with him.

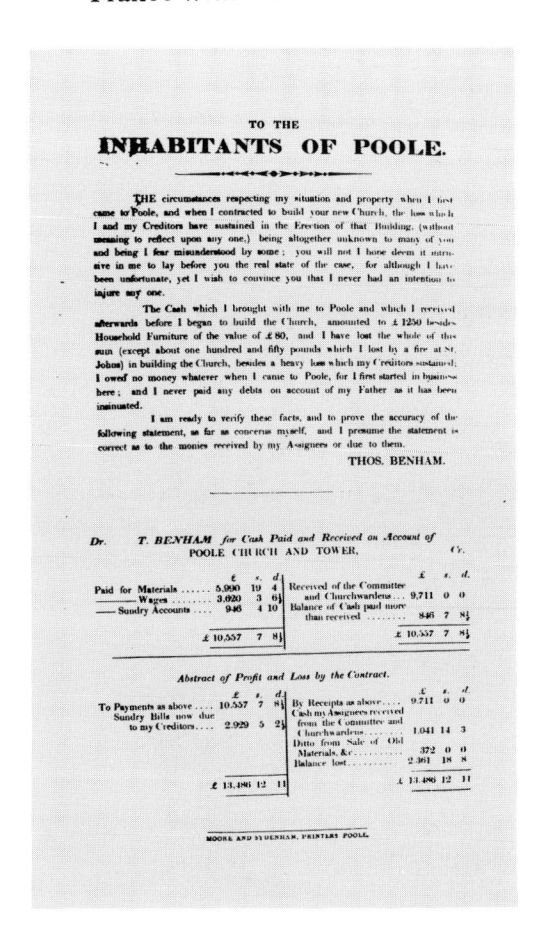

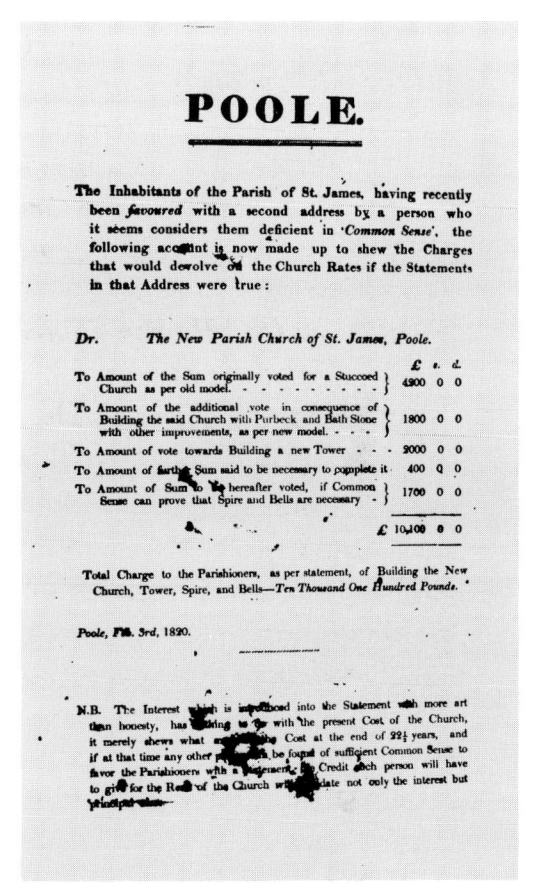

Disputed costs of building the new St. James

As a forerunner to the bitter rivalries that characterized the town in the 1830's and 1840's, the conduct of parish affairs in the early 19th century was the subject of many disputes published in numerous hand bills and open letters.

The fixing of the 'Poor Rate', the appointment of Charity Commissioners, and even the rebuilding of St. James, occasioned charges and countercharges. The new church (present one) was reconsecrated in 1820 and contains the many gifts and memorials of the major personalities who were active in the town at this time; a sculpture of the

St. James Church before rebuilding

royal arms of England, presented by George Ledgard in 1821, an organ presented by Benjamin Lester in 1799, among others, and memorials of the Thompsons', Jolliffes', Seagers', Hydes', Slades', Phippards', Brices', Parrs', and Spurriers'.

Meanwhile, George IV had died in the June and had been succeeded by his brother, William IV, an elderly and more popular man and, at the Election that year, the Whigs who had then recently espoused the cause of the Reformers were suddenly a party of popular interest. The Whig votes, supplemented by those of the Reformers, many of them composed of nonconformists and of the rising middle-classes, who felt they should have a say in government commensurate with their new standing, won the day. The Tories were ousted from power after fifty years of government despite their ownership of the great majority of the "rotten boroughs".

But in Poole it was only the old Burgesses of the Corporation who voted in the election of the Members. They had already returned two Members in favour of reform and there was consequently no change. Benjamin Lester Lester and the Lord of the Manor of Canford and Poole, William Francis Spencer Ponsonby, were elected again as they **both had been in the previous election.**

Thus Poole's two representatives in Parliament elected only by the old corporators (as the freemen of the Corporation called themselves) were among those Whigs in Parliament who, in 1830, voted for the first Reform Bill which passed the Commons with a majority of one. This vote, however, was insufficient to force such an important measure on the House of Lords who were known to be against the Bill.

Lord Grey persuaded the new King to dissolve the Parliament and hold further elections. Poole's Whig Lord of the Manor and its old trusted Merchant, B. L. Lester, were duly returned again and a Whig majority in the new Parliament was 136 and there was country-wide rejoicing as though the battle had been won.

But the rejoicing was premature. The Bill had still to be re-drafted and still had to pass both the Commons and the Lords before it could become law.

Map of the Town of Poole 1821

In the National Commercial Directory of 1830 Poole was described as:

"A Borough — Town and sea-port, is 113 miles from London, 27 from Dorchester, 16 from Blandford, and six from Wimborne. It takes its name from the bay, on the north side of which it is situated; and is a peninsula, adjoining the parish of Canford, connected by an isthmus or neck of land. This is the most considerable port, and most populous town, in the county. In general the buildings are respectable, and many very handsome. The principal trade from Poole is to Newfoundland, which at one time was very considerable: its exports consist of provisions nets, cordage, and all sorts of wearing apparel — in short, of commodities of every kind for the supply of Newfoundland. The manufactures of the town and neighbourhood embrace rope, twine, and sailcloth: here are also ship-building yards, which employ many hands; and the corn-trade is very considerable, both in its imports and exports. The importations besides are cod and salmon, for foreign markets; and oil, seal-skins and cranberries, principally for home consumption. The oyster-trade here employs a great number of boats; large quantities are sent to the London market; and other fish are taken in the harbour in great abundance, amongst which the plaice and herrings are esteemed particularly. Queen Elizabeth made Poole a corporate and free town, and formed it into a distinct county, by the title of "the county of the town of Poole" appointing its own sheriff, in the same manner as the county and town of Southampton. The corporation consists of a mayor, four aldermen, and 28 burgesses. The mayor is chosen out of the burgesses, and is always a justice of the peace; and when his year is expired commences alderman, and is senior bailiff and justice of the peace for the year ensuing; he is also admiral within the liberties, and was anciently mayor of the staple. The right of election of members of parliament is lodged in the mayor, aldermen, and burgesses within and without the town; and the indenture is executed by them, and the sheriff, who is the returning officer. The present representatives are Benjamin Lester Lester Esq. of this town, and the Hon. William Francis Spencer Ponsonby, of Canford Magna. The mayor and senior burgesses hold a court, in the guildhall, for the recovery of debts; and sessions are held for the borough, by the mayor, four times a year.

The public buildings are, the church, four chapels belonging to the dissenters, a very neat meeting-house for the society of friends; the town hall, the market-house and the prison. The church is a beautiful modern edifice, rebuilt in 1821, at an expense exceeding £20,000; it is dedicated

The Parish Church of St. James rebuilt in 1821

Rev. P. W. Jolliff
Minister of the Parish Church of St. James

Engraving of the Independent Chapel, Poole circa 1821

to St. James: the living is a rectory, in the gift of the corporation; the Rev. P. W. Jolliff is the present incumbent. The charities of Poole are free-schools and alms-houses, with periodical gifts dispensed to the poor, arising from bequests and benefactions. In the vicinity of Poole are several seats and tasteful marine residences, which contribute most essentially to improve the aspect of the country, naturally hilly and barren; but the bay-view, with its several islands and vessels, presents an interesting and animated appearance. In the 30th of Henry III, Poole obtained the grant of a market on Thursday; and two fairs annually — one on the feast of St. Philip and St. James and seven succeeding days, and another on All Souls' day and seven days succeeding: there is also a small market held on Mondays. The population of the town and county of Poole, in 1821, was 6,390".

"Post Office — Letters from London arrive every morning at a quarter-past ten, and are despatched every afternoon at half-past four. Letters from Wareham arrive every morning at a quarter-past four, and are despatched at half-past ten".

In this same Directory there were listed 75 men as "Nobility, Gentry and Clergy" among whom were Capt. Stephen Adey; Edward Doughty of Upton House; Capt. Henry Festing of Ponsonby Place, Parkstone; Joseph Garland of the Mansion House, Thames Street; George Garland of Standley Green Cottage; Francis Penton Garland of Longfleet; George Hancock of Fish Street; Rev. Peter Jolliff of Sterte; William Jolliffe of Bayhog Lane; Charles Hiley of Planefield House; George Kemp of Market Street; James Kemp of 69 High Street; Benjamin Lester Lester (M.P.) of 65 High Street; George Lockyer Parrott of West Street; Richard Pinney of Hamworthy; James Seager of West Street; Isaac Steele of 21 Parade; Thomas Strong of Seldown House; Gilbert Tulloch of Skinner Street, and Joseph Wadham of 40 High Street.

Many of these "Gentry and Clergy" were to be the **dramatis personae** of Poole's future dramas. There were, however, others differently listed. There were, for instance, under "Agents" George Penney on the Quay; under "Attorneys" Thomas Arnold; Durant and Welch with offices in Hill Street and High Street; John Foot, the Town Clerk with offices in West Street; Robert Henning Parr and Richard Parr in Fish Street, as well as Sharp and Aldridge at 166 High Street. John Conway and William

Green were two of eighteen "Bakers and Flour dealers". Among the three Bankers we find Fryer, Andrews and Co., at the "Old Bank" High Street and Ledgard, Welch and Co., the Poole Town and County Bank, also in the High Street.

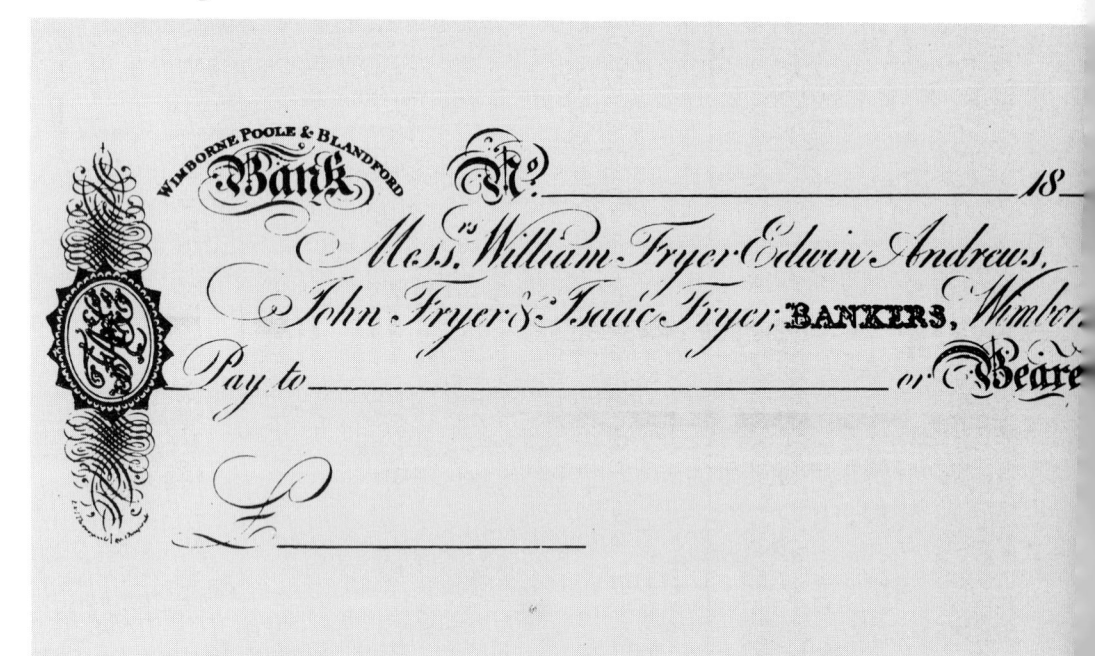

Specimen of the type of cheque issued by Fryer, Andrews and Co.

There were no less than thirteen ship and boat builders listed — firms whose ships had been the mainspring of Poole's prosperity — the Garlands, Spurriers, Slades, Barters and Manlaws and Messrs. Fryer, Gosse and Pack. There were just two printers who were later to be kept so busy with Poole's internecine strife: John Lankester at 92 High Street and Moore and Sydenham at 105 High Street.

Rather surprisingly there were 14 Boot and Shoe Repairers, and, perhaps showing the effect of the supplies once going from Poole to Newfoundland, there were 13 linen drapers, ten of them clustered together between 82 and 147 High Street. There were, too, 5 Brewers and Maltsters, headed by Thomas and William Adey, and among the Coopers was Benjamin Wadham and George Major. The Corn Merchants comprised James Aldridge on the Quay and Tom Rickman — also a maltster and seedsman — in North Street.

Opposite: 'The Angel' Tavern, Poole

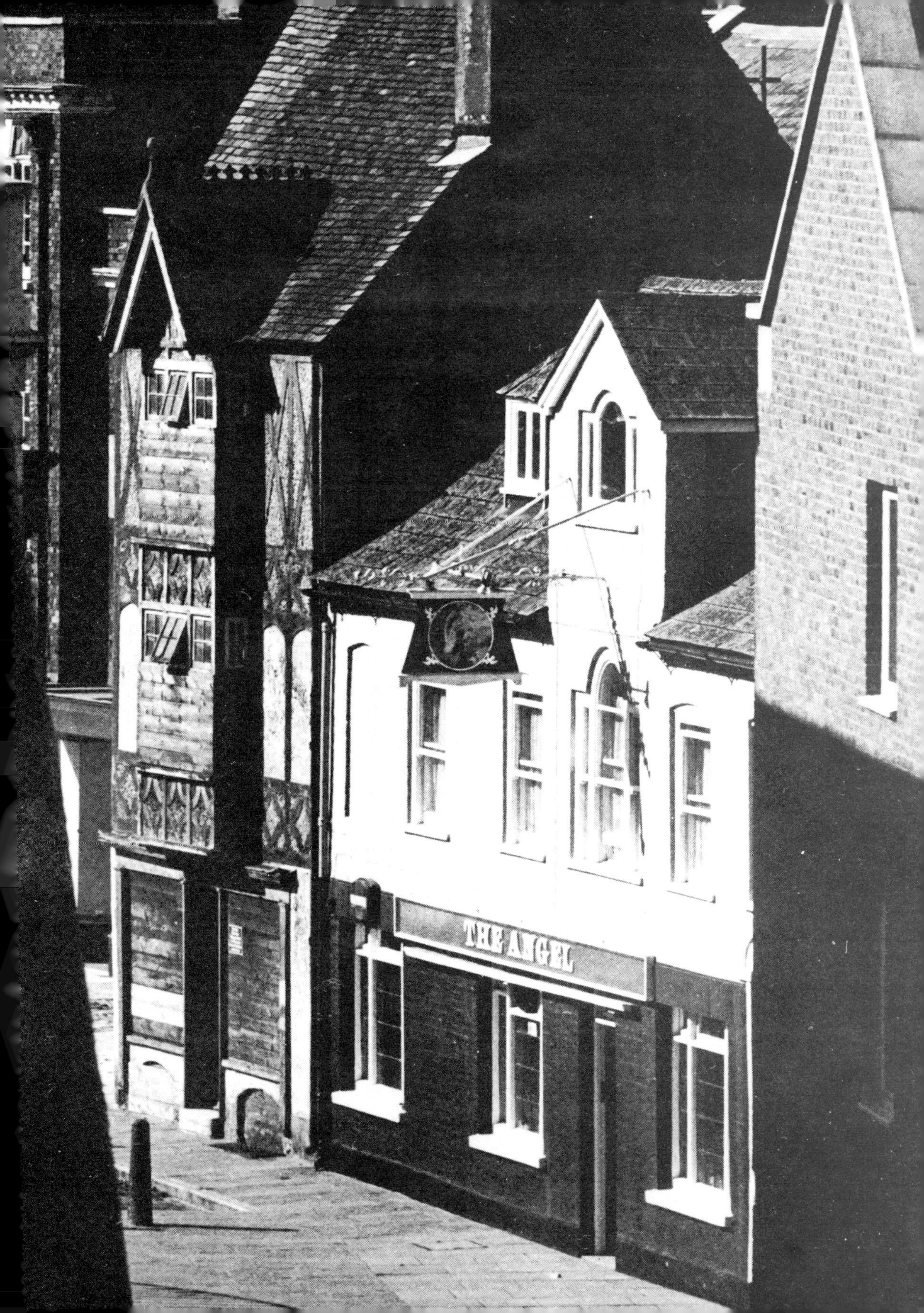
THE ANGEL

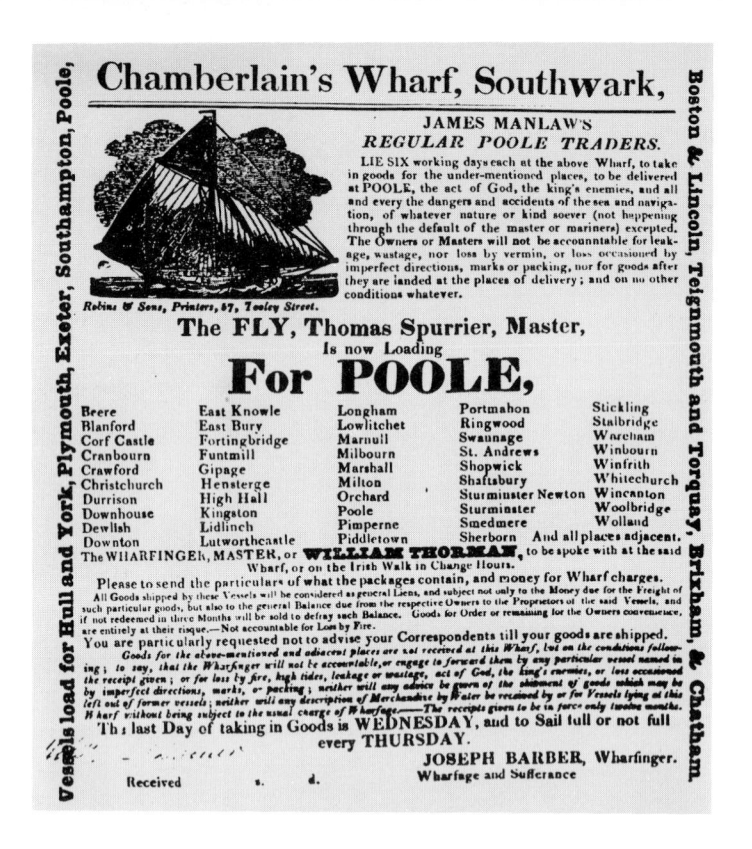

There were then in Poole four Inns and Hotels — the Angel in Market Place at the side of the Guildhall; the Bull's Head at 97 High Street, and the two more important ones, the Old Antelope at 162 High Street and the London Tavern (now the Old Harry) run by Richard Roope Linthorne at 84 High Street.

Finally, there were the ubiquitous taverns and public houses — 36 of them, one tavern for each 200 men, women and children! The list was headed by the "Air Balloon" in West Street and no less than eleven actually on the Quay — the Coach and Horses, the Dolphin, Eight Bells, Jolly Sailor, King and Queen, King's Arms, Lion and Lamb, Lord Nelson, Poole Arms, Portsmouth Hoy and the Two Brothers.

It was from public houses that carriers picked up goods for transit in their horse-drawn wagons. The Lion and Lamb and the Lord Nelson on the Quay were used in this way but probably more often it was the New Antelope, the Bulls Head or the Crown. There were 21 carriers of goods in Poole in 1830 and they made between them no less than 33 regular runs every week, not only to nearby towns such as Christchurch, Wimborne and Ringwood or to Dorset towns such as Shaftesbury, Bridport and Gillingham, but to places as far away as London and Bristol.

But the main form of carriage of goods was still by sea. Even the slow sailing ships were preferable and cheaper than transport by horse-drawn wagons over the sketchy roads of the time and there were a dozen Poole ships sailing regularly between Poole and London, half of them owned by James Manlaws and half operated by J. Barter Bloomfield. There were, too, five vessels sailing regularly from Poole to the Channel Isles, three ships a week to Portsmouth and one to Southampton, as well as a regular delivery of coal from vessels to and from Newcastle.

Perhaps, though, the regular passenger coaches shed the most interesting light on the activities and importance of Poole at the time. Although it was always possible then to hire a horse and carriage for the day or for a special journey, the ordinary form of travel inland was by coach. In Poole these coaches always started at the Angel or the Old Antelope. "The Age" coach set out each morning at 6 o'clock from the Old Antelope to go to London via Wimborne, Ringwood and Southampton. Three times a week "The Wellington" set out for Bristol via Wimborne, Blandford, Shaftesbury, Gillingham, Stourhead and Frome, and "The Independant" called in each day at 1.30 p.m. on its journey from Weymouth to Southampton or its counterpart's journey back from Southampton to Weymouth. There was, too, a coach three times a week from the Angel going to Salisbury.

One of the usual sights of Poole in those days was still the dog-cart. The Newfoundland dogs were considered the best dogs for this and Poole was the centre for such dogs. One, two or three dogs were harnessed to a shallow cart of about two feet wide and a yard long and these dogs were used for local haulage and domestic work around the narrow streets of Poole as well as for fast relays in the delivery of fresh fish to towns along the south coast and even to London.

It wasn't until 1850 that Parliament made illegal the use of dogs in this way but the practice died hard in Poole for a Mr. James Bugden was prosecuted in the Guildhall and fined for using a dog cart in 1853.

The Royal Mails departure from the General Post Office, London

The Mail for Poole leaving the Gloucester Coffee House, Piccadilly

The Brig 'Robert' of Poole John Hall, Master

From the late 17th century until 1815 Poole had been enjoying a prolonged period of prosperity due to the pre-eminence which the Poole Merchants had been fortunate to achieve in the Newfoundland Trade. Barnstaple, Bideford and other Western ports, which had once ranked as 'great towns' among the western adventurers, had drawn out, and only Dartmouth had remained with a share of the trade in fish, whale meat, oil and furs in which Poole was the 'metropolis'.

Throughout the 18th century Britain was dominant on the high seas, the European countries were short of food and Poole ships could sell at high prices as much of their dried cod fish as they could deliver. Owing to the innumerable continental wars, wine was in short supply in England, and the Poole ships bartered their fish for wine and on reaching London or Poole, this in turn, fetched high prices. By the time of the Treaty of Amiens in 1802 Poole had amassed a fleet of over 350 ships and trade had not been as great, or as profitable since the 'High Medieval' period of the 14th and 15th centuries.

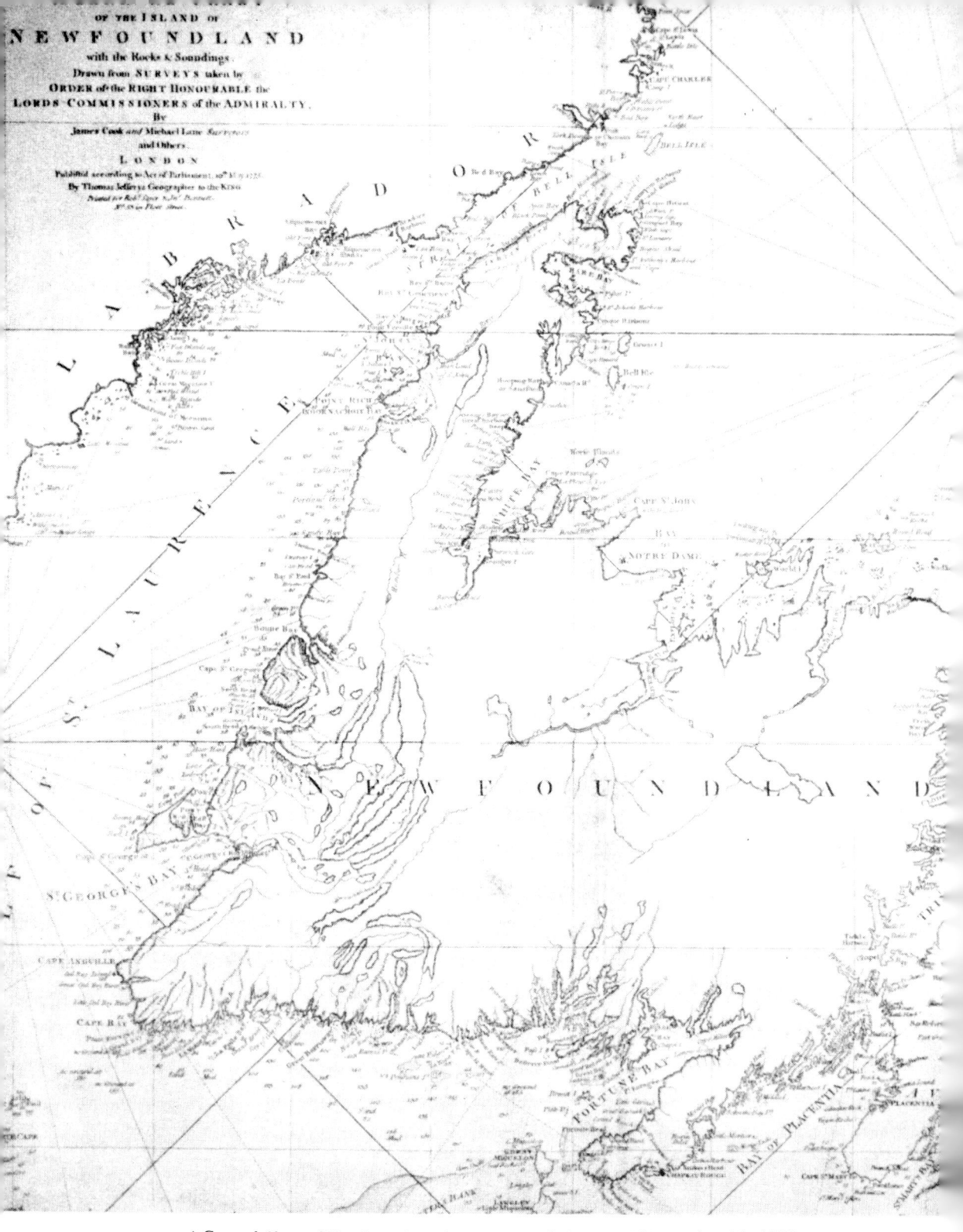

A General Chart of Newfoundland from a book of Charts and Plans printed in 1778

John Bingley Garland 1791–1857
Mayor 1824

The firm of 'Harrison, Slade and Co.', were called the "millionaire firm of Poole", while the Kemps, the Spurriers, the Lesters, the Garlands, and others had similarly thrived in the 18th century, many of them becoming 'Merchant Princes' and living accordingly. George Garland had moved to Stone House at Wimborne; his son Joseph Gulston to Leeson House on his estates at Langton Matravers; while the Spurriers had built Upton House in the midst of the 900 acres of the Upton estate. Others like the Lesters had been content to build their mansions in Poole; such as Benjamin Lester at the Mansion House, Robert Slade at Poole House, and George Kemp who had purchased probably the finest property in Poole, the Thompson House in Market Street (now Market Close).

The news of the victory over Napoleon had come to Poole in April 1814 and had been celebrated in the grand manner, with more than 5,000 people being dined in the streets on roast beef, strong beer and plum pudding. It is unlikely that many of the 5,000 were not dependent for their livelihood in some form or another on the Newfoundland Trade, and yet the event they celebrated was the event which brought their prosperity to an end.

Mansion House, Thames Street, North East front once the residence of Benjamin Lester

Upton House. The Entrance, North front

The Treaties between the nations following the Wars allowed the French and the Americans to fish the Newfoundland Banks, and allowed the other countries of Europe to compete with the Poole traders in the supply of goods to the Newfoundland settlers. The enormous continental armies were disbanded, and as a result European agriculture revived, and the countries gave preference to their own nationals in supplying fish. The demand for Poole fish slumped and the price of what could be sold was halved, and by 1817 the trade was in the doldrums.

With their establishments in Newfoundland and agencies in the main European and Baltic ports, Poole merchants had become almost totally committed to this trade, and no longer, as in older recessions, was it easy to switch into other commodities or start trades in new countries. The Trade had a slight recovery in 1824, but by 1828 the Newfoundland Banks were again deserted, in that year only 10 British ships fished in the Newfoundland waters.

Beech Hurst, High Street frontage built for Samuel Rolles in 1798

By 1830 things looked black for Poole, and in August of that year the town was stunned to hear that the great firm of Spurrier had gone bankrupt. The Spurriers had been foremost in the grand style of the Poole 'Merchant Princes' with their establishment at Upton House. They had acted as bankers to the trade and had maintained a near monopoly of trade in the south of the island with their own ships purpose-built for the fishing and sealing activities in Newfoundland, while William Spurrier had been the Naval Officer at Oderin. In 1824 the firm registered in Poole owned one of the largest of the Poole ships, the Upton of 320 tons, as well as eight other ships.

Christopher Spurrier had married Amy, the daughter of George Garland and the latter and his son, John Bingley Garland, were made Trustees in the bankruptcy, and since there was no limited liability then, Christopher Spurrier's settlement on his wife of £33,333 Consols was sold for the creditors. The three partners of the bankrupt concern were Christopher Spurrier, Peter Jolliffe, and William Jubber Spurrier, and the Trustees assured the creditors that there would be a surplus on the personal estates of the partners, and thus a good dividend.

However, despite this serious recession, by 1830 there were already some more hopeful signs. The midland potteries had begun to gear up for mass production, and they considered that Purbeck clay was the best for some of their products. The Purbeck pits were extended and the most convenient means of transportation was by sea to Liverpool and thence by canal to Stoke. A tramway was laid down to Middlebere from some pits and from others at Godin, a railway was laid to take the clay to Goathom pier.

A series of barges then ferried the clay from Middlebere and Goathorn to Poole for shipment to Liverpool. The Corporation even provided a Clay Cellar on its land between the Wills, Cheritt and Willis shipbuilding yards and the then appropriately named Shipwrights Arms, to store clay. By 1830 this trade already amounted to 30,000 tons a year and had every prospect of increasing.

Poole also had a further standby in the ancient grain trade, in which some merchants, notably the Garlands, had previously been largely involved. In 1798 Cruttwells Universal Directory had reported of Poole that "the spacious and airy granaries for corn stood

In the matter of CHRISTOPHER SPURRIER, PETER JOLLIFF, and WILLIAM JUBBER SPURRIER, Bankrupts.

of

in the island of Newfoundland, in North America, Planter, maketh oath and saith, that CHRISTOPHER SPURRIER, PETER JOLLIFF, and WILLIAM JUBBER SPURRIER, of the Town and County of Poole, Merchants, Dealers, and Chapmen, against whom a Commission of Bankrupt hath lately been awarded and issued, as this Deponent hath been informed and believes, and is now in prosecution, were at and before the date and issuing forth of the said Commission, and still are justly and truly indebted unto him this Deponent, in the sum of

upon Balance of Accounts, for money lent and advanced by him this Deponent, to the said Christopher Spurrier, Peter Jolliff, and William Jubber Spurrier, and for money had and received by them to and for the use of this Deponent, for which said sum of

or any part thereof, he this Deponent, hath not, nor hath or have any other person or persons for his use, to his knowledge or belief, received any security or satisfaction whatsoever.

Sworn at

in the island of Newfoundland,

this   day of

One thousand

eight hundred and

the same having been read over and duly explained to the said

Before me,

Creditors Application Form

Clay barges unloading onto ships at the quay

as a conspicuous proof of the spirit of these times". The merchants had exported barley from Dorset and surrounding counties, and had imported great quantities of wheat and other cereals from Northern Europe. This trade also revived and Sydenham was able to report in 1838 that "great quantities of corn are shipped here for the London and other markets".

In 1834 Poole still received about 100 ships with foreign cargoes and despatched a slightly greater number in return, and coastal shipping had much increased with over 800 ships in and out of the harbour with coastal cargoes. Poole also acted as the distribution centre for Newcastle coal, with the Corporator William Jolliffe as agent, and Canadian timber was still extensively imported.

However, the main trade of Newfoundland with its large profits to which the whole economy of the town had become geared, had slumped. In 1833 "bankruptcies were everywhere", for in the height of the trade twenty years previously 350 ships of Poole and 2,000 men had been directly employed in it, and by 1833 this had been reduced to 70 ships and 440 men.

No. 87 High Street built in 1704 as a single large mansion house

As a further consequence of the Newfoundland slump, Poole's famous oyster beds were threatened. Oyster dredging had always been one trade on which Poole's fishermen could rely for two months' reasonable employment each Spring when in the 'fishermens harvest', the forty or so sloops dredged up the oysters from the harbour.

The timing of the dredging operations and the size of oysters taken were strictly controlled by the Corporation through their Admiralty jurisdiction. But, in the recession of Poole's trade, the lack of money tempted the unemployed Poole fishermen to dredge for oysters illegally.

As early as 1820 the Corporation had found it necessary to pass a byelaw prohibiting the dredging of oysters at night, and by 1830, the position had got worse. Since fishermen were convicted and fined they were often unable to pay the fines imposed, the Corporation was driven to pass a byelaw in 1830 giving itself the power to distrain on the goods of such fishermen and to sell their goods to pay the fines.

The final blow to the oyster-beds came with the Municipal Corporations Act 1835 which abolished all exempt admiralty jurisdiction in the Corporation.

The juries of senior pilots, who used to perambulate the harbour to make their 'presentations' to the Mayor as Admiral of the Port came to an end, leaving only the ceremonial Beating of the Bounds of Poole Harbour and the Mayor of Poole's appointment as Admiral of the Port as an honorary title.

Meanwhile with no powers of control and the new Council otherwise engaged, the famous Poole oyster beds were dredged to extinction.

Poole never again rose to anything like the prominent position as a trading port that it held in high medieval times and which it had recaptured in the late 18th and early 19th centuries due to the trade with Newfoundland. One of the reasons for this was the silting of the channels and the Corporators had real fears that with the coming of steam propulsion, ships would inevitably become larger and that Poole would not be able to accommodate them.

In 1827 they had funds in the Quay Account and thought that a good investment might be to build out a pier into the harbour from the eastern end of the Quay. Before doing so they called in the advice of a Plymouth Engineer, a Mr. Rendel, for his report.

Poole Quay at the turn of the century

Mr. Rendel came to Poole in April, 1827, and spent some days with Mr. Knight the Harbour Master, and the four senior pilots completing "the circuit of the extensive estuary upon which Poole is situate, and also visited the Sea Bar at high and low water" and he met the Corporation's Committee.

Mr. Rendel reported to the Committee that he thought the proposed new Pier would be useful to the Harbour and that it should be carried out at an angle of 22° with the line of the Quay, "or bearing SE by compass to an extent of from 80–100 yards". He then said that he wished to make a full report on the Harbour and went away to find time to prepare it. He finally completed this on 5th May and this report must have given the merchants of the Corporation some pause.

His report was a long and diffuse document. His main worries for the Harbour was the silting up of the channels and the movement and increase of the Bar at the Harbour entrance.

In regard to the silting, he cited as an example that "not many centuries" previously vessels of "dimensions little inferior to those which now frequent Poole could navigate as high up as Wareham, while at present it is with difficulty that a 20 ton barge can approach that place....."

"We also find from some old Charts", Mr. Rendel reports, "and from the information of the Pilots that the channel from North Haven Point to Bar Buoy has within their recollection been gradually moving to the westward and that there is, on the average of the year, from 3–4 ft. less water on the Bar than there was 40 years ago....."

"I would observe that a sufficient depth of water for the accommodation of shipping alongside Poole Quay and for the keeping open a navigable Channel between the Quays and the Diver buoy, must wholly depend on the scour of the ebb tide from Longford Bay".

The whole of this Bay, Mr. Rendel remarked, is mudlands, rapidly approaching the level of the highest spring tides. There was no river emptying into the Bay and therefore when the mudlands of the Bay rose to keep the seawater from entering there would be no flow of water through the Quays to scour them.

"The consequences to the immediate Haven of Poole from the destruction or even considerable reduction of the capacity of Longford Bay for the reception of Tidal waters are too evident to require much comment, indeed we may boldly assert that it would be completely choked up, not even enjoying the advantages which Wareham now does, wanting as it would the assistance of a fresh water river".

Mr. Rendel thought the first priority for the Corporation was to tackle in the Harbour, were "evils which are taking place at its entrance". "Indeed", he says, "it would be childish to talk of internal improvements unless in connection with the removal of external evils, for what possible use, I would ask, are Wharfs, Warehouses, etc. etc. in the absence of a proper entrance for shipping to get at them?"

The Pilots had informed Mr. Rendel that the sea bar had moved half a mile to the westward since 1800. The pilots thought this had been caused by a vessel which had sunk at the old entrance — but Mr. Rendel thought that "to attribute such a change to so simple a cause most unphilosophical".

Perhaps worse than the Bar moving westward to Mr. Rendel's mind was its gradual increase in height. There was from 3—4 feet less water over the Bar in 1827 than had been there in the recollection of the Pilots.

If something wasn't done, Mr. Rendel said, "these evils will continue..... till nature had accomplished her work of entirely shutting up the Harbour so that nothing will remain but Channels sufficiently capacious to carry off the two small rivers which now enter the Estuary below Wareham".

Mr. Rendel described the works which were "absolutely necessary for the preservation of the Harbour".

The backwaters had been so reduced that it had become necessary to make up in power what had been lost in quantity. In other words, the reduced quantity of backwater would have to perform the office of the greater quantity required to keep the channels clear and the bar reduced by making the water travel faster.

First a straight channel should be dredged from the western river buoy to the south-east point of Brownsea Island and turn into this channel the waters of the Wareham and Witch Channels and the water from Longford Bay. This would increase the velocity of the water and increase its scouring capacity.

To aid this process Lytchett and Longford Bays should be converted to reservoirs and provided with sluice gates and the water penned up in flood tide and let out at low water to produce their maximum scouring effect.

The Port of Poole circa 1857

To stop the penned waters filling up with mud Mr. Rendel said that Lytchett and Longford Bays should be united by the construction of a Canal across the Isthmus provided with sluices for running water from one Bay into the other.

Then, said Mr. Rendel, another pier should be run out from the end of the Quay on the Hamworthy side of the Harbour towards the end of the Pier the Corporation had proposed and then provided with gates for the admission of ships and for running off the waters to act as a scour down the whole length of the Harbour.

"Supposing the works here recommended to be executed I have every good reason to believe that from the advantages which Poole offers for a general trade that her commercial wealth would increase and that the capacities of the Harbour would afford accommodation for vessels of from 5—700 tons and that to almost any extent".

"On the contrary I cannot but express my firm persuasion that if the present evils so powerfully at work within this Estuary are neglected or even slightly remedied that within the course of a few years Poole will to a certain extent undergo the same necessitudes as Wareham and many other Harbours upon the southern coast of England....."

The report had been asked for as a result of the meeting of the Corporation in March 1827 when a Committee had been set up to decide how best the £800 in the hands of the Treasurer of the Quays could best be spent for the benefit of the Port and the pier from the town quays had been proposed.

The Corporation appealed to the Government for financial help in vain. By 1830 they asked Mr. Rendel to tell them what they should do "taking into consideration the means in their hands" towards deepening the water at the bar and scouring and improving the Channels from the Quay to Brownsea and to preserving the depths at the Quay.

Mr. Rendel said their money was insufficient to improve the amount of back water flowing out to effect the necessary scouring.

He computed that Poole Harbour contained 9,637 acres and contained 34,855,845 tons of water and he went to long lengths to show the

Corporation that if over 1M tons of water in Lytchett Bay could be used to scour the Quay and Channels it would have a most beneficial effect. If sluice gates were provided to let the water out with a rush at low water it would be even more beneficial. The Corporation was urged to do two things first:

To cut a Canal across the Isthmus to unite Lytchett Bay and Upton Bays and construct the sluices and lock for	£6,550

and secondly,

To make an Embankment at the entrance to Lytchett Bay and construct the Sluices and Dock for	£7,500
Total	£14,050

The Corporation should borrow the money by mortgaging the tolls. But if the Corporation thought this too much to borrow at one time, said Mr. Rendel, they should start with the formation of the proposed Canal to link the two Bays and complete the sluices and embankment when they could get further funds.

These frightening reports of the Corporation's expert had a lot to do with the subsequent quarrels in Poole over the building of the Bridge to link Poole with Hamworthy.

The Corporation had always had the Ferry rights for transporting Poole people from the Great Quay to the Chapelry of Hamworthy and the workers to the shipbuilding yards and the Ballast Quay which were on that side of the Channel. The ferry boat could take up to 70 persons and ran from opposite the "Great Cellar" to the side of the appropriately named Shipwright's Arms. Each family in Poole paid one penny each quarter and could travel free, otherwise there was a charge of ½d. each way.

The question of building a bridge had become a political matter in the elections of Poole's Members of Parliament at that time and Mr. Ponsonby had always said he favoured the building of a bridge and would facilitate it as far as he and his land owning was concerned.

The Town Cellars, Poole Quay

In July 1833 the Corporation had considered the question and had resolved that "a Bridge from Poole to Hamworthy would be of great public utility, more especially to the inhabitants of this town". The Corporators were then really "the city fathers": if there was to be a bridge it never crossed their minds that anybody or person but themselves would be the sponsors of it and would decide its size and situation. However, they were then concerned with the provision of gas lighting and the condition of the harbour and hardly had the financial resources to contemplate such a structure with trade as it was..... Mr. Ponsonby wrote to them early in February 1834 and asked them if they would concur in the raising of subscriptions to the cost of the Bridge and contributing from the Corporation or Quay funds to it. The Corporation's resolution was short and definite:

"Resolved that the Corporation have no funds to subscribe towards the proposed Bridge and that therefore this meeting be adjourned **sine die**".

According to repute it was Mr. Ponsonby's steward, Mr. Easton, meeting Mr. Martin Kemp Welch in Poole when they had gone to see Poole's street lamps lit for the first time in 1834, who hit upon the idea of promoting a Bill in Parliament to authorise the construction of a privately-owned bridge and that they later obtained Mr. Ponsonby's personal interest and enthusiasm for the scheme.

The Harbour Office, and Custom's House, Poole Quay

Thomas Slade, the Sheriff, was duly called upon to have a Sheriff's Meeting of the inhabitants. The meeting, held in the Guildhall, in March 1834 passed a resolution in the same terms as the resolution of the Corporation of the previous July.

However, when the matter came back as a positive proposition, a majority of the Corporators changed their minds. The fact that by now Mr. Ponsonby, no longer M.P. for Poole, had taken over the proposition apparently to build it at his own cost caused considerable suspicion following his recent letter to the Corporation that he had no funds for such a project. The Lord of the Manor's excursions into Poole town's affairs was always looked on askance by the Corporation, fearing that it would somehow be used as a means of infiltrating on their hard-earned powers. There is little doubt that the thought of the bridge being owned and controlled by the Lord of the Manor was a worrying thought to the Corporation.

There were, too, many other fears. The householders of Poole at the time were rated for poor law relief at an effective rate of about 5/- in the £ but as at the time nearly two-thirds of the householders were excused from payment on account of the poverty of the occupiers the burden of rates fell on the Merchants' establishments and the shopkeepers. There was, too, a church rate of 1/6d. in the £ levied under an Act of Parliament to pay off the debt incurred in building St. James Church and which was to continue until 1856 as well as a further rate of 9d. in the £ to cover the running expenses of the church. Moreover the Corporator Merchants were then rated on their stock-in-trade and on the goods imported and exported from Poole. The Corporation, therefore, suspected that if the bridge was built it would be a standing temptation to the Merchants to take their establishments over to the Hamworthy side and thereby avoid the Poole rates as well as to throw any improvement or development occasioned in Poole on to the Lord of the Manor's lands in Hamworthy where he had a few years earlier laid the foundation stone of a new Church.

There was, indeed, a substantial change of opinion in the town. Many suddenly heard that a turnpike road was to be built from the other side of the proposed bridge and they became concerned at the thought of traffic being diverted through the High Street to get to the bridge, and would make the old town into a thoroughfare for with the bridge built, the distance between Poole and western towns such as Wareham and Dorchester would be reduced by two miles.

Opponents of the bridge called a vestry meeting only a few days after the Sheriff's meeting and resolved "That it is inexpedient to have a bridge from Poole to Hamworthy, no good reason for it having been offered and that such a measure would be attended with unnecessary expense".

But the sponsor's of the Bill and their local solicitor, Martin Kemp Welch had been able to move quickly and, within six weeks of the vestry meeting the town suddenly heard that the Committee appointed to hear objection to the Bill were to sit. The Corporation reversed their decision about the bridge and sent Robert Parr, the town clerk, and witnesses to oppose the Bill in Committee. What was more, the Rector of Poole, the Rev. Peter Jolliffe and George Kemp, the leader of the reform party in Poole and the deacon of the Congregational Church in Poole, scurried off to London one Sunday towards the end of April 1834, to speak against the passing of the Bill on behalf of some of the residents.

However, there were others, mainly of the reform party, despite George Kemp's efforts to obstruct, who did wish the Bill to go through. The Town Clerk and his witnesses, the Rector of Poole and the Congregational deacon made no impression on the Committee. It was perhaps hardly likely that they would, for of all people, the Chairman of the select committee was none other than Sir John Byng who had taken over from Mr. Ponsonby as Junior Member for Poole when Mr. Ponsonby had resigned in 1831 and had since become the senior Member for Poole on Benjamin Lester Lester having not put up for election in 1835. To be fair to him, though, the general question of the erection of a bridge had been a matter of debate at Parliamentary elections in Poole and both Mr. Ponsonby and Sir John had always said that they were in favour of such a project.

However, the Corporators were never ones to give up a fight. Their own worries had really been about the possible effect of the bridge on the scouring of the Quays and the Harbour. Mr. Rendel's reports were frightening. If the bridge were built, cutting off the end of the Great Quay just past the Slade's counting house, its abutments would have to be constructed in the main channel of the Quay and must make the scouring effect on the Quays even worse than Mr. Rendel had reported. They made one last effort to mitigate this likely evil to their Quay. They said that they would withdraw their objection to the Bill if Mr. Ponsonby would undertake to carry out that part of Mr. Rendel's recommendation to link Holes Bay with Lytchett Bay to ensure that the high water from both would flood through the Quays.

Engraving of Poole Bridge circa 1855

The sponsors of the Bill had now got into too strong a position to buy off any opposition. The Bill went through both Houses of Parliament just as it stood and Royal Assent followed on 16th June, 1834. Mr. Ponsonby opted for a wooden bridge with a steep and rather awkward gradient to cost £9,600 and it lasted until 1885 as a toll bridge.

The Corporation felt they had lost a serious battle and their old antipathies against the Lord of the Manor were again raised. Even then, though they didn't know that within a few months they would be fighting for their very existence.

They passed the following resolution on 19th March, 1834.

"Resolved that the decrease of the Tidal Waters within the Harbour of Poole, arising from the rapid growth of the mudlands and other causes of obstruction had long been the subject of great anxiety to this Corporation as Conservators of the said Harbour, and therefore they cannot but regard with alarm the attempts now making by Individuals to obtain an Act of Parliament to enable them to erect a Bridge across the said Harbour for their own private benefit and advantage fully aware that it is impossible to erect such a Bridge as the Act contemplates without constructing such abutments thereto as must obstruct the free ingress and egress of the tidal waters to that part of the Harbour which is essential for cleansing and scouring the Harbour generally but especially between the Quays".

A Committee was appointed of the Quay Committee and seven others, including G. L. Parrott with all powers to prevent the passing of the Bill as then drafted but with power to withdraw the Corporation's opposition "provided the framers of the Bill will insert a Clause to compel the shareholders to inclose Lytchett Bay and turn the waters thereof into Poole Harbour in the manner recommended by Mr. Rendel....."

Thames Street circa 1880 showing the New Inn and the quay

The Corporators living in Poole had up to the early 1800's been composed mainly of Tories who were known in the Corporation as the "Ministerial Party". Their majority even among the "in-Burgesses" (as those Corporators living in the Town were called) was getting very slim in the early 19th Century and, in elections for Parliament, when the "out-burgesses" were allowed to vote, Poole Corporation generally returned Whig members.

Up to 1810, however, the Tories had managed to keep control of the Corporation by controlling the appointment of the Mayor and his chief officers by means of a Corporation Byelaw which specified that 'the Mayor and his brethren' (i.e. the present and past mayors) would nominate two or three Corporators for such offices and only these Corporators were eligible for election.

When John Strong was elected Mayor on this system for the second year in 1810, however, the dissatisfied Corporators issued a Writ of Quo Warrento against him and the Judge of Assize at Dorchester declared the election illegal and void as being contrary to the system of election of the Mayor of Poole as laid down in Elizabeth I's Charter.

After 1810 the system was adopted whereby the Sergeant-at-Mace, gave all the Corporators due notice at the meeting held each year on the Friday before the feast of St. Matthew the Apostle, that the election was open to any of them, by his cry of "Oyez! Oyez! Oyez! Does anyone here offer himself for the office of Mayor for the succeeding year?" (There was, of course, no one present at meetings of the Corporation but Corporators). The Sergeant-at-Mace repeated this invitation three times to ensure that all Corporators had a full chance to offer themselves for the office, and a Poll was taken of those offering their services of all the Corporators present, so long as they were living in Poole. (This old custom was taken over by the new Council elected in 1835 but as years went by and first the Press and, later, the public were admitted to Council meetings the old custom of the Sergeant-at-Mace making this invitation was hardly apposite, however hallowed it was by tradition. It led, in the early 1950's, to a member of the public, announcing his willingness to serve as he came from the public gallery into the Council Chamber, only to be told lamely by the town clerk that any motion to elect him had to be moved and seconded by a member of the Council).

But the recision of the Byelaw was not the end of the incipient reformers of the Council who were mainly Dissenters. As such Dissenters could not take office in the Corporation. The Test Act and the Corporation Act prohibited Dissenters from holding any office of State or in a Corporation. The check of a qualified Churchman was that he had taken the sacrament within 12 months of his election.

Unitarian Meeting House, Hell Street, built in 1704

By the 1820's many of the Corporators had become extremely concerned with their own businesses in the great recession of trade in Poole following the Treaties ending the Napoleonic Wars. They had less relish for the Corporation's offices, the duties of which took time and attention, to say nothing of the very considerable personal expenditure involved in carrying out the duties of the office.

At the election for Sheriff in 1821 William Jolliffe and William Adey were nominated. Mr. Jolliffe addressed the meeting and told them he had not received the Sacrament for a year or, for that matter, he had never received the Sacrament. He was, therefore, ineligible for election and therefore "any votes for him would be as good as thrown away". Despite this statement by Mr. Jolliffe, the Burgesses proceeded to a Poll and he was elected and the Sergeant-at-Mace proclaimed his due election. But when the Mayor as Presiding Officer called on Mr. Jolliffe to take the oath Mr. Jolliffe replied that, as he was unqualified, he could not conscientiously do so. The Mayor threatened that the Corporation would prosecute him for a penalty of £500. Mr. Jolliffe retorted he would submit to a fine of £50. The Mayor thereupon promptly demanded it but Mr. Jolliffe, equally promptly, replied he would pay it, but only after 'due process of Law', and stalemate was complete.

There seemed nothing more to do for the time being than to elect another Sheriff for the following year which they then proceeded grudgingly to do. Mr. Adey, the other candidate was, not surprisingly, elected and the Sergeant-at-Mace proclaimed his due election. However, Mr. Adey, had forestalled the Corporation. He had, to quote the report of the day, "left the Hall anterior to his having been put in nomination". The Sergeant-at-Mace was promptly dispatched to tell him of his new honour and get him back to the Guildhall to be sworn. But Mr. Adey had completely disappeared. The Sergeant-at Mace had finally to return to admit his failure to find Mr. Adey, and the Mayor had finally to capitulate. He managed a last flourish by apparently lapsing into the outlook of his other office of the Chief Magistrate: he ordered Mr. Adey "to be called in Court three times" and Mr. Adey not appearing and "the other business of the meeting being over, it was dissolved".

A special meeting of the Corporation was later called to try to solve the problem of appointing a Sheriff. The Mayor overlooked the point that they had elected Mr. Adey when he saw that Mr. Jolliffe had attended the second meeting and he again formally asked Mr. Jolliffe to take the oaths of office. Mr. Jolliffe again refused. On this Mr. Adey was again called to do so and he also blandly refused. If it could be legally imposed, he said, he, too, would rather pay the fine.

This was a new experience for the Corporation. It reflected the fortunes of the town in this new experience of Corporators feeling a reluctance to take on the duties.

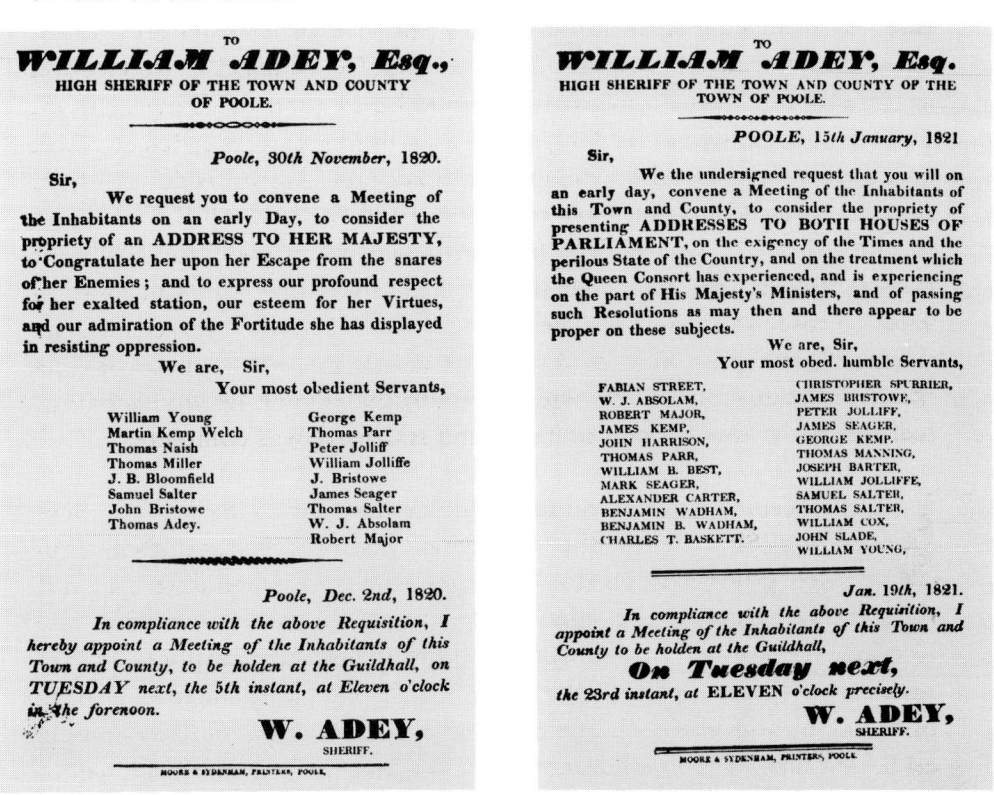

TO
WILLIAM ADEY, Esq.,
HIGH SHERIFF OF THE TOWN AND COUNTY OF POOLE.

Poole, 30th November, 1820.

Sir,

We request you to convene a Meeting of the Inhabitants on an early Day, to consider the propriety of an ADDRESS TO HER MAJESTY, to Congratulate her upon her Escape from the snares of her Enemies; and to express our profound respect for her exalted station, our esteem for her Virtues, and our admiration of the Fortitude she has displayed in resisting oppression.

We are, Sir,
Your most obedient Servants,

William Young	George Kemp
Martin Kemp Welch	Thomas Parr
Thomas Naish	Peter Jolliff
Thomas Miller	William Jolliffe
J. B. Bloomfield	J. Bristowe
Samuel Salter	James Seager
John Bristowe	Thomas Salter
Thomas Adey.	W. J. Absolam
	Robert Major

Poole, Dec. 2nd, 1820.

In compliance with the above Requisition, I hereby appoint a Meeting of the Inhabitants of this Town and County, to be holden at the Guildhall, on TUESDAY next, the 5th instant, at Eleven o'clock in the forenoon.

W. ADEY,
SHERIFF.

MOORE & SYDENHAM, PRINTERS, POOLE.

TO
WILLIAM ADEY, Esq.
HIGH SHERIFF OF THE TOWN AND COUNTY OF THE TOWN OF POOLE.

POOLE, 15th January, 1821

Sir,

We the undersigned request that you will on an early day, convene a Meeting of the Inhabitants of this Town and County, to consider the propriety of presenting ADDRESSES TO BOTH HOUSES OF PARLIAMENT, on the exigency of the Times and the perilous State of the Country, and on the treatment which the Queen Consort has experienced, and is experiencing on the part of His Majesty's Ministers, and of passing such Resolutions as may then and there appear to be proper on these subjects.

We are, Sir,
Your most obed. humble Servants,

FABIAN STREET,	CHRISTOPHER SPURRIER,
W. J. ABSOLAM,	JAMES BRISTOWE,
ROBERT MAJOR,	PETER JOLLIFF,
JAMES KEMP,	JAMES SEAGER,
JOHN HARRISON,	GEORGE KEMP.
THOMAS PARR,	THOMAS MANNING,
WILLIAM B. BEST,	JOSEPH BARTER,
MARK SEAGER,	WILLIAM JOLLIFFE,
ALEXANDER CARTER,	SAMUEL SALTER,
BENJAMIN WADHAM,	THOMAS SALTER,
BENJAMIN B. WADHAM,	WILLIAM COX,
CHARLES T. BASKETT.	JOHN SLADE,
	WILLIAM YOUNG.

Jan. 19th, 1821.

In compliance with the above Requisition, I appoint a Meeting of the Inhabitants of this Town and County to be holden at the Guildhall,

On Tuesday next,
the 23rd instant, at ELEVEN o'clock precisely.

W. ADEY,
SHERIFF.

MOORE & SYDENHAM, PRINTERS, POOLE.

Requisitions to convene meetings to William Adey Sheriff

The Corporation knew this and was concerned about the new situation as, if they allowed Mr. Jolliffe and Mr. Adey to get away with their refusals, they felt that other Corporators could easily avoid the duties simply by omitting to take the Sacrament for a year. It would, in any case, be difficult to find future Sheriffs, for a considerable proportion of them were genuine Dissenters. The only hope of enforcing an election was to be able to fine them for not accepting the office a greater sum than it would cost them to carry out the duties, — and the last case the Corporation had taken on this ground in 1775 the Burgesses had been "amerced" only £50 for not qualifying themselves for the office, and this would not be enough to achieve their object.

The Corporation took Counsel's opinion on their predicament. They got no comfort from this. The statute of Charles II barred Mr. Jolliffe from the job. The Corporation could prosecute Mr. Adey but, if the case was contested it would lead to expensive litigation, they were warned, and, if a fine was imposed, it would hardly be likely to be as heavy as the cost of executing the office of Sheriff.

The only remedy, Counsel advised, was for the Corporation in future to make sure in electing Corporators that they were capable and willing to perform the duties of the various offices to which they might be elected.

A similar position and refusal to take the oaths occurred at the election of the Coroners in 1829 when Mr. William Absolem said he could not conscientiously take the oaths as he was a Quaker.

Society of Friends Meeting House

In early 1830 the Corporation tried a new tack to achieve their ends. They passed a Byelaw to the effect that no Burgess was to be Mayor or a Magistrate unless he had first served as Sheriff, and he was not qualified to be Sheriff unless he had first served as Water Bailiff or Coroner.

However, in 1828, Sir John Russell's Bill to repeal the Test Act and the Corporation Acts prohibiting Dissenters from National and Local Corporation offices had passed the Commons and the Tory Leaders Peel and Wellington persuaded the Lords to pass it. Dissenters such as William Jolliffe could then hold offices in the Corporation and William Jolliffe had been elected Mayor that same year of 1828 without having been Sheriff.

Meanwhile the reform movement was also causing other dissentions among the Burgesses. Five of them had written to George Welch Ledgard, the banker, a staunch King's man, who had been Mayor many times and a magistrate for many years. They wrote as follows:

Poole, January, 1827

Sir,

The measures which have been pursued for the extension of education, having given increased and great facilities to the attainment of knowledge, and led to an enquiry into the Nature of Civil Rights of Mankind, it is not surprising that an anxious desire is evinced to obtain possession of them.

The wisest Monarchs and greatest Statesmen of the Age, contemplating the probable consequences of this expansion of intellect and knowledge, and the dreadful effects of a struggle for Power between Sovereigns and the people, have immortalized their names by voluntarily surrendering the arbitrary power handed down to them by their Ancestors, and bestowing on the People, Constitutions, which, whilst they secure to themselves the necessary Power and Dignity, admit the People to such a participation of them, as is compatible with the general welfare.

At a moment when such events are taking place — at a moment when Great Britain has taken up arms in defence of Constitutional Liberty, we turn our attention to the affairs of our own Town and find those Rights and Privileges, which we consider should be participated generally in the Inhabitants, in possession of comparatively few. The injustice

Poole, January, 1827.

Sir,

"The measures which have been pursued for the extension of education, having given increased and great facilities to the attainment of knowledge, and led to an enquiry into the nature of the Civil Rights of Mankind, it is not surprizing that an anxious desire is evinced to obtain possession of them.

The wisest Monarchs and greatest Statesmen of the Age, contemplating the probable consequences of this expansion of intellect and knowledge, and the dreadful effects of a struggle for Power between Sovereigns and the People, have immortalized their names by voluntarily surrendering the arbitrary power handed down to them by their Ancestors, and bestowing on the People, Constitutions, which, whilst they secure to themselves the necessary Power and Dignity, admit the People to such a participation of them, as is compatible with the general welfare.

At a moment when such events are taking place—At a moment when Great Britain has taken up arms in defence of Constitutional Liberty, we turn our attention to the affairs of our own Town, and find those Rights and Privileges, which we consider should be participated generally by the Inhabitants, in possession of comparatively few. The injustice of this is obvious. In imitation of the noble example before us, we wish to repair it by the admission of our fellow Townsmen to the enjoyment of that to which we consider them fairly entitled.

To consider the propriety of this, we request you to convene a meeting of the Corporation."

Respectfully We are, Sir,
Your obedient Servants,
JOS. BARTER,
WM. JOLLIFF,
H. G. KNIGHT,
H. K. FURNELL,
R. R. LINTHORN,

To G. W. LEDGARD, ESQ.
Mayor,

The original copy of the letter to G. W. Ledgard

of this is obvious. In imitation of the noble example before us, we wish to repair it by the admission of our fellow Townsmen to the enjoyment of that which we consider them fairly entitled.

To consider the propriety of this, we request you to convene a meeting of the Corporation.

Respectfully, We are, Sir,
Your obedient Servants,
Jos. Barter
Wm. Jolliffe
H. G. Knight
H. K. Furnell
R. R. Linthorn

The Mayor bent to no explanation of his concern of these philosophies of democracy or of any counter-thoughts of his own for the solution of the prevailing unrest. He replied promptly as follows:

Poole, January 15th, 1827

Gentlemen,

I have to acknowledge the receipt of your letter without date. In reply, I deem it my duty to decline acceeding to your request.

If however you should consider it a violation of your Principles to continue Members of a body which you deem chargeable with such injustice, I beg to add, I am ready to convene a Meeting of the Corporation at any time you may request, to receive your Resignations.

I have the honour to remain
very respectfully, Gentlemen,
Your most Obedient Servant
(sgd) G. W. Ledgard

Whether it was some compromise on this proposition or arising the Corporators' difficulties in filling some of the offices of the Corporation, — or simply to raise money for the various road and town improvements then being carried out by the Corporation, we shall probably never know, but in 1830, despite Mr. G. W. Ledgard's early opposition, the Corporation decided to let each of its 49 members then living in Poole to nominate two further Burgesses.

It was mainly the new Corporators elected under this resolution who were those who, later, were to fight so long and so strongly among themselves. It is also surprising, in view of the strong views so soon held by many of them, that it was the Whig and reform-supporting M.P. of Poole, Benjamin Lester Lester, who nominated the ardent Tory, Robert Slade; John Foot, the Whig town clerk, nominated the other Robert Slade as well as the future town clerk James Churchill; Samuel Clark, a merchant rope-maker and Tory, nominated the later notorious reform councillors George Lockyer Parrott and Tom Rickman who, five years later, were to put up their colleagues against Mr. Clarke in the first Council election; Joseph Orchard nominated Robert Henning Parr who was to become the most notorious ex-town clerk in England, and Joseph Garland nominated Robert H. Parr's brother, the curate at the then new Hamworthy Church, Rev. James C. Parr.

Prior to this grand election there had been one Slade in the Corporation — afterwards there were no less than eleven of them, four of them minors, which was quite a good representation even for the "millionaire firm of Newfoundland". Of the other great firms there were, prior to these elections, 6 Garlands and three more of the family were added. But by this time there was only one of the great merchanting family of Spurriers living in Poole, Thomas Henry Spurrier, who nominated his son to join the Corporation. Robert Wills nominated his ship-building partner, Richard Stanworth, and John Garland nominated the Chief Clerk of his Poole "Counting Office", Edward Lisby. Perhaps the strangest nomination of all in view of future events, was the radical William Jolliffe's nomination of the last of the three high Tories called Robert Slade.

Even so at the end of the election of September 1830 the number of effective Corporators living in Poole had only risen from 49 to about 90, for 37 of the newly elected freemen were minors and could not be admitted until they were 21 years old and some 20 of them were non-resident in Poole with only the right to vote in the election of Poole's members of Parliament.

To which the Mayor thought proper to make the following reply,

Poole, January 15th, 1827.

Gentlemen,

"*I have to acknowledge the receipt of your letter without date. In reply, I deem it my duty to decline acceding to your request.*

If however you should consider it a violation of your Principles, to continue Members of a body which you deem chargeable with such injustice, I beg to add, I am ready to convene a Meeting of the Corporation at any time you may request, to receive your Resignations."

I have the honor to remain
very respectfully, Gentlemen,
Your most Obedient Servant,
G. W. LEDGARD.

To Messrs. JOS. BARTER,
WM. JOLLIFF,
H. G. KNIGHT,
H. K. FURNELL,
R. R. LINTHORN.

Even before the advent of the many new Corporators in 1830, the old Corporation had often expressed a wish for Parliamentary reform. However at the meeting of the Corporation on 10th March, 1831, the following resolution was passed on the motion of William Jolliffe and seconded by Peter Jolliffe.

"Resolved unanimously that this Corporation regards with feelings of gratitude and respect the efforts of His Majesty's Ministers to redeem their sacred and patriotic obligations which they had voluntarily contracted touching the great and restorative measure of Parliamentary Reform.

And Resolved unanimously — That this meeting do forthwith address both Houses of Parliament desiring humbly and respectfully to implore their mature deliberations and unceasing endeavours so to perfect the great masure now submitted to their united and accumulated wisdom that by the blessing of Divine Providence the British Constitution may be preserved in all its force and purity and still be pre-eminent for the magnitude of those blessings which it bestows and secures to all classes of His Majesty's subjects....."

This minute was signed by Joseph Garland, the Mayor, the Jolliffes, James Seager, Thomas Spurrier, G. L. Parrott, Robert H. Parr, Joseph Barter, John Harrison and five others.

But when the Bill came to be drafted the Whigs declined to enforce a secret ballot. The open method of voting favoured the squire's political control over his tenants; and there were other provisions which surprised the Poole corporators, particularly the provision to add areas to the Borough.

Despite all the premature rejoicings at the return of the Whig majority in the Commons, the Lords threw out the Bill in October 1831. They were later prevailed upon to pass an amended Bill which deleted many provisions, including those abolishing the rotten boroughs. Lord Grey resigned yet again and threw the country into worse turmoil. Work stopped in the factories and, in the knowledge that the Lord Bishops had voted as a body to throw out the Bill, Bristol Bishop's Palace was pillaged. Gold was withdrawn from the Bank of England and the general reaction throughout the country led to a general fear of revolution. In the face of this fear, the Duke of Wellington, the leader of the Tories felt incapable of forming a government and the King had to ask Lord Grey to come back into office and in so doing, to promise him enough new Whig Lords to carry the Bill through the House of Lords. The Bill came before the Commons again and the Tories capitulated. They boycotted the debate and the new Bill was passed by 106 votes to 27. The Poole Corporators soon had a sight of the provisions of the Bill and were horrified. The bill included all the old provisions which they and other Corporations had once persuaded the Lords to delete, including the extension of the Poole electorate for Parliamentary elections to owners and occupiers of property in Hamworthy, Longfleet and Parkstone. Only the Lords again stood between the Bill gaining the status of an Act of Parliament.

William IV

Contemporary caricature of the Duke of Wellington

The Mayor urgently called a special meeting of the Council on 20th February, 1832, and passed the following:

"Resolved 1st — That the meeting have heard with extreme surprise and regret that it is intended to alter the ancient limits of the Town and County of Poole and thus violate the avowed intentions of the contemplated measure of Reform and subvert the best interests of this Town and County.

2nd — That the undermentioned Persons be a Committee to draw up an address to both Houses of Parliament and a Memorial to the Government embodying the just, reasonable and incontravertible objections of this Corporation to any change in the Boundaries of this Town and County....

3rd — That such Committee be desired to submit such address tomorrow morning at 11 o'clock.

4th — That the Members for this Town and County and for the County of Dorset be most earnestly importuned to support the aforesaid Address....."

The Address was duly ready for the following morning's meeting, prepared by the Ledgards, Jas. Seager, James Churchill, Robert Slade, William Jolliffe and others, and was sent off.

The petition left no doubt as to the Poole Corporation's views on the Act. "We cannot allow such a species of corruption as this to be foisted upon the county in the name of reform without some little exposure" it boldly proclaimed. "We hope the inhabitants of Poole will continue the course they have begun, and testify their opinion boldly and firmly on such an attempt to impugn the high respectability of their town, to crush their independence, and to render that extension of the elective franchise, which (if confined to the inhabitants) they ought in justice to possess, a mere cloak for corruption and nomination".

The state of things in Poole then can be shown by the following extract from the Dorset County Chronicle of 23rd February, 1832. It reported the position as follows:

"A very general feeling of dissatisfaction has been expressed in this town at the contemplated alteration of the boundaries of the borough, in the bill just introduced to the House of Commons. This alteration will considerably extend the constituency, as it will embrace great portions of the neighbouring tithings of Longfleet, Parkstone and Hamworthy. We are at a loss to imagine why this proposition has been made. Poole is a place of no mean importance, and surely when it is found, by the last census, that it contains about eight thousand inhabitants, it cannot be said that there is any deficiency of numbers; in point of respectability, also, few towns surpass it. Why therefore, is this insult heaped upon the inhabitants? Why are the landmarks which their forefathers have set up, and which have been ratified and confirmed to them by monarch after monarch, to be thus uprooted? Why are they not considered possessed of sufficient intellect and discrimination, to choose their representatives without assistance? Why is this measure proposed which cannot but tend to excite a feeling of rivalry and animosity between the town and its suburbs, where before nothing but cordiality and peace have prevailed? The project is far from being complimentary to the town, whilst it would place the inhabitants of the suburbs in no very enviable situation. But these are not all the objections for "worse remains behind"; inasmuch this alteration will be a mere job, as, if carried into execution, Poole will lose that independence which now characterises it, and renders it one of the most respectable and influential boroughs in the kingdom, and will become eventually a nomination borough in the hands of the Lord of the Manor of Canford. This appears to be the light in which it is views in the town generally, as yesterday (Tuesday, February 21st, 1832), a public meeting of the inhabitants was held at the Guildhall, at which the Sheriff, Robert Slade, jun., Esq., presided, when it was resolved that petitions on the subject should be immediately forwarded to the House of Lords and Commons. At a meeting of the Corporate Body it was also resolved to petition the Legislature against this extension of the boundaries..... for we cannot allow such a species of corruption as this to be foisted upon the country under the name of Reform, without some little exposure..... we hope that the inhabitants of Poole will continue the course they have begun, and testify their opinion boldly and firmly on such an attempt to impugn the high respectability of their town, to crush their independence, and to render that extension of the elective franchise, which (if confined to the inhabitants) they ought in justice to possess, a mere cloke for corruption and nomination".

To the Inhabitants
OF THE
TOWN AND COUNTY OF POOLE.

The Surveyors of the Highways, anxious at all times to perform the duties which devolve upon them, according to the best of their abilities and the means placed at their disposal, feel, at the present Juncture, a peculiar solicitude that nothing should be omitted on their part, that can keep the Town in a state of cleanliness and thereby preserve the health of the people; They therefore take the liberty to call the attention of the inhabitants to *the condition of the gutters,* which in consequence of the level state of the Streets, can only be kept clean and wholesome by a plentiful supply of water. *They therefore respectfully, but earnestly request that every householder will cause six buckets of water (at the least) to be thrown into the gutter opposite his house, every morning* AT NINE O'CLOCK.

JAMES SALTER, *Surveyors:*
TITO D. HODGES.

POOLE, July 24th, 1832.

LANKESTER, PRINTER, POOLE.

The public meeting referred to was the Sheriff's meeting which was the system adopted by the old Corporation for taking the views of the inhabitants. The meetings of Corporators were, of course, private and, in fact, secret, as each Corporator had to take an oath not to divulge what happened at meetings of the Corporation. However, if ten of the old Corporators called upon the Sheriff he was obliged under the custom of the Corporation to hold a meeting in the Guildhall at which the views of the inhabitants on matters of public concern could be taken.

However, despite the views of the Corporation and the public as expressed at the public meeting, they were not the unanimous views of the people of Poole or at least one of Poole's Members of Parliament. Mr. Ponsonby, the Lord of the Manor and it may well have been this strongly expressed feeling of the Corporation and the public meeting which led him, shortly afterwards, to resign his Poole seat to fight the election in the County of Dorset against Lord Ashley.

And so, finally, notwithstanding these petitions from Poole, the Reform Act of 1832 was passed which, with the Boundaries Act, left the Poole electorate consisting of the old Corporators plus everyone in Poole, the tithings of Longfleet and Parkstone and the parish of Hamworthy having the occupation of a house, warehouse or shop of the yearly value of £10 with a vote for Poole's members. In January 1833 Benjamin Lester Lester was re-elected with Rt. Hon. Sir John Byng, another Whig, as Poole's Member.

It was at this time that Poole's Corporators had still the spirit of adventure to set up one of the very earliest of gas works in the south of England. Mr. G. W. Ledgard, with a number of others of both Parties in the town had formed a Company to manufacture gas and for the Corporation to light the Quay and main streets with gas lamps. The Corporation had never charged its Members for the privilege of electing them as the old rotten boroughs had done. This might have been due to lack of certainty as to the result more than an innate morality because individual members of the Corporation had willingly accepted bribes of all sorts in return for their votes. However, they had usually managed to extract a present from its Members if only as an encouragement perhaps, for their further election. Benjamin Lester Lester and Mr. Ponsonby had, for instance, in 1830, been prevailed

THE BURGESSES OF POOLE

ARE respectfully requested to adhere to their original determination to maintain the Independence of the Borough, by refusing their support to any *Treasury Candidate,* as a highly respectable and influential Gentleman of a neighbouring Family, who is engaged in Mercantile pursuits, who will SUPPORT the Great Measure of

REFORM,

and is entirely unconnected with the Government or any Party, is hourly expected in Poole, to solicit their Suffrages.

POOLE, 26th Sept., 1831.

MOORE AND SYDENHAM, PRINTERS, POOLE.

upon to provide a library at the side of Mr. Lester's house at the bottom of High Street where the present offices of the Harbour Commissioners are.

The Corporation therefore felt it appropriate in 1834 for its newly elected M.Ps. to make a further contribution to the town's welfare — for, to be fair, the 'gifts' were usually for the general benefit of the town — and the provision of gas lighting for the town could hardly be more appropriate. This was especially so as the Corporation had already itself let land at Pitwines to the new Company on very long leases at nominal rents which were later, in 1881, by the Conveyancing Act of that year, converted into freeholds (which left the Corporation having to buy back some of the land in 1973 at industrial land prices).

The wind of change, though, had now swept through the parliamentary scene. The Members of Parliament were no longer subject to the Corporator's votes which were now in a considerable minority in the Poole electorate, as is shown by the following resolution and correspondence with its Members of Parliament in 1834:

RESOLVED — That a letter be addressed to Members intimating that the Corporation of Poole have subscribed £200 towards the expenses of Providing Lamps and Posts, the £200 the remainder is to be made up by subscription —

The reply from Sir John Byng, Kt. —

London, January 13th, 1834

Sir,

I have to acknowledge the receipt of a letter signed by you dated the 9th instant but with the Poole Post Master of 10th in which you give me a copy of the proceedings of a meeting of the Committee appointed by the Corporation for the purpose of raising funds by subscription towards paying for Lamp Posts &c &c &c to which I conclude your letter purposes to apply for my subscription.

I beg leave to write in reply that when I was last in Poole I heard that there was much difference of opinion among my constituents on the subject of Lighting the Town with Gas to which I suppose this subscription has reference and as I could not hope to reconcile it I have considered it most becoming to avoid any interference whatever either in impeding or assisting the Progress of the Works.

I have the honor to be,
Sir,
Your faithful Servant
(sgd) J. Byng

To Rt. Parr, Esqre.

The High Street with Gas Lighting

The reply from Benjamin Lester was —

Sir,

I have been unwell for this day or two past or I should have before replied to your letter of the 9th instant with a copy of the resolution from a Committee of the Corporation met for the purpose of raising a fund to defray in part the expenses of the Pillars, Lamps &c necessary for the intended new Gas Lights, calling on me with others for a subscription for that purpose.

It appears to me if I am correctly informed the Corporation claim all interest in the Lamps, Pillars &c which I think they ought to do — and therefore it is my opinion they are the parties to pay the whole expense particularly as they have the power under an Act of Parliament to levy sums for watching and lighting the Town to which the Inhabitants are rated. If I am correct in the above I do not think that any of the Inhabitants of Poole ought to be called on to contribute to a property which will exclusively belong to the Corporate Body and I must decline giving my name. I have not heard Sir J. Byng's Sentiments on the subject I therefore know nothing as to what he purposes to do. And

I remain, Sir
Your most obedient
(sgd) B. L. Lester

R. H. Parr Esq.,
Poole   Stone, Saturday

Following these replies the Committee asked its Chairman, George Hancock, to write to the members again and explain to them that no difference of opinion had been known to exist in the town as to the lighting of the streets with gas but only as to who should be the contractor. He was, too, to explain to Mr. Lester that the Mayor and Magistrates were to be the proprietors of the Gas Lamps only for the purpose of protecting them but would have no beneficial interest in them and the rate levied on the inhabitants was not sufficient to enable that fund to contribute to the expenses. The Chairman was no more successful than the Town Clerk. The patronage of the Members of Parliament was sadly at an end.

The Committee, "in consequence of the determination of the Members feel it useless to apply to the Inhabitants for subscriptions".

From the name of the recipients of the two letters from the Members to the Corporation it is apparent that one other notable event in Poole's history had occurred: Mr. Robert Henning Parr, a Solicitor, a Poole Corporator from the 1830 election, had been elected Town Clerk of Poole.

The Town Clerk was usually elected from one of themselves and always a solicitor. There were three Solicitor Corporators at the time, Robert Parr, Thomas Arnold and James Churchill. The previous Town Clerk, John Foot, who had died, was a Whig and so was James Churchill. The other two Corporators, Robert Henning Parr and Thomas Arnold, were Tories. The Tories were concerned that if both Mr. Parr and Mr. Arnold put up for election the Tory vote might be split and Mr. Churchill might get elected. The Corporator Mr. Harrison suggested to Mr. Parr that he should come "to some accommodation" with Mr. Arnold in order to avoid such a split of Tory votes. Mr. Parr agreed to pay Mr. Arnold £100 of his fees for his agreement to stand down from the election. Mr. Arnold did not contest the election further and Mr. Parr won the election, receiving 44 votes to Mr. James Churchill's 19.

Portrait of Robert Henning

Mr. Parr was elected Town Clerk on 24th July, 1833, and the Corporation applied to the King for his consent to this appointment which was necessary under the Poole Charters before Mr. Parr could take up his office. The reply came back four days later on 29th July, 1833:

"We being well informed of the Loyalty and Fidelity of him, the said Robert Henning Parr, have thought fit to condescend to the Corporation's request for approval....."

It was ironic that this approval of the King was given on his behalf by Lord Melbourne, later the Whig Prime Minister who, if he did later get on speaking terms with his brother-in-law, the Lord of the Manor of Canford, would have been regaled with many stories of the iniquities of that town clerk and the amount of money in law fees he was costing the Lord of the Manor.

The Lord of the Manor of Canford Magna was the feudal lord of the great tract of land stretching from the Manor House at Canford, past "the lawns" on the south of the house, east to Kinson and Knighton and west to take in Upton and Hamworthy as it swept on to the harbour, the sea and, of course, Canford Cliffs.

The Lord's sovereignty was much more than a mere ownership of land. He had despotic control over all the activities carried on in his manor and an effective dominance over the lives and activities of all who lived there under his 'protection'.

The achievement of any powers by the Merchants, therefore, to trade in Poole, to build ships, quays, warehouses or manufactures had to be by way of a grant from, and a diminution of the powers of, the Lord of the Manor. Happily for the Poole merchants the lords of the manor were often absent from the area and the Merchants had carried on a trade from Poole long enough for them to be able to claim that they had exercised these rights 'from time immemorial' which, indeed Hutchin's Dorset History says had, in fact, happened, and this to some extent gave them some defence to any subsequent lord's challenge to their activities. But, without the formal acceptance by the Lord of the Merchants' privileges, they were always at risk. The Lord could always challenge their rights in the King's courts or, as likely as not, by main force.

With the powers and privileges of the Poole merchants — later the Poole Corporation — being always basically at the expense of the overall sovereignty of the Lord of the Manor it was inevitable that the thrusting Poole Merchants would often be in conflict with the Lord.

The first Charter which the merchants ever obtained reads today more like a confirmation of the Lord's overall sovereignty than a grant of privileges to the Corporation. However, it is obvious that the merchants of that day knew that the Lord's agreement to appoint a reeve; his acknowledgment of their rights to trade from the Harbour, and the Poole residents' rights over the common lands and wastes of the manor was worth a great deal to them. They paid 70 marks for this Charter, which shows that they had already been trading most successfully from Poole. For all that, they would never have got William Longspee to have granted them these rights had he not then been in dire need of cash to equip himself and his entourage to join Louise IX in his disastrous Seventh Crusade that year of 1248.

The Longespee Charter circa 1248

This antagonism between the Poole Corporation had continued off and on over the centuries right up to the beginning of the 19th century, but at last, with the death in 1797 of Sir John Webb, the fifth in succession of his family to have been the Lord of the Manor, there had arrived at least the possibility of the end of these quarrels, for Sir John left no male heir.

Sir John had left his estate in trust for his great grandchild and appointed Edward Arrowsmith as trustee with full powers of management and improvement. Sir John's only child, his daughter Barbara, was life tenant of the estate. She had married the fifth Earl of Shaftesbury and it was her only daughter, Lady Barbara, who had married William Francis Spencer Ponsonby. Thus, on the death of Edward Arrowsmith in 1825, Mr. Ponsonby became the trustee of the estates through his wife's inheritance from her mother, and it was Mr. Ponsonby who then assumed the Lordship of the Manor.

In the interim, while Edward Arrowsmith had been trustee, the last batch of quarrels and law suits between the Manor and the Corporation — which had started as long ago as 1781 when Sir John promoted a Bill in Parliament to enable him to embank, enclose and reclaim great areas of the mudlands of the harbour — had at last been settled.

Those quarrels had started with the Corporation passing its usual resolution, on hearing of Sir John's activities, "to save harmless and keep indemnified the Mayor, Benjamin Lester" in authorising him "to pull down or cast down any Hedges, Ditches or Fences of any Inclosure of Heath or Wastes belonging to the Manor of Canford Magna". The quarrels had spread. Both sides had had their successes and defeats and, finally, in 1812 their quarrels had all been settled by a grand carve-up of all the common and waste lands of the Manor between the Lord of the Manor, the Corporation and other freeholders of Poole. This was all done by legislation under the Enclosure Act and Commissioners were appointed who, after inquiry, awarded various allotments of land to the different claimants. The Lord of the Manor, like the other allottees of land, was then enabled to enclose his lands free of any rights of herbage, turbary and the like.

In this way the Corporation had a sudden accretion of land ownership both inside the old town and in the surrounding districts. Their allotments of land totalled over 350 acres. Other areas had been allotted to the Inhabitants of Poole, the Church and the other, fairly numerous freehold owners of land who, not surprisingly, were mainly the members of the Corporation in their personal capacities. These awards of lands were eventually published by the Commissioners in 1822 and one of the few of these allotments of land still retained by the Corporation after its subsequent financial troubles is the reversionary interest of the long leases in Upper Parkstone. The title to this ownership is still the "Canford Award of 1822". There was a considerable activity in the Poole area in 1812/20 with the owners of these newly acquired lands in them erecting ring fences or embankments. The great expense of embankment and fencing proved a great strain even on the Corporation's finances at the time.

To JOHN CLARK, Esq., Sheriff.

SIR,

WE, the undersigned, do request the favor of your convening a Meeting of the Freeholders and other Inhabitants of this Town, interested in the *Canford and Poole Inclosure*, for the purpose of taking into Consideration the propriety of adopting such Measures as may tend to a completion of the Award.

JAMES KEMP.	JOS. GARLAND, Junr., Mayor.
M. K. WELCH.	J. W. ORCHARD.
G. KEMP, Junr.	THOMAS MANNING.
PETER JOLLIFF.	GEO. W. LEDGARD.
M. SIMMONDS.	JAS. SEAGER.
B. L. LESTER.	SAML. WHITE.
RICHD. PENNEY.	JOS. BARTER.
J. COLBOURNE.	D. LANDER.
JOHN BROWN.	GEORGE KEMP.
SAML. WESTON.	

Poole, January 5th, 1820.

In consequence of the above Requisition, I hereby appoint a Meeting for the purpose therein mentioned, to be held at the Guildhall, on Monday next, at 11 o'clock.

JOHN CLARK,
SHERIFF.

Poole, 7th January, 1820.

Moore and Sydenham, Printers, Poole.

At a MEETING of the Freeholders and other Inhabitants of the Town and County of POOLE, interested in the CANFORD and POOLE INCLOSURE, held at the Guildhall, in the said Town and County, this 10th day of January, 1820, it is

RESOLVED,

That after the repeated assurances of the Clerk to the Commissioners under the Canford and Poole Inclosure Act, that the Award should long since be executed, thereby preventing any Measures being adopted agreeable to the Resolutions of the 6th November, 1818, it is a matter of great surprise to this Meeting that the same has not yet been completed.

RESOLVED,

That if the Award be not executed by the 15th March next, or sufficient cause shewn why it should be further delayed, application be then made to the Court of Chancery to compel the Commissioners to complete the same.

RESOLVED,

That these Resolutions be signed by the Chairman on behalf of the Meeting, and that he be requested to forward a Copy thereof to each of the Commissioners.

RESOLVED,

That this Meeting be adjourned to Monday the 27th March next, at 11 o'clock.

JOHN CLARK,
Chairman.

RESOLVED,

That the thanks of this Meeting be given to the Sheriff, for his ready compliance in convening the same, and for his conduct in the Chair.

MOORE & SYDENHAM, PRINTERS, POOLE.

Handbills relating to 'Canford and Poole Inclosure'

However, it did mean that the greatest bone of contention between the Corporation and the Lord of the Manor had now been finally and amicably settled. The centuries of distrust and enmity between the Corporation and the Lord of the Manor would take many years to be finally eradicated, but at least no Lord of the Manor had ever taken over his estates at a more propitious time, at any rate in the debilitating series of quarrels and law suits with the Corporation, than did Mr. Ponsonby in 1825 when he took over his wife's inheritance.

Moreover, Mr. Ponsonby with his new acquired wealth and estates, decided that he would live at Canford. The old manor house at Canford had been let for many years to the English nuns of Teresa of Avila who had gone there from Hoogstract to escape from the dangers of the French revolution. It was one of the few old English manor houses left in the country and, what with the sight of this ancient grey house and the interest of seeing nuns exercising in the grounds, it had been a favourite recreation for the people of Poole to walk or ride out to Canford to "The Nunnery".

However, with the advent of the new Lord of the Manor and his wish to live at Canford in style the nuns were very soon embarking at Poole Quay on their way back to Holland. A short time afterwards the historic old mansion house was being demolished, apart from the old kitchens, to make room for the rather grandiose new mansion of Mr. Ponsonby, who had it built in the rather eccentric Elizabethan style which can still be seen there housing Canford School. Thus, a year or so after succeeding to the estates, Canford again had their lord, Mr. Ponsonby and his family, living amid his vast estate of over 16,000 acres in his new Canford House. But Mr. Ponsonby was no ordinary 'Mr.', in fact as the third son of the Earl of Bessborough, he was officially "the Honourable Mr. Ponsonby". His family had come to England with William the Conqueror. They had been awarded a tract of land in Cumberland which included the manor of Ponsonby, and it was from this that the family took its name. Moreover, the family had later been granted the honour of giving personal service to the King which, it was thought, had given rise to the family crest composed of three combs.

It was, therefore, only natural for Mr. Ponsonby to be a most ardent Whig in the great tradition of the landed aristocracy. In fact his aunt was none other than the Duchess of Devonshire, the **grande dame** whose social activities at Devonshire House were the very hub round which the high society of the Whig peerage revolved.

Canford Manor, Exterior from South-West

Mr. Ponsonby's family connection with the Devonshires was very close indeed. When his mother, the Countess of Bessborough was taken ill a year or so after his birth, his sister Caroline, only about a year older than him, had gone as a child to be brought up by the Duchess of Devonshire at Devonshire House. It was here some fifteen years later that Caroline Ponsonby, as a young woman, met William Lamb and from Devonshire House she eventually married him. It was this William Lamb who was later to inherit the title of Lord Melbourne and who in 1834 became Prime Minister.

It was, too, this same Caroline Ponsonby or, rather Caroline Lamb, for she had been married to William for over four years then, who had set the gossip of London's high society throbbing with her quite scandalous conduct with Lord Byron which even the Ladies Devonshire, Bessborough, Melbourne and the rest of London's Whig society could not camouflage, let alone stop. Eventually at a fashionable ball at which Byron ignored her, Caroline Lamb gashed her naked arms with a glass she had broken. After this even the ingenuity of that high society with its genius for permissive but apparently decorous living was utterly shocked. Caroline Lamb had outraged them sufficiently to be forced to leave the London society altogether.

It was about the time that William Ponsonby inherited Canford that his sister, who had caricatured her Byron love-affair in subsequent affairs, finally drove even Lord Melbourne to suggest divorce. Lord Melbourne, in suggesting a divorce had offered Caroline an alimony of £1,500 a year. Caroline was horrified at such a meagre offer. She wrote to all her family and friends complaining. She alleged Lord Melbourne beat her, had driven her to distraction by his cruelty — but they all knew Caroline, her tantrums and her outrages of the truth. That is, all but her brother William Ponsonby.

He wrote forthwith to Caroline's husband. He was not going to see his sister trampled on, he stormed, by such as Lord Melbourne. Lord Melbourne owed his sister a great deal for her having deigned to marry one like him of such inferior social position.....

Portrait of Lord Melbourne

Lord Melbourne, it was said, could never bring himself to answer the bombastic Lord of the Manor of Canford and Poole whose judgment, to say the least, seemed hasty and imperfect. Lord Melbourne left the answer to his sister Emily, Countess Cowper. She said that Poole's new Lord was "reckoned an ass and a jackanapes by everybody" and took over the duty of replying which, she said, she had fulfilled by 'bullying the bully'.

However, it is not surprising that Mr. Ponsonby should feel interested in politics and that it should seem appropriate to have a seat in the House of Commons on behalf of Poole. It so happened that Parliament was dissolved in 1826 and John Dent, the junior member for Poole for the past nine years or so, decided or agreed not to stand again for re-election. First to declare his candidacy was Henry Charles Sturt, on behalf of the Tories, whose address was given as Portman Square in London, though his professed earlier connections with Poole must surely have been through the Sturt's county estate, Critchell House near Wimborne which Charles Sturt had leased, when first built in 1796, to the Prince Regent where the Whig Prince had entertained Lady Jersey.

TO THE

BURGESSES

OF THE

TOWN AND COUNTY OF

POOLE.

Gentlemen,
      The encouraging support I have uniformly experienced since I first declared myself a Candidate for your favor, induces me to look with confidence to the approaching Election for the accomplishment of my hopes, by obtaining the honorable distinction of a seat in Parliament as one of your Representatives.

      Accustomed in my early days to a frequent intercourse with the Town of POOLE and its immediate vicinity, I have always felt an attachment to it, and entertained a wish to cultivate a more intimate connection with your ancient and respectable borough, whenever a fit occasion presented itself. An opportunity has offered that has enabled me to indulge this desire without disturbing your long established political connection, and without a wish to interfere with any of your local interests.

      If I should have the good fortune to succeed in this object of my ambition, and be associated with the honorable and worthy Member who has so long and so faithfully watched over your interests, it will be my pride, as it will be my duty, to co-operate with him in promoting the future welfare of the Town, and by my personal exertions, to aid his more extensive commercial knowledge and practical experience in protecting the mercantile and local interests of the Inhabitants, while at the same time, I devote my best abilities to the service of the country at large.

I have the honor to be with respect and esteem,
Gentlemen,
Your faithful obedient Servant,

HENRY CHAS. STURT.

Portman Square,
May 30th, 1826.

TO THE

BURGESSES

OF THE

TOWN AND COUNTY

OF

POOLE.

GENTLEMEN,
      The Dissolution of Parliament at length affords me the opportunity I have anxiously looked for, of offering myself as a Candidate, for the honour of representing your ancient and opulent Borough in Parliament; and soliciting the favour of your support for the attainment of that object.

      Deeply lamenting the cause, which has induced your late worthy representative Mr. DENT, to announce his intention of retiring from public life, I beg leave to assure you, that had you not been thereby called upon to select some other Gentleman for the distinguished post of representing you in Parliament, I should not have attempted upon any account to disturb the unanimity which subsisted between the Electors of POOLE, and those representatives whom they had honored with their confidence. But as no Gentleman in the remotest degree connected with the Town had been named to supply the place of Mr. DENT, I ventured to hope that the ancient connexion of the Borough of POOLE, with the Manor of CANFORD, and the community of interests which must ever subsist between them, would possess some weight with you in my favour; whilst the manly and independent character which has always distinguished this Borough, rendered the honour of representing you an object most peculiarly worthy of my ambition, and congenial to my views in becoming a member of Parliament. The kind and flattering reception which I have experienced, ever since I first presented myself to your notice last autumn, proves to me that I have not been mistaken and I will only farther assure you, Gentlemen, that should the efforts of those friends who have honoured me by their support, be crowned with that success which I confidently anticipate, no exertions will be spared by me in the discharge of those duties, which I consider to be incumbent upon every member of the House of Commons, whilst I should feel a pride and satisfaction in more particularly devoting my attention to your local interests, and promoting the welfare of this important commercial Town by every means in my power.

I have the honor to be with great respect,
Gentlemen,
Your faithful and obliged Servant,

W. F. S. PONSONBY.

Canford House, June 3rd, 1826.

Mr. Ponsonby was only a day or two behind. He had his message to the Corporator-voters printed and circulated in the town. "The kind and flattering reception which I have experienced, ever since I first presented myself to your notice", he announced, had led him to feel his candidature would be "crowned with that success which I confidently anticipate". He ended by promising that "no exertions will be spared by me in the discharge of those duties..... in promoting the welfare of this important Town".

His confidence was not misplaced. Benjamin Lester Lester, Poole's senior representative in Parliament for 17 years was top of the poll with a near-unanimous election. He got 82 votes — though, to be fair, no less than 11 of these were from his own family of the Garlands. The Lord of the Manor got 52 votes and Mr. Sturt 33.

Mr. Ponsonby succeeded in the subsequent two elections in Poole, and was its junior member from 1826 until 1831 when he applied for the stewardship of the Chiltern Hundreds and retired from his representation of Poole to fight the vacant seat in the Dorset county elections.

The County election was held throughout the County, including Poole, in October of that year and Lord Ashley was the Tory candidate in opposition to Mr. Ponsonby. Judging by the previous county election and the euphoria surrounding the Whigs and the great popularity of their reform programme, Mr. Ponsonby had every reason to expect success. He had, too, the other great benefit of his position as Lord of the Manor of a considerable part of the eastern end of the County for, with open voting, it took a brave man even in 1831 to let his Lord of the Manor know he had voted against him or, for that matter, had even desisted from voting.

The county elections in those days was polled at eleven stations (two at Bridport, two at Dorchester and one for 'Cerne and Poole') and was spread over fifteen polling days between 30 September and 17 October, even though there were only about 4,000 electors in all. There was, however, no equivalent to a register of electors, and Assessors were appointed to adjudicate on whether or not those proferring their votes were really freeholders in the county and thus entitled to vote. The adjudication was a difficult and complicated matter and, as he was entitled to do, the Assessor frequently postponed his decision, often

STATE OF THE POLL

At the Election of two Representatives in Parliament,

FOR THE

TOWN AND COUNTY OF POOLE,

June 12th, 1826.

CANDIDATES,

BENJAMIN LESTER LESTER, Esq. 82
The Honble. WILLIAM FRANCIS SPENCER PONSONBY. . 53
HENRY CHARLES STURT, Esq. 33

	L.	P.	S.		L	P	S
Absolam, William James	—			Jolliffe, William	—	—	
Adey, Thomas	—			Joyce, Thomas	—	—	
Adey, William	—			Kidd, Benjamin	—	—	
Aldridge, George	—	—		Knight, Henry Gillingham	—	—	
Aldridge, George Olive	—	—		Lander, William	—	—	
Aldridge, James	—			Ledgard, George Welch	—		—
Bartlett, Thomas			—	Leer, Humphrey	—		
Bavly, James			—	Lester, Benjamin Lester	—		
Biddle, Waring			—	Linthorne, Richard Roop	—	—	
Bird, Thomas Young			—	Linthorne, Thomas	—		
Bloomfield, Joseph Barter	—	—		Major, William	—		
Brice, George Tito		—		Major, Robert	—		
Brooks, Joshua Mauger			—	Manning, Thomas	—	—	
Buck, Richard, jun.	—	—		Noble, George	—	—	
Clark, John	—		—	Noble, George James Luke	—	—	
Clark, Samuel	—		—	Oke, William	—		—
Clark, Robert	—	—		Olive, Joseph	—		
Driver, Samuel White	—	—		Olive, Joseph jun.	—		
Driver, Charles Burrell	—	—		Orchard, Joseph White	—	—	
Durell, David	—	—		Page, Robert	—	—	
Ferris, James	—	—		Pitt, William Morton	—		
Ferris, Thomas	—	—		Pointer, James	—		
Foot, John	—		—	Salmon, Thomas	—	—	
Furnell, Henry Knight	—			Seager, James	—	—	
Furnell, William	—			Seager, Mark	—		
Gaden, Thomas		—		Sharp, John	—		
Garland, George	—			Slade, Robert	—		
Garland, Augustus Lester	—			Spurrier, Christopher	—	—	
Garland, Francis Penton	—			Spurrier, William Jubber	—		
Garland, John	—			Spurrier, Thomas Henry	—		
Garland, John Bingley	—	—		Stansmore, William	—		
Garland, Joseph	—			Strong, Samuel Spratt	—	—	
Garland, Joseph, jun.	—			Strong, Samuel Spratt, jun.	—	—	
Garland, Capt. Joseph G. R. N.	—			Strong, Thomas			—
Garland, Thomas	—		—	Thompson, Thomas			
Garland, Joseph, tertius	—		—	Wadham, Benjamin	—	—	
Haly, Richard Standish	—	—		Walker, Samuel	—	—	
Hancock, George	—		—	West, Young	—		—
Hancock, Thomas Gregory	—	—		Weston, Samuel	—	—	
Hayward, James			—	Whitewood, William	—	—	
Hayward, John	—	—		Wills, Richard	—	—	
Hayward, Richard		—		Wills, Robert	—	—	
Hyde, Revd. George Hooton	—			Wills, William Green	—	—	
Jolliff, Peter	—	—		Wise, Richard	—		—
Jolliff, Christopher	—	—		Wise, William	—	—	
Jolliffe, Rev. Peter William	—	—		Young, Samuel	—		
Jolliffe, Cornwall	—	—		Young, William	—	—	
	42	**24**	**18**	**Total**	**82**	**53**	**33**

MOORE AND SYDENHAM, PRINTERS, POOLE.

for days after the polling stations had closed.

The responsibility for the election was that of the High Sheriff of Dorset. Unfortunately he was too ill at the time of the election to take any part in it. Mr. Damer, the High Sheriff, had to delegate all his duties to deputies and the troubles started immediately with Mr. Ponsonby taking exception to the Under-Sheriff. According to Mr. Ponsonby, the Under-Sheriff, Thomas Fox of Beaminster, was an undisguised partisan of Lord Ashley and, as such, should have no part in the election. To add to the early quarrels Mr. Fox appointed Phillip William as Assessor at the election despite Mr. Ponsonby's vehement protests. In fact, Mr. Ponsonby thought little of any of the persons concerned in the election for he alleged that Mr. Stone, the Clerk to the County Council, was "an active paid agent to Lord Ashley".

When the fifteen days' of polling were over the result of the election was still not known. The weight of objections and counter-objections to the qualifications of many of the voters had led to a great back-log of adjudications on the qualification of voters. There were still over 400 votes awaiting the decision of the Assessor and the whole result of the election depended on the result of this adjudication. Of those votes declared valid after the poll had closed on 17 October, Lord Ashley had 1,847 votes and Mr. Ponsonby 1,811 and there were 424 votes awaiting adjudication.

Mr. Ponsonby and his supporters had already decided that Mr. Williams, the Assessor, had already shown partiality in favour of Lord Ashley. When Mr. Williams was interviewing voters for Mr. Ponsonby (for it was already known which way these voters wished to cast their votes, and if all were allowed Mr. Ponsonby would win by 26) he had intimidated Mr. Ponsonby's supporters by delivering to them a dissertation on the meaning and consequence of perjury in their claims to be freeholders. Moreover, they said, Mr. Williams had employed as his clerk an attorney who was employed by Lord Ashley and this appointment was persisted in despite of Mr. Ponsonby's objections. Mr. William's partiality was also shown, they said, in that he had already turned down the claims of twice as many of Mr. Ponsonby's supporters as he had of Lord Ashley's.

Mr. Ponsonby and the Whig-radicals knew they were going to be cheated.

In fact, they said, Mr. Ponsonby had already been cheated, for mere squatters, encroaching on land at Charmouth had been wrongly allowed to vote, to say nothing of the inmates of almshouses at Weymouth and Wimborne being allowed to vote. Lord Ashley, they claimed, was in danger of being elected "on the votes of these miserable dependents on charity".

The Western Times spelt all this out — and more — and then added that it "may be wrong to say much at present" as Mr. William's conduct was "shortly to be the subject of an investigation in the House of Commons"!

"While such tyrrany exists in the country", it went on, "it requires the strong energy in the friends of Reform to assert their liberties — they have done much — they will do more — they will assert their right in this election —" and the ever-to-be-repeated, confident assertion so often later heard in Poole's troubles, — "they will succeed".

The result at the end of the 15 days of polling was certainly tight and the announcement of Mr. Ponsonby's defeat caused riots in many places in the County as well as in Poole. In Poole a mob descended on, and wrecked, Longfleet House, the home of Thomas Gaden, an active opponent of reform. It went on to Parkstone where it attacked the King William Public House and then thought of Robert Parr. The mob uprooted the sign post of the King William and carried it all the way to Fish Street to use it to batter off its hinges the stout door of Robert Parr's offices and house there, — and this despite the fact that in Cerne and Poole Mr. Ponsonby had been shown to have received 211 votes out of the 316 which had been cast.

Following this result came what John Sydenham, writing a few years later, contented himself with saying led to Mr. Ponsonby's "celebrated and protracted contest with Lord Ashley". But despite the riots, the violence and the inquiries and the law suit — Mr. Ponsonby finally lost this election.

However, no one was found, either wealthy enough or foolish enough to contest with Mr. Ponsonby the subsequent Dorset County election. Mr. Ponsonby was then returned unopposed. Lord Ashley found a quieter seat.

Thomas Parr's house Fish Street

It should, however, have served as a warning for all those connected with election in which Mr. Ponsonby was concerned to watch the technicalities of future elections. And Mr. Ponsonby was to be very concerned with future municipal elections in Poole.....

Harbour Office, Town Cellars and Customs House

The arguments for the reform of most town corporations in 1834 was incontravertible. The population of England in the previous few decades had increased substantially and there had been a great migration of population into the towns from the country. This was particularly so in the rising industrial towns of the north which had mushroomed without any regard to sanitary control or aesthetic considerations. Many of the old town corporations did not even feel themselves responsible and those that did had insufficient powers to deal with the problems.

Conditions were relatively good in Poole; it could be genuinely claimed by the Poole Corporators that they had done well by the town. Their views as to what were their responsibilities could be, and later were challenged, but by and large, it would have been agreed that they managed their funds and powers well and, generally, to the benefit of the people of Poole. They had, for instance, in the years prior to the Reform Act 1832 widened High Street and Market Street, widened and straightened Corkscrew Alley and Pritchetts Alley. They had either given or bought land to extend and widen the Quay. They had been instrumental in the building of a larger school at Perry Gardens to replace the old one in Thames Street and in having a subscription library built at the bottom of High Street, as well as arranging for an extension of the Town House (now Harbour Office). They had, too, made byelaws to stop the display of goods from shops on the sidewalks, to stop dogs frequenting the Market and firm action to protect the oyster beds. An example of their efficacy can be seen in their action in the 1831 Cholera scare. The notice issued by G. W. Ledgard from the Committee composed of J. Gulston Garland, John Gosse, Robert Slade, Thomas Gaden, Robert Slade, D. O. Lander and P. Jolliffe, the Rector, sounds the acme of good sense today.

But the Poole Corporators were hardly likely to be made an exception to the general rules for reform. Whatever might be said on their behalf the Corporators of Poole were still a self-perpetuating oligarchy, and this was an affront to the ideal of representative government which had swept the country and the pressure from the newly-enfranchised 'Ten Pounders' of Parliamentary elections. The Poole Corporators were lumped with the other "shabby mongrel aristocracies" of Town Corporations due for reform and, to give them their due, most of the Corporators did not disagree in principle.

The Government turned its attention to this problem in 1833 and appointed Commissioners to inspect and report on each of the Corporations. In January 1834 each Corporation was asked to answer sixteen questions.

The Corporation's answers to the questions summarises the position of local government in Poole in 1834. The return for the Poole Corporation was prepared by James Seager, Mark Seager, James Churchill, George Penney and John Hooper. It was as follows:

TO THE

INHABITANTS

OF THE

TOWN AND COUNTY OF POOLE.

It is to be feared from the reports contained in the Public Papers, that the Cholera Morbus, which has proved so fatal in Asia and various parts of Europe, has made its appearance in England. It becomes, therefore, the Duty of every one to exert himself to prevent, if possible, the introduction of this direful Disease into his own Family, Town, or Neighbourhood.

By Order of Government, a BOARD OF HEALTH has been formed in this Town, consisting of the Magistrates, the Sheriff, the Parochial Minister, the Collector and Comptroller of the Customs, and the Gentlemen of the Medical Profession; who will at all times be ready to afford any information, or receive any communication that may tend to promote the Health of the Inhabitants.

The Board of Health have endeavoured to obtain the best information as to the most effectual means of Preventing the Introduction or Spread of this Disease, and they beg to call the attention of their fellow Townsmen to a few suggestions which they earnestly beseech them to adopt, believing that if they do so, they will prove efficacious (under the divine blessing) in preventing the Introduction or spread of the Cholera Morbus in Poole.

First. The Board recommend constant attention to EXTERNAL CLEANLINESS. That the Streets, Lanes, and other Highways of the Town, be kept free from Dirt, Filth, or Stagnant Water; and they hope that every Householder will cheerfully co-operate with the Scavengers in endeavoring to accomplish this important object; and as there are but few public Pumps, that they will cause a few Buckets of Water to be daily thrown into the Gutter opposite their respective Dwellings, in order to prevent Noxious Exhalations arising therefrom, which are at all times very prejudicial to health.

Second. The Board recommend INTERNAL CLEANLINESS. That no accumulation of Dirt, or Decayed Vegetables or Fruit, be allowed to remain in or about their Habitations, but that every care be taken to keep their Houses Clean and well Ventilated. A free circulation of Air is of much importance, the Windows should therefore be opened as often as Weather will permit.

Third. PERSONAL CLEANLINESS. It is very important that Parents should pay particular attention to their Children being kept clean, and sufficiently Clothed to protect them from the Effects of Cold and Damp Weather, and those who from extreme Poverty are unable to do so, should make known their situation to their Wealthier Neighbours, whose liberality they may be assured will be manifested as on all former occasions.

Fourth. The Board earnestly recommend a strict regard to Habits of Temperance and Sobriety, as nothing tends to predispose the human frame to disease, more than intemperance. *All immoderate use of Spirituous Liquors should especially be avoided.*

Fifth. The Board desire to impress on the Inhabitants, the great importance of the earliest possible application to Medical Aid, should any person be attacked by any disease that may resemble the Cholera Morbus. This is a matter of much moment, and cannot be too powerfully urged on the attention of all classes, as the progress of this disease is generally so rapid, that it is only by an early application of Medical Skill that beneficial results can at all be relied on. *That the Poor may be encouraged so to do, the Medical Gentlemen have kindly promised their services to them gratuitously.*

Lastly. While the Board have felt it their duty to place these Remarks before the Inhabitants by way of Caution and Guidance, they feel pleasure in encouraging them to hope and believe that such is the Climate of England, that if general attention be paid to Cleanliness, Ventilation, and Sobriety, together with timely application for Medical advice and assistance, the continuance of this Disease in England will not be long, but that our Country will speedily, by the blessing of God, be freed from its direful consequences. All unnecessary Fear and Anxiety should therefore, be avoided, under the full assurance that if we invoke the Protection of an invisible but Almighty Guardian, and diligently use the appointed means of safety, he will crown our endeavours with his blessing.

ON BEHALF OF THE BOARD,

G. W. LEDGARD, *Mayor,*

CHAIRMAN.

11th November, 1831.

Municipal Corporations Commissioners

	Questions	Answers
1.	The local limits of the Corporation	The local limits of the Corporation on Land and co-extensive with the only Parish in the Town and County of Poole (Saint James) bounded on the North East by part of the Tithing of Longfleet in the County of Dorset on the North West and South East and South and South West by the Harbour of Poole on the West by part of the Parish of Hamworthy in the County of Dorset.
2.	The Charters by which it is constituted	The Corporation is founded by prescription and is now constituted by the several Charters enumerated in the Answer to the next Question.
3.	The Title of the Corporation a Copy of the Governing Charter and the data of all other Charters	The Title of the Corporation is "The Mayor, Bailiff, Burgesses and Commonalty of the Town of Poole" The principal Charter Governing the Corporation of Poole is one granted by Queen Elizabeth dated 23rd June in the 10th year of her reign (1568) a printed translation of which accompanies this. The dates of the other Charters are as follows:— William Longspee Charter (sans date) William Montacute Charter dated 10th June, 45 Edward 3 (1372) Thomas Montacute Charter 12th Henry 4, 8th July, 1412 Henry 6th Charter Anno Regni 11 (1433) Henry 6th Charter Anno Regni 31 (1453) Edward 4th Charter Anno Regni 1 – 20 Jany 1461 Henry 8th Charter Anno Regni 3rd – 20 June 1512 Henry 8th Grant for cutting wood in Southampton and Sussex 17 Feby 1521 Arthur Plantaganet's Charter 18 Henry 8th, 1527 Queen Elizabeth's confirmation of the Grants of William Longspee and William Montacute and Ratification of Thomas Montacutes Charter Anno Regni 18th Jany 1559 The Charter of Charles 2nd Anno Regni 18 (1678) The Charter of James 2nd Anno Regni 4 (1689) Winchelsea Charter granted in 1365
4.	The several officers	The Mayor and Mayor of the Staple Elected

of the Corporation. How and whom appointed or removed the time for which they hold their respective Functions and Privileges and their salaries and incidental emoluments.

annually by a majority of the resident Burgesses from among themselves. The Mayor is ex-officio a Magistrate and presides in the absence of the Recorder or his deputy at the Quarter Sessions.
Admiral of the Port
One of the judges at the weekly Court of Record.
Clerk of the Market.
He has no salary.
The only incidental emoluments are a Bushel of Corn from every Vessel bringing corn from Foreign Parts. And a contribution of Fish from all Fishermen not belonging to the Port bringing Fish for Sale.

The RECORDER is appointed on a vacancy occurring by a majority of the Resident Burgesses. His appointment is for life and is confirmed by the King.
He is ex-officio a Justice of the Peace and when present presides at Quarter Sessions.
He has the power to appoint a Deputy.
He has no salary nor any incidental emoluments.

The ALDERMEN become so after having served the office of Mayor.
They with the Mayor Elect the Sergeants at Mace and they or two of them are directed by Charter of Charles the 2nd to be present when the Mayor Recorder and Justices of the Peace are sworn.

The SENIOR BAILIFF is elected annually in the same manner as the Mayor.
He is a judge of the Weekly Court of Record and is generally elected one of the four justices of the Peace.
He has no salary nor any incidental emoluments.

JUSTICES. Four Justices of the Peace elected annually in the same manner as the Mayor. They hold the Quarter Sessions and have an Exclusive jurisdiction within the Town and County.
They have no salaries.
The only incidental emoluments are the usual fees of office paid to the Town Clerk as their Clerk.

The SHERIFF. The Sheriff is elected annually in the same manner as the Mayor.
He has the exclusive execution of all writs and Processes within the Town and County except

those issuing from the Weekly Court of Record (which are directed to the Sergeants at Mace).

He has power to hold a monthly Court and in all other things the same power as the Sheriff of any County.

He holds an Annual Court called his Tourn at which a Jury is sworn and examine all weights and measures.

The Sheriff has no salary but an allowance from the Corporation for his Quietus of Twenty Guineas. He has the usual fees of office.

The TOWN CLERK & CLERK OF THE PEACE. The Town Clerk is elected in the same manner as the Recorder.

He is also appointed for life and his appointment is confirmed by the King.

He is also Prothonotary of the Weekly Court of Record.

He has a salary of Twenty pounds a year from the Corporation for attending their meetings and recording the Proceedings.

The Town Clerk has annually a Bill on the Corporation for General legal business done by him.

He receives the Fees as Clerk of the Peace upon the same terms as the Clerk of the Peace of the County.

He is also Clerk to the Magistrates.

The WATER BAILIFF. The Water Bailiff is elected annually in the same manner as the Mayor.

He has the execution of Process within the Admiralty Jurisdiction.

No salary but the same incidental emoluments as the Mayor.

TWO CORONERS. Two Coroners elected annually in the same manner as the Mayor having exclusive jurisdiction within the Town and County.

They have no salary but the usual fees of office.

CONSTABLES OF THE STAPLE. Two Constables of the Staple are annually elected in the same manner as the Mayor who have no duties, salary or emoluments.

KEY KEEPERS. Key Keepers — The Mayor and Justices are annually elected Key Keepers and Overseers of the new Almshouses but there are no duties, salaries or emoluments attached to either of these offices.

FOUR CONSTABLES. Two Constables are elected Annually in the same manner as the Mayor and two others are appointed annually at Easter Quarter Sessions.
Their duties are those generally attached to the office. One of them is appointed as Sessions High Constable with a salary of Ten Pounds a year.
They all receive the general fees of their office. The Corporation have the Power to appoint Brokers, Carmen, Watermen, Porters and Packers.

CORN METERS are annually appointed and receive no emolument from the Corporation.

SERGEANTS AT MACE. Two Sergeants at Mace are appointed by the Mayor and Aldermen as Vacancies occur.
Their appointment is General and they continue in office during the pleasure of the Mayor and Aldermen.
They are the Bailiffs of the Weekly Court of Record and execute the process of that Court.
They receive a salary of Ten pounds each per annum besides fees.

5.	The mode by which persons become free. Their duties privileges and emoluments. The number of resident and non-resident Freemen.	There is no Body denominated Freemen. The Burgesses are admitted by election of a Majority of the resident Burgesses. The duty of a Burgess is to attend all meetings appointed by the Mayor. Those elected previous to the 1st March 1831 have the right of voting for representatives of Poole. They have as already stated the right to elect the Mayor and other officers out of the Corporation. They receive no emolument. There are 91 resident and 71 non-resident.
6.	By whom and from whom the ruling body of the Corporation is Elected.	There is no ruling Body in the Corporation distinct from the rest.
7.	Fees paid on admission to the	A Fine has been paid to the Mayor for the general purpose of the Corporation on the admission of

Freedom or any Office in the Corporation and to whom paid.	each Burgess which has varied in amount but which has of late years been £25. The fees paid are as follows:—

Town Clerk   £2. 2. 0.
His Clerk   5. 0.
Sergeant at Mace each 10/6d. £1. 1. 0.
                           £3. 8. 0.

besides the stamp. There are no fees paid on the Admission to any other offices.

8. Courts, Criminal and Civil. The officers or Magistrates presiding or otherwise acting in them. The extent of their Jurisdiction. Whether exclusive or otherwise. The nature of their process. What fees are paid in them and to whom And Tables of Costs.	QUARTER SESSIONS held before the Mayor, Recorder or his Deputy and the Justices of the Peace. An exclusive Jurisdiction over all cases arising in the Town and County. The Process at the Court is nearly the same as in Dorset and other Sessions. No Tables of Fees have been made but they are regulated by the County fees. There is a Weekly Court of Record held before the Mayor and Senior Bailiff having an unlimited but not an exclusive Jurisdiction over all Pleas comprised in Pages 20, 21 and 22 in the printed Charter of Elizabeth. The Admiralty Court is held by the Mayor as Admiral whatever Occasion required. A Jury is empannelled usually of Old Ships Masters and Pilots who generally perambulate the boundaries of the Harbour and present all nuisances and Incroachments. The Sheriff holds his County Court whenever it is necessary. And an annual Court called his Tourn when a Jury are appointed to examine Weights and Measures in the Town. The fees received in the Weekly Court of Record are regulated by ancient Custom and are very trifling in amount. The fees in the County Court are the same as in other County Courts. There are no fees attached to the Admiralty Court.
9. The Juries Grand and Petty— Criminal and Civil. By whom & from whom selected.	The Juries at Sessions Grand and Petty consist of 24 each and are selected by the Sheriff under a Precept from the Mayor and Senior Bailiff from the respectable Householders of the Town. The Jurors in the Court of Record have been

A LIST OF

BURGESSES

IN THE CORPORATION OF THE TOWN AND COUNTY OF POOLE,

Admitted September the 16th, 1830,

AND BY WHOM NOMINATED.

BURGESSES.	NOMINATED.	
Absolam, William James	Isaac Steele,	John Hooper
Adey, Thomas	John Adey	Charles Hiley
Adey, William	Stephen Adey	Stephen Adey, jun.
Aldridge, James	Henry Mooring Aldridge	Joseph Crabb
Barter, Joseph	Thomas Barter	George Penney
Barter, Henry	John Miller Bloomfield	James Barter, a. Lawrence
Bayly, James	William Scaplen Bayly	John Tulloch
Bayly, John	John Slade	Robert Standley Slade
Bird, John	Thomas Slade	Isaac Notley
Bloomfield, Joseph Barter	Joseph Barter Bloomfield, jun.	John Strong Adey
Clark, Samuel	Tom Rickman	George Lockyer Parrott, R.N.
Durell, David	Robert Tito Durell	Robert Durell
Durell, John Nicholson	David Durell	Francis Edwards
Foot, John	James Churchill	Robert Slade
Furnell, Henry K.	Thomas Lamport	Martin K. Welch
Furnell, William	Robert Henning	George Masterman Henning
Gaden, Thomas	Benjamin Skutt Gaden	Caleb Jackson, R. N.
Garland, Joseph	James Salter	Revd. James C. Parr
Garland, Joseph, jun.	Joseph Hare Garland	Thomas Arnold
Garland, Capt. Joseph Gulston, R.N.	Thomas Salter	John Harrison
Garland, John Bingley	Lester Garland	Richard Penney
Garland, John	John Gosse, jun.	Edward Lisby
Garland, George	George Vallis Garland	Thomas Slade, junr.
Hancock, George	William Parr	George Hancock Gutch
Hancock, Thomas Gregory	George Holland	John Pitt Gutch
Hayward, James	Jeremiah Olive Hayward	Thomas Strong Hayward
Jolliffe, William	James Jolliffe, a. Bethell	Robert Slade
Jolliff, Peter	William Jolliffe Barter	Robert Poole Slade
Joyce, Thomas	Joseph Joyce	Charles Weeks
Knight, Henry Gillingham	Joseph Knight	John Durant
Keates, Thomas William	William Gosse	John Williamson
Lander, David Osmond	Frederick C. Lander	Alfred Robert Lander
Lander, John	Robert Henning Parr, jun.	James Turtle
Ledgard, George Welch	Richard Ledgard	James Revans
Ledgard, George	Nathaniel Polhill	John Turpin
Leer, Humphrey	John Slade	James Slade
Linthorne, Richard Roope	James King,	Joseph King, jun.
Lester, Benjamin Lester	Robert Slade	Tito D. Hodges
Orchard, Joseph White	Robert Henning Parr	Richard Weston Parr
Seager, James	James George Gaden Seager	William Green
Seager, Mark	Edward Seager	William Seager Green
Slade, Robert	David Slade	Thomas Slade
Spurrier, Thomas Henry	Thomas Henry Spurrier, jun.	James Bristowe, jun.
Strong, Samuel Spratt, jun.	Samuel Henry Strong	John Gosse
Thomson, Thomas	Samuel Vallis Thompson	Richard C. Hopkins
West, Young	John Wickens West	Thomas Ellis
Whitewood, William	Robert Turtle	James Sturmey
Wills, Robert	Richard Stanworth	John Kendall

MOORE AND SYDENHAM, PRINTERS, POOLE.

heretofore selected by the Sergeants at Mace under the Precept of the Judges of the Court. In the last instance they were selected by Prothonotary and approved by the Judges of the Court.

10. The Management of the local Police & general regulation of the Town.

By the Mayor and Magistrates.

11. The Superintendence of Gaols by whom exercised and under what control

The superintendence of the Gaol is exercised by the Magistrates.
The Sheriff exercises jurisdiction over the Debtors Ward.

12. Fines imposed by the Corporation on their own members and others

There has been no recent Instance of the Corporation fining their own Members but have the power and have heretofore exercised it. They impose various small Fines under Byelaws for the Good Government of the Town and Fisheries.

13. The nature of the Property the amount of the Receipts of the Corporation, from whom derived, by whom received, to what purposes and by whom applied, how and to whom accounted for.

Freehold Lands and Tenements and Tolls of Markets and Fairs. Interest of Money advanced to the Scavengers for improving the Streets.
Fines paid on admittion of Burgesses.
The amount of Receipts averaged at 15 years.

Rents	£350
Tolls	£230
Interest	£ 15
Fines on admissions	£150

Received by the Mayor and by him applied to the following purposes —
Widening the streets and other public improvements in the Town
Repairs of Almshouses and Public Buildings
Salaries of officers
Legal expenses
Interest on money borrowed
Salary of £20 to the Organist and Annual Dinner on appointment of officers
Four Sessions Dinners and celebrating the King's birthday.
The receipts and expenditure are accounted for to the Corporation at large yearly at a special meeting for the express purpose of Auditing and Vouching the Mayor's Accounts.

The Corporation are also Lay Impropriators of the Tithes of Parkstone and Longfleet which have produced on an average of 15 years £342 per annum and which has been received by the Mayor for the time being and the Corporation have disposed of the same in salaries to the Minister of Saint James and his Curate and payment of an annual quit rent of £12.16.0d. and in payment of interest on Incubrances thereof.

The Tithes are accounted for in the same way as the Mayor's General Account at an Annual meeting. The Corporation are also Trustees of the Quay Fund under the Local Act and they Apply the proceeds as requested to the repairs and improvement of the Quays and Harbour as directed by the Act.

14. The Patronage Ecclesiastical and and other Exercised by the Corporation through whom dispersed.

The Corporation are the Patrons of the Church of Saint James and is dispensed by a Majority of the Corporation. The Corporation are also Patrons of divers Charitable Institutions.

15. A Schedule of the dates and Titles of the local Acts of Parliament relating to Municipal Government or local taxation

An Act of 29 Geo 2nd 1756 for the better ascertaining recovering and collecting certain duties payable upon the importation or exportation of Goods and Merchandizes into or out of the Harbour of the Town and County of Poole. And also of Ballast and Boomage duties payable in respect of Ships and Vessels coming into and going out of the said Harbour and for keeping in repair the said Harbour and the Quays and Wharfs and for providing a proper place for keeping Gunpowder in or near the said Town; and for establishing and regulating the nightly watch and enlighting the streets of the said Town.

16. The general state and prospects of the Town

We deem it advisable not to answer on our own responsibility.

signed: James Seager.   Mark Seager.   George Penney.
          John Hooper.   Jos. Barter.   Jas. Churchill.
          Robt. H. Parr, Town Clerk.

Edward Gambier, one of the Commissioners, came to Poole late in January 1834 and the Corporation asked the town clerk to attend him at the Guildhall and 'to answer the interrogatories'.

The report of the Commissioners reinforced the Government's views on reform and a Bill for the reform of local government was drafted, and passed its first reading in June 1834.

At the meeting of the Corporation on 24th June the Corporation heard of some of the provisions of the Bill and did not like them. They had heard from other Corporations which thought little better of the Bill. The Poole Corporation

"Resolved, That a Committee be appointed to watch the progress of the Bill..... and to appoint a deputation to meet in London other deputations from other Corporations and to co-operate with them as may be deemed necessary for the benefit of the Borough".

The Committee consisted of William Adey, George Hancock, Joseph Barter, Thomas Arnold, John Adey and the town clerk and £300 was put at their disposal to carry out the terms of the resolution.

George Hancock was made Chairman and he reported back to the Council rather hopefully on 1st July to say that the Committee had appointed Robert Parr, the town clerk, as its deputation. He had been to London and had reported that he thought the Lords would receive evidence against the objectionable clauses in the Bill and the Committee felt that they should formally petition the Lords, giving them the views of the Corporation and asking for their witnesses to be heard at the bar of the House.

The Committee prepared such a petition which was approved by the Corporation later that same month. It started by setting out the Corporation's "Rights and Immunities under its fourteen Charters", and went on:

"That your Petitioners have in pursuance of their Charters been elected for life and possess as they conceive a Right to their privileges as indefeasible as the right of any Peer or office Bearer of the realm and they humbly demand Protection of your Right Honourable House for this their Constitutional Right".

"That your Petitioners desire to express their readiness to adopt and carry unto executions any plan of Reform which may be thought conducive to the good government of their Borough".

"That your Petitioners regret to find in the Bill before your Right Honourable House for the Regulation of Municipal Corporations it is proposed to displace the present Governing Body in each Corporation. That your Petitioners are not aware of the slightest charge having been brought against them".

"That your Petitioners also observe with regret that in the proposed Bill the inchoate Rights of Freemen preserved by the Parliamentary Reform Bill are now to be taken away and that the various local Charters which are founded for the Benefit of Freemen and their Children will cease with the Existing Generation. They appeal to your Right Honour-

View of the town from Constitution Hill

able House whether it is just to condemn without accusation or to deprive without a hearing and whether it is consistent with the Constitutional practice in these Realms to condemn the innocent with the Guilty or to apply a general Confiscation as a remedy for individual crime".

"That your Petitioners submit to your Right Honourable House that the proposed Plan of annual Elections and triennial Tenure in Town Councils is in nowise adapted to the Genuis of the British Constitution and they avow their deliberate conviction that such a plan will be productive of excitement and party strife in every Borough rather than conducive to quiet and peaceable local government".

"Your Petitioners would further submit to your Right Honourable House whether if the Burgess Franchise be extended to every Householder connected with a three years Residence and payment of Rates the issue of the Elections ought not to be made to depend upon the Amount of Rates paid by voters. Your Petitioners would deny to no Rate Payer the right of expressing his opinion but they submit the effect of that opinion upon the local government should not be more than equal to his share of the local Burdens. That a numerical Majority of Householders in the Borough if taken from the lowest class of dwellings would be found in its aggregate Payment to the Poor Rates not to equal a fourth part of the Total Amount of Poor Rates paid, within the Borough. Your Petitioners therefore submit that the Body who will be authorised to lay on the new Borough Rate should be chosen by those who have the greater part of it to pay and that it would be equally unjust and inexpedient to place the Municipal Power in any other Hands than those who really pay the Municipal Burdens".
"Your Petitioners would also submit that if it should seem to your Lordships inexpedient to regulate the Elections by the amount of Rates the only alternative which remains to do anything like Justice to the Ratepayers of the Borough would be to confine the Municipal Franchise to the same class as now possess the Parliamentary Franchise. This would also prevent the Expense of a Separate Burgess Roll and would in the Opinion of Your Petitioners conduce to the Peace and good government of the Town".

"That the proposed Annexation of the Parliamentary District to the Borough for Municipal purposes is highly objectionable".

"That the Patronage of the Church now in the Hands of the Corporation who are principally Churchmen will be thrown into the Hands of Ratepayers the Majority of whom are non-conformist to the Establishment".

"That the Corporation of Poole possess an Admiralty Jurisdiction which has been found highly advantageous to the Port and the Fisheries belonging to it and which Admiralty Jurisdiction is not proposed to be preserved by the Bill".

On 5th August the Corporation were told that if their witnesses attended the House of Lords on 7th August they would be heard.

The Corporation sent two witnesses. Joseph Barter, an assistant overseer and vestry clerk, was the only Corporator witness. In principle, he had always been in favour of the reform of urban government. In fact he had been the first signatory of the letter to the Mayor in January 1827 asking the Corporations themselves to consider a wider constitution for the Poole Corporation. He now, however, seemed to have decided that the old Corporation was better than a Council elected as proposed in the Bill. The other witness was George Billows whose firm, Messrs. Billows & Son and Turpin, had just previously made the pillars and lamps for Poole's new street lighting.

Lord Stafford led the questioning of the Corporation's witnesses from the Whig point of view. The Whig Lords had been well briefed on Poole Corporation's activities. They inferred the Corporation's wrongful actions in supporting the interest of the Poole fisherman, Tilsed, in Sir Charles Chad's action against him for fishing in Poole waters over which Sir Charles claimed exclusive rights of fishing; they inferred the Corporation had wasted a great deal of money in opposing Mr. Ponsonby's Bridge Bill. Mr. Barter was even questioned as to the amount of Mr. Parr's legal bill on the Corporation for 1834.

The Duke of Wellington who knew something of Poole from having stayed in Poole at the Antelope's best room early in his military career, himself took some part in the matter but Joseph Barter can only be credited as doing moderately well in his evidence. Perhaps the most prophetic statement came from George Billows at the end of his evidence. He said that Poole merchants, mariners and traders on the one hand and the residents of Parkstone and Hamworthy on the other were "Parties so different in their interests (that they) will never be able to unite cordially in the Municipal Government of the town".

Lord Lyndhurst and his brother peers, however, were sufficiently impressed by the case of the Corporations, including Poole, of course,

POOLE REFORM ASSOCIATION.

At a Meeting held at the London Tavern, Poole, on Thursday, June 11th, 1835, pursuant to notice, for the purpose of forming a BRANCH ASSOCIATION;

GEORGE KEMP, ESQ., IN THE CHAIR :---

It was Resolved unanimously.

1. That an Association be formed, to be called the " POOLE BRANCH REFORM ASSOCIATION," for the purpose of superintending the Registration of Voters for the Borough and District of Poole, and for the County of Dorset residing within such Borough and District, and for securing to the Electors the free use of their Rights and Privileges.

2. That all persons subscribing 2s. 6d. per Annum or upwards, or making a donation of one guinea, be constituted a member of this Association.

3. That the business of the Association be managed by a Committee of Twenty-one persons, to be chosen annually by the members of the Association.

4. That the Committee meet as often as may be necessary, to transact the business connected with the Association, and that Five Gentlemen do form a Quorum.

The Chairman having left the Chair---

A vote of thanks was passed unanimously for his able conduct therein.

which had given evidence before them for them to amend the Common's Municipal Corporations Bill out of all recognition. Their action precipitated another Parliamentary crisis between the two Houses but finally early in 1835 Sir Robert Peel persuaded the Duke of Wellington to order the Tory peers to retreat from their opposition and, shortly afterwards, with some slight modifications the Bill was passed by both Houses and received Royal Assent on 9th September, 1835.

The Reformers had anticipated the passage of the Act by three months. In June the Reform supporters had had their meeting at the London Tavern. They had taken over from the Whigs of Poole. They elected George Lockyer Parrott by acclaim, displacing George Kemp, the leader of the Poole Whigs. They had nominated candidates for all the anticipated 18 seats on the new Poole Council. The Poole Tories, furious that the Reformers should nominate 18 candidates instead of coming to a gentlemanly agreement between the parties as to who should be nominated, themselves nominated 18 candidates of their own and a free-for-all election was ensured for the first Poole municipal election and a feeling of animosity already arising between the parties.

At the meeting of the Corporation following the news of the passing of the Act there would have been some talk of their own, now certain, demise on 31st December that year. The minutes of that meeting, however, are eloquent of the feeling of numbness which must suddenly have afflicted the Corporators. The minutes of that historic meeting were as follows:

Town & County of Poole   At a monthly meeting of this Corporation held at the Guildhall the 7th October 1835

Nothing done.
(sgd) **Robert Slade, Mayor**

The Poole Corporation, in its 268th year since its formal establishment in Elizabeth's Charter, was in its last three months of existence.

The Corporators felt sore and cheated. Each of the freemen living in Poole had in 1830 each nominated two new freemen. 92 new freemen had paid £2,300 between them for the privilege of membership of the Corporation. Many of these were the minor sons or other relatives of Corporators who had been promised free membership on coming of age. The Corporation would now be unable to carry out that promise.

Some of the Corporators recovered their spirits sufficiently to call a special meeting of the Corporation later in October to consider "the propriety of refunding in every instance the sum of £25 being the price paid on nomination of each Minor as a Burgess of the Corporation in order that they should be elected free Burgesses on their attaining their respective majorities, the Corporation having now no power to fulfil such contract".

The meeting resolved "to repay the sums accordingly".

Some of the Corporators disagreed with this decision. William Jolliffe, Tito Hodges, James Seager, George Penney, G. Lockyer Parrott, James Churchill, James Salter, and R. C. Hopkins signed a letter to the Mayor saying that they felt it their duty to protest "because it appears to us illegal and involving a serious and dangerous breach of trust and also because such an appropriation of the Corporate funds ..... is a direct variance with and against the spirit of the Municipal Reform Bill".

In this very early quarrel among the Corporators themselves lays the very kernel of the quarrels which were later to be developed. The older Corporators looked upon the Corporation as the creation of their ancestors and themselves, with its funds being essentially their funds. They had bought and fought for the Charters and privileges; despite the power to do so they had never levied a rate. The Corporation's possessions and funds were theirs. The newer Corporators looked on the old Corporation's possessions and funds as belonging to the townspeople as a whole because the Corporators' actions and ownership of lands or funds were or should have been on behalf of "the commonalty" as much as the Corporators themselves. It therefore did not matter to the Reform members that funds had been received from the individual Corporators, they were received on behalf of the commonalty on trust for them and should only be expended on their behalf. The two sides could never appreciate the other's viewpoint.

Town and County of Poole.

At a numerous Meeting of the Electors of the Borough of Poole, held at the Antelope Hotel, on Tuesday, June 16th, 1835, to form a CONSERVATIVE ASSOCIATION of Persons, who, although friendly to the Redress of Real Grievances, and the correction of all proved Abuses, are nevertheless resolved to use all lawful means to preserve unimpaired the fundamental principles of the British Constitution in Church and State,—

W. THOMPSON, Esq., in the Chair;

THE FOLLOWING RESOLUTIONS WERE PROPOSED AND UNANIMOUSLY AGREED TO

FIRST,
That an Association be now formed, and that the following Declaration be adopted, embodying the principles of this Association.

We whose Names are hereunto subscribed, declare our fixed determination to maintain the tried and ancient principles on which the Constitution of our Country is founded; and we hold ourselves pledged to resist all measures, by which the necessary connexion between the Established Church and the State may be severed; by which the dignity of the Monarchy may be impaired, or its existence endangered; by which the privileges of the House of Lords, as an independent branch of the legislature, may be virtually annihilated, or the deliberative powers of the Commons House of Parliament become fettered or controuled; as we are convinced, that, on the united and energetic support of these authorities, depend the continuance of social order, the security of property, and the interest of religion.

SECOND,
That all persons residing in, or connected with the County of Dorset, or the Town and County of Poole, who entertain such principles, be invited to enrol themselves as Members of this Association.

THIRD,
That the Association be conducted by a President, a Vice-President, a Treasurer, two Secretaries, and a Committee of Ten, to be elected at the Annual Meeting, with power to fill up vacancies.

FOURTH,
That ROBERT SLADE, Esq., (Mayor,) be the President of this Association.

FIFTH,
That ROBERT SLADE, Jun., Esq., of Parkstone, be the Vice-President.

SIXTH,
That ISAAC STEELE, Esq., be the Treasurer.

SEVENTH,
That J. HAIRBY, Esq., M. D., and G. LEDGARD, Esq., be the Secretaries to this Association.

EIGHTH,
That Donations be received, and that all Members of the Association subscribe not more than One Pound, nor less than One Shilling; and that the money so raised shall be applied to the legitimate expenses incidental to the Registry and to Elections, and to the general purposes of this Association, subject to the controul, and under the direction of the Committee.

NINTH,
That Meetings of the Committee be summoned by the Secretaries, under the direction of the President, Vice-President, or Three of the Committee, and that Public Meetings be called at the discretion of the Committee.

TENTH,
That the above Resolutions be printed in the Dorset County Chronicle, and the Standard Newspapers.

W. THOMPSON, Chairman.

RESOLVED UNANIMOUSLY,
That the thanks of this Meeting be presented to the Chairman, for his kindness in taking the Chair, and his great attention to the business that has been brought before him.

J. SYDENHAM, TYP., POOLE.

These members opposing the repayment took legal advice which supported their contention. J. Campbell, a barrister of the Temple, wrote to them at the end of October saying that before the Municipal Corporations Act "Corporations might squander their funds or appropriate them to the use of their own members without responsibility or control" but he thought the Poole Corporation's proceeds were made illegal by the Act and could be set aside if "the New Council should corruptly refuse to set aside the mortgage".

The old Corporation even refused to enter the Protest in their Records as they had been requested to do. Instead, they resolved at their subsequent meeting on 4th November not only to repay the amounts, but that the repayment of money received from the minors took "precedent of any other payment".

The Committee appointed to watch the progress of the Municipal Corporations Bill made its last report to say that the Town Clerk had submitted a Bill to them for £331.13.2d. and they had recommended him to accept £300 in full discharge of his Bill.

The very last meeting of the old Corporation took place in the Guildhall at 11 a.m. on Wednesday, 2nd December, 1835. They granted a mortgage of Corporation property to secure the £400 they had been given by Benjamin Lester as an endowment for the organist of St. James Church. To get the money they mortgaged the Shipwright Arms and their Clay Cellars which adjoined it. They then passed the following two last, sad resolutions:—

"Resolved — That at this last Monthly meeting of the old Corporation although we the Corporators are unwilling to revise any of the feelings which animated us whilst we thought there was a chance of effective resistance to the Municipal Corporation's Bill are desirous to testifying our acknowledgments of and gratitude for the countenance and support afforded us in our endeavours to pursue our Rights and Privileges by His Royal Highness the Duke of Cumberland, His Grace the Duke of Wellington, the Earl of Shaftesbury, Baron Lyndhurst and Lord Ashley that our humble and heartfelt thanks be given to them accordingly and that the Mayor be requested to communicate the above Resolution to them".

"Resolved — That the Plate belonging to the Corporation be sold and that the proceeds thereof be laid out in the purchase of Plate to be presented to the Parish Church of Saint James....."

The following Corporators signed those last minutes: Robert Slade, the Mayor; George W. Ledgard, Senior Bailiff; James Seager; Robert Slade, Senr; George Hancock; Samuel Clark; George Ledgard; Thos. G. Hancock; Richard Ledgard, Sheriff; John Adey; James Sturmey; R. Linthorne; Thomas Gaden; Wm. Adey; D. O. Lander and T. C. Sharp.

These sixteen Corporators were the only ones to attend the last rites of the old Corporation. Twenty-nine days later there were no Corporators left, for their office had been abolished.

The old maces and punch bowl of the Corporation of Poole used prior to 1832

Those supporting municipal reform had been made confident of success by the results of the General Election in January 1835. The Poole reformers' confidence had been boosted further by the Poole Parliamentary by-election of May 1835, occasioned by Poole's senior member, the Whig/Reformer, Sir John Byng, having been created Baron Stafford, when his son, George S. Byng, was returned.

The Poole Reformers had immediately started preparing for the inevitable local election to follow the passing of the Municipal Corporations Act.

In those days of 'open count,' voting the parties were well aware of how each voter had voted. Therefore, both parties knew how those voting in the Parliamentary elections had voted. The Reform Party calculated that they would win all nine seats in the South-East Ward, which was

POOLE ELECTION.

NOTICE IS HEREBY GIVEN, that the POLLING will commence To-morrow Morning at NINE o'clock precisely, at the Guildhall.

And in order to avoid partiality, and to prevent confusion and delay, the Sheriff has determined on taking the Votes for each Candidate alternately.

Voters in the interest of the Honorable G. BYNG are requested to present themselves on the *right hand side* of the Table; Voters in the interest of General Sir C. GRANT on the *left hand side* of the Table.

RICHARD LEDGARD.

POOLE, *SHERIFF.*
19th May, 1835.

N.B. No Person will be admitted within the space below the Bench except the Poll Clerks, and the Agents for the Candidates.

J. SYDENHAM, PRINTER, POOLE.

that part of the old town lying south-east of High Street, plus Longfleet and Hamworthy. They were less hopeful of the North-West Ward, which included the merchants' houses of West Street and Market Street, plus Parkstone, but they thought that if they put up three of their strongest candidates there they would win at least one seat there which would be sufficient to give them a majority on the new Council. With even a single seat majority they would be able to elect 6 aldermen who were to be elected by the Councillors. They would then have complete control of the new Council.

The division of political opinion in Poole had never been clear-cut. This was probably because the Tory party had been supreme in Parliament for half-a-century and the division of opinion within the Corporation had been referred to as the 'Ministerial' or, sometimes, 'Mayor's Party' and the opposition, vaguely in favour of the Whigs. With the Whigs having adopted the Reform programme the combined party were in Poole variously referred to as the Radicals, the Reform Party and in later years, the Liberals. The Mayor's Party or Tory Party gradually became over the following decade the new Conservative Party, through the Poole Conservative association which was formed at a meeting held on 16th June, 1835. This meeting elected its first President, Robert Slade, the Mayor; its first Vice-President, Robert Slade, Junr.; its first Treasurer, Isaac Steele. Its Joint Secretaries were Dr. J. Hairby and George Ledgard and the Chairman of this inaugural meeting was W. Thompson.

But, in those early days, no one knew quite how to refer to the new party which had come about by the Whigs adopting the members of the reform movement. John Lankester, for instance, the first witness in the later inquiry by the Select Committee of the House of Commons, when asked to define the two parties in Poole, said, "I feel great difficulty in describing them; I know there are two parties, but I hardly know how to describe them". Even when the leader of the party, George Lockyer Parrott, was asked to which party he belonged, he answered, "To the party opposed to the Mayor; that is the best description I can give you".

But however the party was referred to, it had one overriding ambition: to carry through the reform of municipal government and to oppose the remnants of the old corporation's oligarchical control, personified

Borough of Poole.

At a Public Meeting of the Inhabitants of the Borough, this 24th day of June, 1835, at the London Tavern, pursuant to notice; GEORGE KEMP, Esq., *in the Chair* :---

It was Resolved unanimously,

THAT this meeting, viewing with pleasure the prospect of important improvements in our local Institutions afforded by the introduction into Parliament of the just and liberal measure of Municipal Reform now under discussion, is desirous of expressing its cordial approval of that measure in all its details.

Resolved unanimously,

THAT although the proceedings of a Meeting of the Corporation held this morning; abstractedly are not calculated to interrupt the progress of the Reform Bill now pending in Parliament; yet the sending a Deputation to London, on the part of such meeting, to co-operate with other Deputations personally interested in clinging to the present state of Municipal abuses, ought to stimulate the Inhabitants of this Borough to express, by a suitable Petition to Parliament, their disapprobation of any attempt on the part of the Corporation of Poole, to prevent by Combination of Town Clerks, or other agency, this great and necessary Measure from passing unimpaired into a Law.

Resolved unanimously,

THAT Petitions be presented to both Houses of Parliament, founded on the preceding Resolutions,— and that a Committee be appointed to prepare such Petitions.

Resolved unanimously,

THAT the Petition to the House of Commons be forwarded to our Representatives, CHAS. AUGUSTUS TULK, ESQ., and the Right Honorable GEORGE BYNG; and that to the House of Lords, to the Right Honorable LORD STRAFFORD, for presentation.

Resolved unanimously,

THAT this Meeting returns its most cordial thanks to the Gentlemen of the Corporation who opposed the proceedings at the Corporation Meeting held this day.

Resolved unanimously,

THAT the Resolutions of this Meeting be printed and circulated, and that they be advertized in the Sherborne Journal and Hampshire Independent.

The Chairman having left the chair—

Resolved unanimously,

THAT a Vote of thanks be tendered to GEORGE KEMP, ESQ., for his able conduct in the Chair.

The following is the Petition adopted by the Committee :—

"TO THE HONORABLE THE COMMONS OF THE UNITED KINGDOM OF GREAT BRITAIN AND IRELAND IN PARLIAMENT ASSEMBLED.

"The Petition of the Inhabitants of the Borough of Poole.

"HUMBLY SHEWETH

"That your Petitioners, viewing with pleasure the prospect of important improvements in our local Institutions, afforded by the introduction into Parliament of the just and liberal measure of Municipal Reform now under discussion, beg to express to your Honorable House their cordial approval of the principles of that great and necessary measure; and their full confidence that no combination or exertions of interested parties will be allowed to arrest its progress or prevent its passing unimpaired into a law.

"And your Petitioners will ever pray."

The Inhabitants are informed, that Petitions to both Houses of Parliament, are NOW READY FOR SIGNATURE AT THE LONDON TAVERN, and will remain till FOUR o'Clock, FRIDAY AFTERNOON.

LANKESTER, PRINTER, AND BINDER, HIGH STREET, POOLE.

in the Mayor.

On this basis the party, perhaps best described then as the Reform Party, nominated its 18 candidates for the election to be held later that year and, as such, were nearly all men who were to have much to do with the destiny of Poole over the coming decades.

In the Ward in which they were certain to do well they nominated **William Green**, a confectioner at 110 High Street; **Richard Pinney** of West Street; **George Lockyer Parrott**, a Master in Royal Navy, of West Street and a Corporator since 1830; **Richard Stanworth**, a Corporator nominated by his partner, Robert Wills, ship-builders and lessees of the yards owned by the Corporation on the Hamworthy side of the Quay; **Tom Rickman**, corn dealer and brewer of Market Street; **Tito Durell Hodges**, a currier and leather cutter of 71 High Street; **Samuel Salter**, a surgeon; and **William Conway**, a clockmaker and gunsmith of 152 High Street.

In the North-West Ward the new leader, George Lockyer Parrott, selected three of his party's best-known and most respected members. They were **George Kemp**, the previous leader of the Whig Party in Poole, a member of the Kemp family, and the Deacon of the Congregational Church. The latter was known as the "aristocratic deacon" from his pedantic and old-fashioned dress of the previous century — "a black coat and small clothes, silk stockings, silver buckled shoes, or Hessian boots, and his silver locks, which were covered by a shovel hat, were tied pig-tail fashion and hung down his back as the fashion was of the last century". His political opponents, on the other hand, referred to him as "old pig-tail". (His brother Martin had been persuaded by his mother's brother, a London banker, named George Welch, to add 'Welch' to his name and had become Martin Kemp Welch).

The other two strong candidates put up by the Reformers to try to steal a seat or two in the North West-Ward were **James Seager** and **William Jolliffe**. James Seager had been a Corporator for many years, he had been Mayor of Poole and like his father, Alderman for many years and was a respected magistrate as well as Treasurer of the Quay funds. William Jolliffe had been Mayor, too, and always anxious for some reform of Parliament and the Corporation and, of course, of an old family of Merchants of Poole.

Poole High Street

The Reform Party confidently expected the election of one at least of these three candidates. They felt no confidence in the election of their other six candidates. They were **James Tulloch**, wine and spirit merchant of 72 High Street; **John Brown**, a shipowner and timber merchant of 90 High Street; **John Williamson**, Linen Draper of 115 High Street; **Joseph Notting**, a tanner and boot-maker of 30 Market Street; **Thomas Naish** of Hill Street; and **Edward Mullett**, a Chemist of 80 High Street. These candidates were not thought to have a chance of election — though Poole was to hear quite a lot of many of them over the coming years.

The Ministerial or Tory Party of the Town for some reason took the gravest offence to the nomination of these eighteen members of the opposition party. They thought, apparently, that there should have been some accommodation made between them for sharing the nominations as had recently been come to when the Corporation had elected Reform Corporators (such as William Jolliffe and James Seager

143

as Mayors). They were startled, too, to hear that the London Tavern meeting had decided that when they had a majority of Councillors they would use this majority to elect all six Aldermen from their followers and throw out the old Corporation Tory officers from their posts.

The Tories, therefore, angrily followed suit and nominated 18 Tories for the prospective Councillor seats on the new Council, at the same time had redoubled their efforts to at least modify the terms of the proposed Municipal Corporations Bill.

They were probably not so clever in the selection of their candidates or, perhaps, their stronger candidates were not willing to face the likelihood of their defeat in the South-East Ward. Their strong candidates were put into the North-West Ward. The Mayor, **Robert Slade**, who lived at Barbers Piles, was put up with the respected Banker, ex-Mayor and patriot, **George Welch Ledgard**, the wine merchant **Samuel Clarke** of West Street, **John** and **William Adey**, Brewers and Maltsters of Towngate Street and Market Street. There were, too, **Robert Slade Senior**, of West Street and the Mayor's son, **Robert Slade** of Market Street as well as **Thomas Slade**, again of West Street and **George Holland**, Coal Merchant of Hill Street. These candidates, or most of them, could expect to be elected. The more unlikely ones selected for the South-East Ward by the Tories were **Robert Major**, partner in Major, Seager and Co., rope-makers; **George Ledgard**, Banker, son of George Welch Ledgard and a Corporator of many years standing; **Joseph Barter Bloomfield** of similar status in the town, a shipowner with business on the Quay; **George Hancock**, another leading Corporator, living at 28 Fish Street, in business previously with George Holland as coal merchants; **William Thompson**, a Clay Merchant of Hamworthy; **William Cox** a merchant shipowner and shipbuilder of Fish Street as well as a **Mr. Gavin**.

The Municipal Corporations Act was not finally passed until 9th September, 1835, and even then there were many details of the impending election not known. Only a few years previously some seats in Parliament had been openly bought and sold. The Act said "upon the first day of November in every year the burgesses so enrolled in every borough shall openly assemble and elect ..... the Councillors of such boroughs". It also enacted that the means of voting would be to deliver to the Mayor "a voting paper containing the Christian names and surnames of the person for whom he votes, with their respective places of abode and descriptions, such paper being previously signed with the name of the burgess voting, with the name of the street, lane or other place in which the property for which he appears to be rated on the Burgess Roll is situate".

The presiding officer had to accept any voting paper tendered as long as the voter, if asked, satisfactorily answered the three questions which could be put to him: was he the person whose name was on the Burgess Roll? Had he previously voted in that election? Was the signature his on the ballot paper which he was tendering?

View of Fish Street looking towards the High Street

Another section of the Act which caused so much bother in Poole enacted that the Mayor and Assessors would, after the close of the Poll, examine the voting papers and declare elected those candidates who had the greatest number of votes and that the Mayor would then cause the voting papers to be kept in the town clerk's office for six

145

months after the election where any burgess could inspect them on payment of a fee of one shilling. The Mayor had to publish the result of the election by 2 o'clock two days after the election.

The first elections under the Act were fixed to be held on Boxing Day, 26th December. The various overseers of the Poor in the four Parishes of the new Poole Borough Council (St. James, Hamworthy, Longfleet and Parkstone) had to prepare their alphabetical list of their Parishioners who occupied or owned a house, warehouse or shop of the annual value of £10 and lived within 7 miles of Poole and who were up-to-date in their payment of the poor rate. These lists were to be printed by the town clerk and exhibited on the Guildhall notice board. Anyone objecting to the inclusion or exclusion of their name had a right to object. In later times these objections were to be settled by the Assessors who were to be elected by the parishes. In that first year there was no time to hold elections of Assessors so the Government appointed a number of barristers to visit towns finally to settle the Burgess Roll after hearing objections.

This procedure did mean, though, that for a long time during the canvassing by the two parties in Poole they were never quite sure who would, or who would not, have a vote. It was, in this first process of compiling the Burgess Roll, demonstrated to what lengths each side would go to to gain an advantage over the other. One of the two overseers of the poor of the Parish of Hamworthy was Richard Pinney, a candidate in the election on the side of the Reform Party. He included in the list he provided Robert Parr, the town clerk, many persons who the Tories considered were clearly not qualified to be in the Burgess Roll. The Tories, on the other hand, were convinced from their canvass that a number of these persons would vote for them so, despite their certainty that they were not properly qualified, they made no representations to the Revising Barrister, and these men finally appeared in the Burgess Roll as being qualified. The Tories found later to their chagrin that their canvass had been wrong. It was them, therefore, not the Reform Party who finally felt cheated.

In this pre-election period rumour fed on rumour through the town, for Poole was a small compact town. It had always been a town in which strong and opposing views were taken on most things whether it was how the Church was built, who should elect the Rector, whether the Bridge should be built ..... and quarrels had always been fought to the death.

The previous quarrels about the Bridge with Mr. Ponsonby had raised old emotions of the old Corporators fearing that the Lord of the Manor was trying to regain the Lord's dominance over the town. He encouraged the Reformers, mostly anti-Corporation, and personal hatreds had grown up strongly again.

On the Reform side, too, there was much feeling between the new Reform Leader, George Lockyer Parrott, and his many supporters — John Lankester, William Green, Tom Rickman, George Penney and others on the one side and the Slade family, the two Ledgards and the town clerk, Robert Henning Parr, on the other.

Mr. Parr, an able lawyer, had with his brother taken over the practice of his father, the very respected Thomas Parr, a master-extraordinary and notary public, in the house in Fish Street at the side of the previous Guildhall which had stood in the middle of the road. In 1836 Robert Parr was 36 years old and a staunch Tory. He had been elected town clerk only in July 1833 on the death of John Foot, the previous Whig town clerk.
Mr. Parr had immediately been thrown into the controversies of the Corporation with Mr. Ponsonby about the Bridge Bill and about the passage of the Municipal Corporations Bill.

It was, therefore, about Mr. Parr rather than the Mayor and George Welch Ledgard, the political leaders of the Tories, that rumours circulated in Poole prior to the first election. It was said and believed that Mr. Parr had advised voters they could put two ballot papers in the ballot box. It was said that he had made a pact with Thomas Arnold for Thomas Arnold to take over as Town Clerk to the new Council and that he, Robert Parr, would get £7,000 compensation under the Act for the loss of his office — and, to make things worse, much of this 'excessive' compensation would be based on his Bills for opposing the Bridge Act and the Municipal Reform Act.

On the other hand there were also rumours that Mr. Ponsonby would eject any of his tenants who did not vote for the Reform side and there was the inevitable feeling among some of those who were to be newly franchised that as parliamentary seats were being openly hawked for sale at large prices only a few years previously it would not be improper to make themselves a little money for their vote.....

But, for all the battles and emotion over the widening franchise in the Poole electorate when the Burgess List was finally issued totalled a mere 384 voters for the two wards — out of a population in the region of 10,000!

The parties had had their ballot papers printed weeks before the election. They had badgered nearly the whole electorate into one camp or the other. Generally they had brought their partisans or converts into their Committee room — the Tories into the upper room at the Globe Hotel in the High Street and the Radicals to the London Inn or John Lankester's shop in the High Street — and they had got the signatures on the ballot papers which they had then kept safe till the Saturday, Boxing Day, the prescribed day of the election. The papers were then delivered to the voters who were often taken to the Poll with the voting paper whose correctness had been ensured in the Committee rooms, or were delivered to them at the "breakfasts" which the parties organised. The Radicals held such a breakfast in the Angel Hotel immediately to the side of the Guildhall in which the poll for the North-West Ward was held and a "feast", later in the day, at the George. The Tories held breakfasts at the Bee Hive, the Sloop and the Antelope.

The Poll opened at 9 a.m. and was to continue till 4 o'clock in the afternoon. The Mayor had appointed the Sheriff, Richard Ledgard, another notable Tory, but not standing for the Council, as his Deputy for the South-East Ward.

The Tories had, of course, heard of the Radicals plan to print their ballot papers in blue ink. They had therefore copied the ballot papers and reprinted their own papers in blue ink. The Act said that the Burgesses should "openly assemble and elect ..... the councillors" by delivering their votes to the Mayor at the booths or rooms appointed and only burgesses should be allowed in the room.

The Tories had been defeated at previous elections of members of Parliament they thought by the crowd of fishermen in the galleries of the Guildhall intimidating their votes. At the election when

Borough of Poole.

MUNICIPAL ELECTION, 1836.

VOTING PAPER FOR THE NORTH-WEST WARD.

I, the undersigned _George Ledgard_ Vote for the following Persons as Councillors for the NORTH-WEST Ward for the Borough of Poole, under an Act of the 5th and 6th WILLIAM IV., ch. 76, entitled, "An Act to provide for the regulation of Municipal Corporations in England and Wales."

Christian Names and Surnames.	Place of Abode.	Descriptions.
William Adey	Town Gate Street, Saint James Poole	Brewer
Samuel Clark	High Street, Saint James Poole	Wine Merchant
William Thompson	Lytchet Minster, Dorset	Merchant

Dated the _First_ day of _November_

In the Year One Thousand Eight Hundred and Thirty-six.

(Signed) _George Ledgard_

of* _High Street, Saint James Poole_

* Name of the Street, Lane, or other Place in which the Property for which he appears to be rated on the Burgess Roll is situated.

Voting paper of George Ledgard

the Tory Mr. Irving had lost, at a signal being given by their friends near the ballot box, the sailors and men in the galleries would hiss and hoot derisively at the voter. At the last election the Tories, to support their candidate, Mr. Tulk, had tried to foil this by filling the hall and galleries with their own supporters. The sailors had then invaded the Guildhall, entering through the windows as well as the doors and dragged out the Tory supporters and "sent them down the steps". The Tories, therefore, claimed that the Radicals, with their distinctive blue papers, were doing this for a ready identification to the crowd of supporters. The Tories, therefore, had had a new lot of ballot papers printed to resemble the Reform ballot papers. The Reformers found this out on Christmas Day and John Lankester had taken all his Party ballot papers back to his printing shop in the High Street and spent Christmas Day endorsing his party's papers with further large blue letters to make them distinctive again.

The arrangements for the election had had to be hurried. The Mayor

'A prospect of an election'

had had two ballot boxes specially made for the occasion with slits at the top so that the papers could be pushed through rather than clipped together on his table, as was the usual custom then at elections. He had given one of the boxes and asked Richard Ledgard to act as his Deputy at the Polling Station. The Election was held in the Boys' section of the School, which only a year before the Corporation had been instrumental in setting up. The room was some 39 feet by 23 feet and was the classroom for some 200 boys. Richard Ledgard had had experience of elections for as Sheriff he had been responsible for the recent Parliamentary election in Poole, but had only been given two days' notice. He had taken a copy of the Act home and had talked over the provisions with his father, George Welch Ledgard, after their Christmas dinner. The Mayor had made his own study of his duties and had been given some help by Mr. James Rickman Justican, Mr. Parr's chief clerk.

Not unnaturally after these long and strenuous days of preparation, most of the electorate had polled by midday on the day of the election. The Mayor and the Sheriff stood by their newly made ballot boxes. There were two agents for each party beside them as well as a poll clerk to check the voter with the Burgess Roll, and Mr. Durant, a solicitor, was with the two Burgesses at the Guildhall, and Mr. Churchill, another solicitor, with Mr. Hodge and Mr. Smith watching the proceedings and deputed on behalf of the Reform Party to see the Mayor and Sheriff put the three prescribed questions.

The Mayor and Sheriff took it as no part of their duty to put these questions to a voter unless one or other of the party agents asked him to do so before the voter had polled his vote. The voters, after a feeble and abandoned attempt by the Sheriff to get Mr. Francis Trimwell Rogers to leave, remained in the room if they felt so inclined and there was, apparently a truce called for the day. A generally pleasant atmosphere prevailed, at least in Richard Ledgard's polling station, — the Mayor had chosen the 'Justice Room' at the Guildhall which was small enough to ensure there was no great crowd present.

Suspicion was, however, not far below the surface. On two or three occasions during the day, for instance, the Radicals saw Justican, the Town Clerk's chief clerk, write notes to the Mayor and the Reformers were most suspicious. A few months later they were able to tax Mr. Justican for an explanation. He agreed that once or twice he had submitted notes to the Mayor and had had notes of reply from the Mayor. He said that the notes were occasioned by messages he had received from the constables. "There was a special constable detained against his consent at Ham in a house; and there was a note received as to the course to be adopted to liberate him. Another was a note received wishing for a warrant to liberate a person of the name of Cole, who was detained against his consent". (His captor, one John Jones, was later alleged to have been brought drunk to the poll on the back of a party supporter).

However, eventually the Poll was closed. Shortly after four o'clock the Sheriff, accompanied by a constable bearing the ballot box, walked to the Mayor's House opposite the Church to deliver it to the Mayor. It was now left to the Mayor to conduct the count and to announce the results by the following Tuesday.

Robert Slade was mainly anxious about the result of the North-West Ward. He had told those at the polling station that he would not sleep a wink before he knew the result. He, therefore, took the box from the Sheriff and locked it in his safe in his warehouse just off the Quay, then went back home to rest and have his dinner.

He had arranged with Mr. Justican to come to his house at 9 o'clock to help him with the count of the North-West Ward. Mr. Justican, however, was delayed and didn't get there till after half-past nine and the Mayor was well on with the count. He had emptied the ballot box and put the votes in three piles. One pile was the "plumpers" for the conservatives; one for Radical "plumpers" and the third for those who had split their votes between the parties.

He had dealt first with the split votes as they had to be listed. He had then counted the Tory votes and last dealt with the Radicals. Here he had found that he had some voting for Radicals which he had already polled for the Tories. He therefore discounted these votes as invalid, and found the voting as follows:—

Robert Slade	110
G. W. Ledgard	104
R. Slade	103
R. Slade	103

G. Holland	101
J. Adey	100
Wm. Adey	100
Samuel Clarke	100
Thomas Slade	100
James Tulloch	93
George Kemp	91
James Seager	91
William Jolliffe	90
John Brown	87
John Williamson	88
Thomas Naish	85
Joseph Notting	84
Edward Mullett	75

Out of an electorate for the North-West Ward of 215, 191 voted, there were 13 'at sea', 4 were ill, 1 had died. Only 7 had refused to vote.

On Tuesday morning the Mayor had arranged with Mr. Justican to come to his counting house on the Quay to help him with the count for the South-East Ward. Unfortunately, Mr. Justican was ill and could not arrive in time. The High Constable Inkpen, however, had attended to extract the ballot box from the safe, which he took to the Mayor who started his count. He had decided to use the same system as he had done with the count of the North-West Ward two days earlier. He first started to sort the votes into three piles: "plumpers" as he called party votes for all 9 candidates for the Conservatives or Reformers, and the third pile for those who had split their votes between the parties. He started with the split votes and marked those on the 18 divisions of a paper he had prepared. While he was doing this, Tom Rickman and Francis Trimwell Rogers called on behalf of the Radical party and demanded to look at the voting papers. After some argument with the Mayor they eventually left and met Mr. Justican who had arrived to help the Mayor. As they continued with the count the Mayor finally came to the pile of Radical 'plumpers'. Here he found that several of the votes, who he had polled for the Conservatives or as split votes, were also 'plumpers' for the Radicals. Those voters he had already counted he discounted as being unable to vote twice and returned them to the ballot box uncounted.

In this fashion he arrived at the result that 7 Radicals had been elected and 2 Conservatives. The 2 Conservatives were George Major and George Ledgard who had by common consent been successful in obtaining a great many more of the split votes than any other candidate. The other successful candidates were Radicals: Green, Pinney, Parrott, Stanworth, Rickman, Rogers and Hodges.

Mr. Justican then left the Warehouse with the list of successful candidates to get 25 copies printed in order that the Mayor's announcement of the result of Poole's first election could be put up round the Borough.

Meanwhile the Mayor put both lots of ballot papers into another box so as to retain his newly constructed ballot boxes for the next election. He was going to retain the papers until 1st January when, he anticipated the new Council would have appointed a new town clerk for Mr. Parr was not, under the Municipal Corporations Act, able to hold the offices of Magistrates' Clerk and Clerk of

Poole High Street

the Peace if he was town clerk and had, the Mayor knew, elected to give up the office of town clerk and take a compensation for this loss of office as provided for in the Act. The Mayor was spending the evening with his brother, James Slade. He went there sometime after 3 o'clock that afternoon and, shortly after he had arrived there, John Lankester, the Printer and bookseller in High Street, Samuel Scott, a clerk with the solicitors Durant and Welch, and Tom Rickman, all leaders in the Radical party knocked at the door and the Mayor answered it. They were, according to the Mayor, "very violent in demanding the voting papers". "The moment I answered the door they immediately had each of their hands in, poking a shilling in my face, demanding a sight of the voting papers and I shut the door in their face".

However, this was enough to persuade him to get rid of the voting papers quickly. He sent them round to Mr. Parr to hold till the new town clerk was appointed, for Mr. Parr was technically the town clerk until 1st January 1836.

Mr. Parr received the box with the voting papers not long after 4 o'clock. He had no option under the provisions of the Act, but it did not please him in the least for he knew from the feeling already in the town that his last few days of office were going to be contentious. There had already been an ugly scene in the town that morning. As Mr. James Slade, one of the Coroners was walking home with the High Constable after holding an Inquest at the Guildhall, a large crowd had jeered them and pelted them with snow, ice and stones from the road. A stone or a lump of ice had split Mr. Inkpen's forehead but at least he had recognised four of the men 'pelting' them whom he later successfully prosecuted.

At Lord Ashley's election as a County Member a year or so previously when the Reform Lord of the Manor had not been successful a crowd had descended on Mr. Parr's house and, according to Mr. Justican, who described the mob's action modestly as having, "broken the windows to pieces and beaten the door off its hinges". In fact, Mr. Justican had in no way exaggerated. At the subsequent election of Poole Members, Mr. Parr had been the agent of the unsuccessful Tory candidate and had taken no chances. He had 200 special constables sworn in to keep the peace. Therefore, as soon as Mr. Parr received the box with all the votes from the Mayor he feared the worst would happen again. He had

'Tory Plumpers'

Borough of Poole.
MUNICIPAL ELECTION, 1836.
VOTING PAPER FOR THE NORTH-WEST WARD.

I, the undersigned _Robert Slade, Sen. of Robert_, Vote for the following Persons as Councillors for the NORTH-WEST WARD for the Borough of Poole, under an Act of the 5th and 6th WILLIAM IV., ch. 76, entitled, "An Act to provide for the regulation of Municipal Corporations in England and Wales."

Christian Names and Surnames.	Place of Abode.	Descriptions.
William Adey	Towngate Street Saint James Poole	Brewer
Samuel Clark	West Street Saint James Poole	Wine Merchant
William Thompson	Lytchet Minster Dorset	Merchant

Dated the _first_ day of _November_
In the Year One Thousand Eight Hundred and Thirty-six.

(Signed) _Robert Slade_

of _West Quay Road Saint James Poole_

* Name of the Street, Lane, or other Place in which the Property for which he appears to be rated on the Burgess Roll is situated.

Borough of Poole.
MUNICIPAL ELECTION, 1836.
VOTING PAPER FOR THE NORTH-WEST WARD.

I, the undersigned _Robert Slade Sen. of David_, Vote for the following Persons as Councillors for the NORTH-WEST WARD for the Borough of Poole, under an Act of the 5th and 6th WILLIAM IV., ch. 76, entitled, "An Act to provide for the regulation of Municipal Corporations in England and Wales."

Christian Names and Surnames.	Place of Abode.	Descriptions.
William Adey	Towngate Street Saint James Poole	Brewer
Samuel Clark	West Street Saint James Poole	Wine Merchant
William Thompson	Lytchet Minster Dorset	Merchant

Dated the _first_ day of _November_
In the Year One Thousand Eight Hundred and Thirty-six.

(Signed) _Robert Slade_

of _Barbers Piles Saint James Poole_

* Name of the Street, Lane, or other Place in which the Property for which he appears to be rated on the Burgess Roll is situated.

immediately set off to get the Magistrates' approval to appoint special constables to guard his office.

As he came back, having got some twelve 'specials' to guard his office that night, he was sure of one thing: no one was going to examine the voting papers that night. True enough, Mr. Lankester and Mr. Scott had soon heard where the papers had gone and were soon in attendance demanding to see the contents of the box. They couldn't examine the box that evening, said Mr. Parr. In fact, he added, he had a list of five applicants to examine the ballot papers and he would add their names to the list and they could see them in their turn.

Mr. Parr gave this list to his chief clerk Mr. Justican after Mr. Scott and Mr. Lankester had left. The office was shut up safely for the night and Mr. Parr was left with his twelve special constables protecting his office which was also his home, for he lived upstairs.

The next morning George Hancock, an unsuccessful candidate and one on Mr. Parr's list attended Mr. Parr's offices to look at the voting papers just before Mr. Arnold, the solicitor, and the man likely to succeed Mr. Parr as town clerk in a few days' time. Mr. Hancock had come to check up on how some of the voters had cast their votes. Mr. Justican had been left in charge of the box. He unlocked the box for Mr. Hancock after receiving the prescribed fee of a shilling. Mr. Justican's orders were that only one person at a time was to be allowed to inspect the votes and they were not to be allowed to take notes. Dr. Hairby, another Tory supporter, was the only other voter who saw the contents of the box that day. Mr. Justican had to leave these persons to attend the office door and carry out other duties.

The following morning Scott and Lankester called at 10 o'clock. They were told Mr. Parr had laid down the time of inspection as between 11 a.m. and 4 p.m. and in any case there were others still who had booked to see the votes before them.

They called in the afternoon, but Mr. Justican had retired home ill to bed and there were no instructions in the office about the papers. They were again unlucky.

They called at 11 o'clock the following morning but the 'papers were engaged'. It was thought they would be free at 3 o'clock. The two men attended at 3 o'clock and waited till 4 o'clock in vain. They returned again on the next day, 31st January, only to find the papers again engaged.

Their patience was exhausted. Mr. Scott, the legal clerk with the reform solicitors, Messrs. Durant and Welch, went away to draft a legal document to serve on Mr. Parr demanding an immediate written appointment for an inspection to be made.

This carefully worded document was delivered the next day. Mr. Parr was on his own in the office. Mr. Justican was still away ill; his clerks were still 'keeping their Christmas'. He found the young Absolam Cole to carry the box of votes up to Mr. Arnold's office and Robert Parr himself walked up with the key. Mr. Arnold received the box but would not take the key until his clerk, Richard Berry, had had time to check and initial all the votes in the box. Thus Mr. Parr left Mr. Arnold's offices still with the key in his pocket, crossing the road to Mr. Lankester's shop, "if you would like to deliver this to Mr. Arnold", he said, handing Mr. Lankester back his carefully prepared notice, "no doubt he will pay every attention to it, for I have been removed from the office of Town Clerk. The Council have appointed Mr. Arnold".

Though Mr. Parr had, no doubt, enjoyed that little interlude with John Lankester he can hardly have thought that that would be the end of it.

Mr. Arnold finally took the papers over on 4th January. He adopted the same rules for inspection as Mr. Parr but, shortly afterwards, requiring help from his chief clerk, Richard Berry, in committee and council meetings in his new duties as town clerk, he cut down the hours of inspection to two hours a day, from midday to 2 p.m. His business, he felt, could not stand his chief clerk being concerned four hours each day with the constant inspections, for which he received only the statutory fee of one shilling.

Parliament can never have intended, in giving the town clerk the duty of preserving the voting papers and any voter the right to inspect them on paying the town clerk the fee of one shilling, that a full examination and recount of them could be carried out by each voter. But it was nothing less than this which would satisfy the Reformers that the election result was correct, and, of course, if only one person was allowed at one time with only one vote at a time in his hand — which was Mr. Arnold's rule — and only two hours a day to carry out this work, — their recount was impossible. They had to take some further dramatic action, somehow, to upset what they were now convinced was a fraudulent election.

The Guildhall, Market Street

Meanwhile events were happening quickly in the new Council, composed of those whom the Mayor had declared to be duly elected.

On the morning of 31st December, before the Radical leaders had seen the voting papers, the new Council had its first meeting.

Robert Slade, the Mayor of the old Corporation and the Returning Officer had declared the following as the result of the election.

For the North-West Ward

To hold office till November 1838:
Robert Slade, Barbers Pile, Merchant (Tory)
George Welch Ledgard, High Street, Banker (Tory)
Robert Slade, the Elder, West Street, Merchant (Tory)

To hold office till November 1837:
Robert Slade, son of Robert, Market Street, Merchant (Tory)
George Holland, Hill Street, Coal Merchant (Tory)
John Adey, Market Street, Wine Merchant (Tory)

To hold office till November 1836:
William Adey, Towngate Street, Brewer (Tory)
Samuel Clark, West Street, Wine Merchant (Tory)
Thomas Slade, the Younger, West Street, Merchant (Tory)

For the South-East Ward

To hold office till 1838:
William Green, Old Orchard, Gentleman (Reform)
Richard Pinney, Hamworthy, Merchant (Reform)
Robert Major, Longfleet, Merchant (Tory)

To hold office till 1837:
Richard Stanworth, Barbers Piles, Shipowner (Reform)
George Lockyer Parrott, High Street, Gentleman (Reform)
Tom Rickman, High Street, Cornfactor (Reform)

To hold office till 1836:
George Ledgard, High Street, Banker (Tory)
Francis Trimwell Rogers, Longfleet, Tanner (Reform)
Tito Durell Hodges, High Street, Currier (Reform)

The results for the North-West Ward were not really unexpected by anyone. All the Councillors elected were for "the Mayor's Party", the anti-reformers, the Tories. The election of two Tories among the others, all reformers, for the South-East Ward, was a bitter disappointment to the leaders of the Reform Party. They suspected that they had been cheated.

However, all the newly elected Councillors — with the notable exception of their leader, George Lockyer Parrott, — attended the first meeting of the Council, and the official record states that the following were unanimously elected Aldermen:

Robert Slade, the late Mayor
Davis Osmond Lander
George Ledgard
George Hancock
Thomas Gaden
Joseph Barter Bloomfield

All these new Aldermen were members of the old Corporation. Only two of the new Aldermen, Robert Slade and George Ledgard, were new Councillors. Two of them, George Hancock and Joseph Barter Bloomfield, were unsuccessful candidates, Messrs. Lander and Gaden had not put up for election. The result of the election of these Aldermen by the Councillors was that the election result of 11 Tories to 7 Reformers had been changed to 15–7. The Reformers spoke against the election of six Tories as Aldermen by the Councillors but the method of minuting adopted by the new Town Clerk, Thomas Arnold, was that, whatever objection or speech might be made by members, he always minuted the decision as being 'unanimous' unless an opposing motion had been formally moved: the minute of the Council reporting the election of the new Aldermen therefore showed it as being 'unanimous'.

This was the only business transacted at the meeting on 31st December 1835. The now fully constituted Council, with its 6 new Aldermen and 16 Councillors met again at noon on the following day, 1st January, 1836.

Robert Slade was 'unanimously' elected Mayor again. Thomas Hancock, Sheriff, and Thomas Arnold as Town Clerk, Clerk of the Peace and Registrar of the Poole Court of Record at a salary of £100 'for his ordinary business'. James Slade was elected Treasurer, and the Watch Committee of six was appointed — all Tories: Benjamin Inkpen, the High Constable of the old Corporation, was re-appointed with the additional duties of Water Bailiff at an annual salary of £20. (Benjamin Inkpen also ran a linen shop and supplied the policemen's clothing for many years). The Council finished its meeting by resolving ('unanimously' crossed out in this minute!) that the 'Mayor and Aldermen wear Gowns as in the late Corporation', and that the Councillors should wear black silk Gowns.

All, according to the official records, was going smoothly with the establishment of the new Council. The election was over. There were now seven Reformers on the Council to sway it to a more liberal outlook and there was a new town clerk in office.

The life of the inhabitants had not yet been disturbed unduly

But the course of Poole's future for a long time ahead was being busily charted and plotted towards the rocks as the printer, John Lankester and Messrs. Durant and Welch's chief clerk, Samuel Scott, and the whole array of scrutineers besieged the offices of the hard-pressed solicitor, Thomas Arnold, who had now the part-time job of the Town Clerk of Poole.

To keep some semblance of order and to retain some help from his chief clerk, William Berry, in the various meetings of the Council and its Committees, Thomas Arnold felt constrained to reduce the hours of inspection to only two hours a day. In view of the even more scurrilous rumours circulating in the town he laid down a rule that his clerk was to show the papers only to individual scrutineers and that they were to have one paper at a time in their hands. He also adopted Mr. Parr's rule that no notes were to be taken by the scrutineer.

Within a few days of the new year the legal battles had commenced. The Parrott-party of Poole reformers had considerable backing as well as influential sympathisers. One was James Seager, a most respected man of standing in the town who had, for instance, been one of the executors of the last of the male Lesters, Sir John Lester. He was an ex-Mayor, a Merchant shipowner of means who had also been a Magistrate of Poole for many years. Others supporting the Reform Party were William Jolliffe and George Kemp. George Kemp had great influence in the town. He lived in 'Poole Mansion', the old Thompson House in Market Street, and had for years past been the colourful and 'aristocratic deacon' of the Poole Congregational Church. More sinister, though, to the emotions of many Poole people and perhaps especially the members of the old Corporation, the Lord of the Manor of Canford Magna and Poole, Mr. W. F. S. Ponsonby, one of Poole's M.P.'s from 1827–1831, and then the Member for Dorset, with his great family connections with the Whig Party, and through them, with the Houses of Parliament, took a most active part in the support of the Whig/Reform faction in Poole. The battles of the old Corporation through the centuries with the Lords of the Manor had in the lifetime of many of the older Corporators been revived by the battles over the recent passage of the Poole Bridge Bill through Parliament. There the Whig member for Poole, Sir John Byng, as Chairman of the Committee set up by the Commons to consider the Bill, to quote Bernard Short, "was able to advocate the scheme in such an effective manner that it was bound to have a definite result upon his hearers".

The battles in Poole started by George Penney taking out summonses for bribery in the election against four Tories, and with the Tories quickly responding with ten summonses for bribery in the election against their opponents.

'Votes for Sale'

The Reformers' next move was to issue Writs against George Ledgard and Robert Major, the two Tory Councillors elected in the South-East Ward. The Writs were those of **Quo Warrento** — a demand for them to prove 'by what right' they were acting as Borough Councillors. The persons bringing this action were the most respected Reformers, James Seager and George Kemp. The basis of their case was that the Reformers had duplicates of the signed voting papers of the Reform Supporters for the South-East Ward which showed that, of the 159 voters in that Ward, 87 voted for George Conway and 88 for Samuel Salter which, in each case, gave him a majority — and yet neither had been elected. The trial was set down for the Summer Assizes at Dorchester.

However, meanwhile, the system of inspection of the ballot papers instituted by the Town Clerk made it impossible to carry out a complete check and recount of the votes and the Reformers considered it their right to be able to do so. They, therefore, started High Court proceedings for an order of the Court to compel him to open his office for a longer period for the inspection of the votes, to allow the whole of the ballot papers to be before them and to be able to make notes of their findings.

Lord Denham, the Lord Chief Justice, in disposing of the case, made remarks which, to the great suffering of Poole, neither of the parties involved took any heed. "It is very difficult to lay down any precise rule on this point", he said, "and whatever rule was laid down, either by the Court or by the Act of Parliament, there must be something of a spirit of mutual accommodation even in the very height of political controversy, or else the affairs of the world cannot go on".

Lord Denham suggested that strictly speaking the town clerk could not be compelled to change his rules, but that it might be convenient to everyone, not least the town clerk himself, to let any voter examine all the votes and, if they wished, to take minutes. The town clerk had said he would be happy to abide by the views of the Court and would act accordingly and no decision of the Court was thought necessary. The case was discharged by consent. This first excursion into legal defence by the new Council had cost it a mere £141.11.10d.

"a spirit of mutual accommodation even in the very height of political controversy"

The Reformers were not willing to wait while the new Council became esconsed in power and authority and, of course, had they been successful they could have redressed the balance of the Council. It is hardly to be doubted that it was through the kind offices of the Lord of the Manor that their leader, Mr. Parrott, had been introduced to Lord John Russell, the Home Secretary in the Whig Government and Mr. Poulter, the Whig member of Parliament for Shaftesbury. Mr. Parrott took up a Deputation from Poole to see Lord John Russell and the upshot of it all was that Mr. Poulter brought forward in Parliament a Bill reciting that as there was no remedy at law "for the gross frauds committed in the Poole election", Parliament should declare the whole election void and order another election of Councillors in both Wards.

Parliament referred the Bill to a Select Committee "to inquire into the circumstances and to report back".

The Committee selected by the Government contained Lord Stanley who was in the rather neutral position of being a Tory who supported reform, but he attended none of the subsequent meetings of the Committee. There were four other Tories, among whom was, surprisingly, Lord Ashley who, after his long fights with Mr. Ponsonby a year or two earlier for the representation of Dorset, must have later felt he had heard much of it all before. The other members of the Committee were six Reformers, headed by the Chairman of the Committee, the very same member for Shaftesbury who had proposed the Bill, Mr. Poulter.

It is difficult to disagree with the Committee's general conclusion that there was much which was questionable that had happened in Poole's first municipal election, but the system of election then with its 'open court' system, with Parties printing their own ballot papers, with voters signing them in duplicate even before they know whether or not they were eligible to vote, gave rise to a situation in which it is difficult to imagine that the result of most elections could have been questioned in some way. Moreover, many of the voters were fearful of voting as they wished, with their tenancies and jobs at stake, and some other, more independent voters, cared more about trying to get a cash payment or personal benefit for their vote than for whom they cast it.

Even more important to any fundamental decision upon the votes in the ballot box was the history of its custody, and the multitude of examinations which the voters had undergone. It was quite impossible for anyone to have remotely satisfied themselves as to the differences which appeared between the Mayor's conclusions and the votes finally found in the box by the Committee. However, it was certain that there had been some irregularities. The balance of probability was certainly that someone had — to put it at its most neutral — unfairly favoured the Tory cause and that, as far as the votes cast was concerned, the result should have been that 9 Reformers should have been elected for the South-East Ward and the new Council formed of 9 Tories and 9 Reformers.

A decision on these lines by the Select Committee was inevitable as soon as the Committee decided that the affidavits of the 88 voters filed in the Kings Bench Court in connection with the case of Attorney-General v Ledgard and Major would be received as **prima facie** evidence but, starting on 7th March, 1836, the Committee spent 8 days examining the twenty-five witnesses, a further day deciding upon the Heads of their report and a further day in approving it. All was complete on 25th March, 1836.

High Street, Poole

The Council's witnesses had been cross-examined severely and were in a weak position for they could offer no explanation for most of the irregularities in the votes. The Mayor could hardly defend his system of counting the votes even if it was difficult to see how he could have justly chosen between two ballot papers both apparently cast by the same person. The Committee even seemed to find that the ex-town clerk, Mr. Parr, had lied and preferred the story of one, Robert Pierce, a tenant of the Lord of the Manor, whose credibility and standing as a witness seemed dubious to say the least. He had, according to Mr. Parr's brother, suggested he could bring in quite a number of votes if he were provided with a horse and cart, — he ended a rabid reformer equipped with a new horse and cart allegedly provided by a Reformer. For all that, the Tory witnesses were, throughout the hearing put entirely on the defensive and their evidence was given with an apparently ingenuous innocence as if they hardly contemplated a possible decision against them.

However, there was no doubt at all that the voting papers for the South-East Ward which were in the box on 7th March when the new town clerk brought them up to the House of Commons from the custody of his chief clerk, did not correspond with the Mayor's declared results. It seems fairly clear that a few of the pre-signed votes had been put in for voters who had probably later changed their minds and that someone, if John Lankester was to be believed, had abstracted four votes even during the time he was carrying out his inspections. It is, perhaps, not surprising to find that these four votes were by voters who had been put on the Hamworthy Parish list by Mr. Penney and considered by the Tories ineligible even though they had raised no objection to their inclusion before the Revising Barrister.

For all that, the Reformers in their evidence were allowed to spend an inordinate time dealing with what they alleged were the reason for the 'frauds'. They paraded what they considered the outrageous decisions of the old Corporation in disposing of their assets before the new Council took over; in the new Council's unreasonable sacking of the most respected James Seager from Treasurer of the Quays and Francis Edwards, the Collector. But, most of all, their anger was directed at the Town Clerk, Robert Parr. The town knew that the Tories had made a plot with him that they would appoint Thomas Arnold in his place and pay Mr. Parr compensation for the loss of all his offices and he would receive the enormous sum of about £7,000 in compensation, — a compensation swollen by the outrageous actions of the old Corporation fighting the Bridge Bill and the Municipal Corporations Act.

The Bridge and Toll Gate

The House of Commons' Committee was on the side of the Reformers in every particular. They even felt competent to opine that the new town clerk, Thomas Arnold, had put "vexacious difficulties" in the way of Messrs. Lankester and Scott for a proper inspection of the voting papers, and that he had raised these difficulties "under the most frivolous pretences". And this was despite the Committee having by then the opportunity of studying the Lord Chief Justice's views on this same case having been argued before him.

Another surprising decision which the Commons' Committee felt was relevant was that "Mr. R. H. Parr, a decided partisan of the new Corporation, being in full practice of his business of an attorney, and in the prime of life, having held the office of Town Clerk for only 2½ years ..... was discharged ..... with a view to compensation, whatever may be its amount, must be an injury to the property of the Corporation and a heavy burden upon its limited finances".

Whatever else may be said of the decision of the Select Committee, however, it was quite clear that the Reform Party in Poole had achieved a most notable victory over its opponents. What was more, they had achieved it at little financial cost to themselves, for their expenses were met from Government funds. On the other hand, however, the expenses of the Council's witnesses of going to and staying in London during these protracted hearings and the legal costs involved must have been known even then to have been very heavy indeed.

The Select Committee's last recommendation was as follows:—

"Your Committee are of opinion that every effort has been made by the Petititoners to obtain all the redress which the courts of law can give, and that the ejection from office of the two Councillors so illegally and fraudulently returned will be obtained at the earliest period which is consistent with the rules and practices of the Court of King's Bench; but this period cannot arrive until next Michaelmas Term about which time the said Councillors would retire from office, according to the provisions of the Act of Parliament; and that in reference to the ulterior consequences of these original frauds in the constitution of this entire Corporation, Your Committee cannot see any other mode of giving the immediate and effective redress required in this very special case than that which can be afforded by an Act of the Legislature".

The House of Commons, however, were curiously unimpressed by this very forthright Report. For more than four months following the receipt of it they vacillated to the great consternation of the Poole Reformers.

In this period of awaiting the decision of Parliament the Council put a brave face on its predicament for it hardly knew from day to day whether it would be brought to an abrupt end. However, it decided to make a petition to be re-granted its Recorder and Court of Quarter Sessions, and it put up its most respected Members to the Home Secretary for appointment as the new Justices of the Peace for the new Borough. They were all Aldermen of the old Corporation, men who had been Mayors of Poole and were: Robert Slade of Market Street; George Welch Ledgard; Robert Slade, son of David, of Barbers Piles; Samuel Clarke; George Hancock; Robert Slade, Snr. of West Street; D. O. Lander and Thomas Gaden.

And it was in regard to these two matters that the Reformers were able to continue the fight. They made a submission of their own to Lord John Russell, the Home Secretary, with whom they had now had considerable dealings over the proposed Poole Corporation Bill. The Reformers put up their own most respectable men to constitute the new Bench and, to the mortification of the Council, the Home Secretary, without consulting the Council, appointed all those recommended to him by the Poole Reform Party and none of the Tory candidates. No doubt Lord John was motivated by the odium which the Select Committee's decisions had brought on the Poole Council and the Tories in Poole, but his decision to appoint the Reform candidates exclusively was certainly another factor in Poole's future quarrels, for the Magistrates Court was given considerable powers under the Act, including the power to appoint Overseers of the various Parishes through whom the Borough's rate, either as a separate rate or as part of the Poor Rate (which these officers had previously collected) was to be enforced.

In fact, however, the Bench was not entirely made up of Reformers even after Lord John's appointment because the Mayor was ex-officio Chairman of the Bench for his year of office and a member for the year following. The Reformers, too, had made one mistake in compiling their suggested magistrates. They had included Capt. Festing, thinking he must be a supporter of their group because at the previous parliamentary election he had voted for George Byng. In fact, however, Capt. Festing had voted for Mr. Byng on the personal basis that Mr. Byng was his commanding officer even though Capt. Festing was more of a Tory than a partisan reformer. The other men appointed by the Home Secretary in April, 1836 were:—

James Seager, previously a Corporator and Mayor of Poole
George Lockyer Parrott, the Reform Leader and Councillor
Tom Rickman, the Cornfactor, also a Councillor
The Rev. William B. Clarke of Longfleet
Nathaniel Brice, a retired lieutenant, R.N.
George Penney, a general shipping agent and a Quaker

A FEW QUESTIONS

TO SOME OF THE

Poole Magistrates.

Who betrayed his native Country that gave his Parents protection? Ask—GEORGE L. PARROTT, Esq.

Who put on the blue Frock and Belt and joined the Revolutionists in Belgium? Ask the Revd. W. Clarke, of Furze Hall, Longfleet, Esquire!

Who fled from Brussels at midnight, in disguise, to avoid his pursuers? Ask the Revd. W. CLARKE, Esquire, of Furze Hall, Longfleet.

Who was CONVICTED of Defrauding the Revenue? Ask TOM RICKMAN.

Who took the Corn out of the Sacks after having Sold it! Ask TOM RICKMAN.

Who was Tried by a Court Martial and found GUILTY of Cowardice? Ask Lieutenant BRICE.

Contemporary Handbill — anonymous

The new Magistrates held their first meeting in May 1836 and their first act was to dismiss Mr. Parr from his post of Clerk to the Magistrates and appoint in his place Mr. Martin Kemp Welch. Whatever the Reformers could say later about Mr. Parr's other claims for compensation, this first act of the Magistrates made certain of the basis for his claim as to the office of Clerk to the Magistrates which led to a claim of £1,200.

The trial of the Writ of **Quo Warrento** against George Ledgard and Robert Major came up for trial at Dorchester Summer Assize on 20th July. The Poole Reformers took every possible care with their case. They themselves put it "here it was that the Burgesses of Poole were suddenly, and in the most astounding manner, called upon to determine whether they would tamely submit to be deprived by a gross fraud of the whole value of a franchise just conferred upon them". "The undisturbed success of one fraud might have acted as a stimulus to renewed exertions of the same character; and have carried us, perhaps, to results still more prejudicial and degrading, and more beyond the reach of remedy".

The Reformers had transported to Dorchester all the 88 Poole voters

Harbour Office and Customs House from the Hamworthy side of the harbour

who had sworn affidavits that they had voted for the Reform candidates but the Judge accepted the affidavits as evidence and, subject to a number of legal points raised at the trial, which he remitted to the Court of King's Bench for decision, instructed the Jury to bring in a qualified verdict for the plaintiffs.

The House of Commons after giving the Poole Corporation Bill a first reading on 20th April had taken until 11th July to attain its second reading. As the Reformers put it in one of their pamphlets, "Owing to a variety of interruptions consequent upon the multiplicity of other business, the forms of the House, etc. the most mortifying disappointments and delays were experienced".

However, on the result of the Dorchester trial being reported, the House was suddenly galvanised into action. The Bill was out of the Committee by 25th July and finally passed by the Commons on 28th by a majority of 44 votes.

The Bill came to the House of Lords on 2nd August, 1836. By this time the Poole Corporation had a Petition from Poole ratepayers in favour of the Bill and the proceedings in the Lords started with Lord Stafford presenting this — followed immediately by Lord Redesdale presenting a Petition from 500 inhabitants against the Bill; these petitioners begged "to represent to your Lordships the great confidence they repose in the present Council....."

The Duke of Richmond then introduced the Bill by referring to the Select Committee's report. "Now, My Lords", he said, "the body so elected, and so illegally elected, they having falsified the voting papers, ... have been guilty of these gross frauds..... Their first step was to remove some of the old officers of the Corporation, to displace others, to give compensation to some, and in short they have been allowed, and there is no means of preventing it, to get the benefit and rewards of their frauds....."

Lord Redesdale opposed the Bill. It would establish a dangerous precedent. Lord Lyndhurst was not prepared to support it on newspaper reports of the Dorchester trial. The Duke of Richmond spoke again in the Bill's favour but, when Lord Wharncliffe, the Marquis of Salisbury and Lord Wynford spoke against it the Bill was lost for all time, despite the official end of the debate being that it was "ordered to be read a second time, that day three months".

The decision of the Lords was a heavy blow to the Radicals of Poole. They had waited impatiently for its passage through Parliament, fretting at the actions of the Tory Council meanwhile and desperate to see the end of the Tory rule in Poole. They had the unanimous recommendation of the Select Committee for the Bill, — a Committee which had on it Lord Ashley and Lord Eastnor — they had won handsomely the Quarter Sessions' case against Robert Major and George Ledgard — and there had been the quick decision of the Commons and a substantial majority for the Bill. Then, suddenly, when all seemed won, they had been deserted. In the Lords' debate not a single Minister appeared and hardly any of the Whig Lords bothered to attend to support the Duke of Richmond's motion and the Bill was lost without a vote being taken.

The effect on the newly-formed Conservative Association of Poole was, of course, one of extreme elation. Within ten days of the Lords' decision they had organised the biggest display of triumph that had ever been seen in Poole or which Poole is ever likely to see, and which can hardly have been without its effect on the further Poole events to follow, especially as the Hon. G. S. Byng had been elected in the place of his father as an M.P. for Poole only ten weeks previously by the narrow majority of 25.

But, for the time being the Poole Tories had won a most notable victory and, to quote the local, Tory-sympathising Paper, "As soon as the noble conduct of the Peers was known in Poole, it became the general wish to celebrate the Conservative — and constitutional — triumph by such a display of public feeling, as should not only mark the popular sense in Poole, with regard to this great event, but also as an incentive to other parts of this and neighbouring Counties....."

The celebrations arranged by Richard Ledgard and his fellow stewards were in the best full-hearted traditions of the old Corporators. On Tuesday, 12th August, 1836, all business in the town was suspended for the day. "Favours of true-blue were worn by all; the ladies wore scarfs and head dresses of the favourite colour; the very poorest of the people contrived to sport the blue ribbon themselves, and to decorate their childred with it".

"At Parkstone a triumphal arch of laurels and flowers was erected, surmounted by a handsome banner inscribed "Welcome". It was at this spot we witnessed the entrance of the following procession into the borough:

Horsemen with flags.

Grand Banner.

Two trumpeters.

Union Jack.　　Union Jack.

Horsemen (near a hundred) : two and two.

Stand of colours, in a waggon, drawn by four greys.

The Band in an omnibus.

The Mayor (R. Slade, Junr. esq.) the late Mayor (R. Slade, esq.)
G. W. Ledgard, esq. and T. Gaden, esq. in a
carriage and four greys.

The Aldermen, in a carriage and four.

The Councillors, in a carriage and four.

Town Clerk and Professional Gentlemen in a carriage and four.

The Committee of Management in a carriage and four.

Burgesses and their Friends, in carriages.

Stand of Colour, in a waggon.

Horsemen, two and two.

Band of Music.

PROGRAMME
OF THE
GRAND STATE PROCESSION
TO THE
Monstre Tory Meeting
DULY ANNOUNCED BY THE BLUE PLACARDS.

A BLUE FLAG supported by a HURDLE.

DEPRIVER DIRTY PEST, SWART,
The quasi **M.P.**, or rather **P.M.** (Petition Monger)

Riding with his respected friend and firm supporter,

MRS. MOKES, (OF CHURCH STREET,)
Reclining in state in white of spotless purity.

MR. SPARKS
(On Horseback)
Smoking a short pipe, and a new Blue suit on.
RABBLE.

SKILLY MARTHA
(On Horseback)
The disappointed and *popular (?)* friend of the Pooleites.
RABBLE.

CHARLES · JOHN FLINT, ESQ.,
OF ELECTORAL AND OYSTER LICENCE PURITY,
Wearing a new Thimble made expressly for this occasion.

MR. PUFF MUFF GRUFF,
Singing the "Bailiff's Daughter," riding on the **Danford Screw**, especially trotted out for this occasion.

A Blue Carriage, drawn by and containing two other
Specimens of the Danford Screw Genus,
CONTAINING:

LADY LOBELIA,
A perfect specimen of apeing popularity.

TOMMY,
The Turncoat's Wife, wearing the unmentionables.

Both taking Afternoon Tea. (It's astonishing the power of a friendly cup of tea, and a walk round the grounds.) Followed by their friends and acquaintances,

MRS. PATHEWS,
The **Truthful** Tory

MRS. BUSTLE,
OF HAM,
Who has saved her **V**ote for the last.

Each in their respective Donkey Carts

THE REVEREND CRACKED PAYTIE,
In a pair of new Giglamps, riding the high grey horse, and reading about his goodness in the *Barset Chronicle*, eating a stick of Celery gathered from the Union Gardens

---

Contemporary Handbill — not all of Poole joined in the general euphoria

"A LIBERAL OF THE LIBERALS,"

(Self-named) with a Blue Flag in one hand and a Box of Pills in the other. He will be accompanied by his former **Partner** of a few days' duration, drinking milk and water to keep up his nerves.

Hanging on behind his brougham, is

THE VENERABLE SNOB,

With the Blue Necktie—The Bell with the big clapper—and his truthful friend

BRICKFORD THE PAINTER,

Drinking Beer that came out of the cask from "The Dolphin."   Bah!

BRINEY SALT, ESQ.,

With a "correct card" of the Expenses

ÆSCULAPIUS CANCER, ESQ., M.D.

Of the Danford Dispensary—the popular and correct accountant.

GEORGIE, the PARKSTONE POTTER

Weeping because his Men won't turn like he has.

JAMES JUST BE I CAN'T, ESQ

The popular and straightforward Electioneering Agent

SIMPLE SIMON,

Singing "Cherry Ripe"

"THE BANNER," borne by MRS. TOM

(WHO MADE IT.)

WOODEN HEADED JIMMEY,

With a Thousand Pound Bank of England Note in his hand. Who was never so rich before.   Is it his own?

CHILDREN with BLUE RIBBON.

More Children with more Blue Ribbon.

TWO HUNDRED WOMEN

Some with Babies—Who have come out to see the fun.

TWO HUNDRED BOYS PAID

to shout.   Followed by

A HEARSE, containing

THE
DEFUNCT SPIRIT
OF
CONSERVATISM
IN POOLE.

It Rests in Peace.

ASHLEY FOR EVER!!

Burgesses of Parkstone & Friends in carriages.

Flags."

"All gentlemen wore blue ribbons, sashes etc; two or three waggons, covered with festoons of flowers and evergreens, and filled with merry female assemblages, joined the rank, which altogether was a full mile in length."

As the triumphant procession reached the Turnpike entrance into Poole there was an arch erected, festooned with flowers and topped with an immense blue banner with a large inscription which belied its two Reform Members of Parliament in proclaiming: "Welcome to this Conservative Borough".

The Parade-proper started at the Antelope in High Street at 11 o'clock. It went up to Parkstone, round the Church, "returning via Brown's Bottom" to Ringwood Road — to Longfleet Church — Hungerhill — Market House — King Street — West Street — Thames Street — round the Quay — Gas Works — "up the road to Mr. Steele's House" — High Street — Antelope. Throughout the morning's proceedings Church bells were ringing and the Quay guns were fired in salutation. The windows of the houses the parade passed "were crowded with ladies, who waived handkerchiefs and blue scarfs". Triumphant arches had been erected at many points of the route with various inscriptions, such as "Church and State", "King and Constitution", "Defeat of Falsehood and Triumph of Liberty", "Defeat of the Radical Faction", "Defeat of the Ham Fraud" and "Where is the Bill? Defeated without a Division". "We never saw so many flags exhibited on any other occasion", the newspaper concluded, and the only signs of dissention to the general rejoicing was "two frantic women in High Street and, at the Quay, some eight to ten along-shore men greeted the procession with a few hisses, which could scarcely be heard against the tumultuous applause of the crowd".

There was such a demand to attend the celebratory dinner that evening that provision was made for over 600. The main dinner was in two rooms at the Antelope but overspill dinners were arranged at the Bell and Crown, the Globe, the Port Mahon, Eight Bells and the Bull's Head.

High Street, Poole

The main dinner at the Antelope started at 4 o'clock. At the head of the main table was a "splendid blue flag on which was painted the Conservative symbol – the Bible and Crown – with the inscription, "In this sign we placed our hopes, and conquered".

After the meal was over and "on the removal of the cloth" the Mayor started the speech by calling on the diners "for a bumper for the King". This was given "with three times three and immense applause". The second toast was "the Queen", followed by "The Princess Victoria and the Royal Family" which was given "with three times three and one cheer more", and afterwards the assembly could get down to the real speeches of the evening.

One of the early toasts, of course, was that given by G. W. Ledgard to the Mayor who, in responding, said that "As Returning Officer at the late Municipal Election, it is highly gratifying to me to witness the proceedings of this day and the complete establishment of the Return I made on that election. The warm reception which has just been given to my name warrants me in the confident supposition that you do not credit the reports that I acted unjustly in that Return (Cheers). In discrediting those reports, gentlemen, you do me but justice..... After seven months of investigation have left (my Return) as they found it....."

In all that evening there were some twenty-six toasts and replies to toasts including one by William Thompson, the Chairman of the Conservative Association of Poole to Mr. Robert Parr, "a gentleman who had been calumnated beyond measure; a man who had been their pilot, and borne them through their difficulties".

Between the speeches there had been what were thought appropriate songs such as "England is the noblest home", "Jack Stedfast", "Glorious Apollo" and "Here's a health to honest John Bull" but, at last, at 9 o'clock it was all over and the diners could leave to walk the short distance to the Quay and join the crowds which had come to watch the display of fireworks over the water of the Channel as they were set off at the Ballast Quay. "The effect was exceeding fine", we are told, and the report ends by reconfirming that "Nothing occurred throughout the day to disturb the general joy".

Despite the Duke of Richmond's statement, there had been no formal decision by the Poole Council, to pay any compensation. Mr. Parr had not in fact submitted his claim and the necessary figures to support it. However, it was not very many days after the Lord's decision that Mr. Parr's claim came into the Guildhall. It was for £4,835 and, of course, included a claim for his newly-lost office of Clerk to the Magistrates. It also included a claim for the loss of all the other offices which Mr. Parr had succeeded to on being appointed town clerk on John Foot's death nearly three years previously. There were Clerk of the Peace, Clerk to the Commissioners of Taxes, Solicitor to the Coroner, Under Sheriff, Solicitor to the Overseers and Guardians, Solicitor to the Surveyor of Highways, Solicitor to the Quay Committee, Solicitor to the Lamp and Watch Commissioners, Solicitor to the Water Bailiff and Prothonotary to the Poole Weekly Court of Record.

The claim by Mr. Parr was considered by the Council on 5th October and deferred to a further meeting on 14th October when it was resolved — "That Mr. Parr appeared to be justly entitled to a fair and reasonable Compensation for all the offices claimed by him in his Memorial, the same being usually held by the Town Clerk" and some items of the claim were then admitted. Consideration of the remainder were adjourned until 9th November — but, before that day, the second Poole Municipal election was held.

While all this was going on Robert Parr had put up for election as Assessor against Mr. Kemp Welch's senior partner, John Durant. Mr. Parr had won and, it was alleged by the Reformers, that he had put on another 80 voters on the Burgess Roll and, in many cases, paid arrears of rates for persons in order to qualify them for inclusion.

Whatever the reason, the second election in Poole was a complete defeat for the Reformers; none were elected. Councillors Francis Trimwell Rogers and Tito Durell Hodges who were put up for re-election were defeated. George Ledgard had been promoted Alderman since the previous election. There were, therefore, three new Tory Councillors, all previously unsuccessful, William Cox, William Thompson and Isaac Steele. The result was that the Reform Party's representation on the Council had dropped to less than one-third. This meant that they could not invoke the provisions of the Municipal Corporations Act which allowed one-third of the Council to refer to any proposed compensation agreement to the Treasury to inquire into and settle.

The new Council considered Mr. Parr's claim for compensation on 9th November. At the same time they considered the claim of the dismissed Collector of Quay Dues, but quickly disposed of his request for them to reconsider their rejection. He was not, they decided, a Corporation officer. They adjourned Mr. Parr's claim to a further meeting on the 23rd but, at that meeting, agreed it at £4,500. On 29th November the Mayor entered into a Bond with Mr. Parr to secure £4,500 payable to Mr. Parr by four yearly instalments with interest at 5% on the amount outstanding at any time.

Meanwhile Councillor Parrott and Councillor Green on behalf of the Reform Party had tried to repeat their success with the appointment of Magistrates by applying to the Lord Chancellor to appoint new trustees for the old Corporation's various Charities, the responsibility for which had not been transferred to the new Council. At the end of September,

1836, Mr. Parrott, J.P., with Messrs. Lankester, Scott, Fricker and Richard Cull Hopkins swore an affidavit that eleven Reformers were 'fit and proper persons to be appointed Trustees' as they were 'substantial inhabitants of great respectability and that their appointment would give satisfaction to the majority of the inhabitants'.

The suggested Trustees were the leading men of the Reform Party: the Rev. Peter Jolliffe, James Seager, J.P., Nathaniel Brice, J.P., Tom Rickman, J.P., Francis T. Rogers, Joseph Notting, Richard Stanworth, John Williamson, Councillor Richard Pinney, Robert Wills and James Burgess Hamilton.

The Chancellor sent a copy of Mr. Parrott's application to the Council for comment and the old Corporator Councillors were appalled. The old Corporation had been commended by the Charity Commissioners in 1835 for the way they had ran their charities. They anticipated that those who had been responsible for administering them in the old Corporation would have been re-appointed on a personal basis. The Council presented a counter-petition and, after hearing the case, the Chancellor appointed six Conservatives and five of the Reform candidates as the new Trustees.

The Council's costs of this further escapade into law came to £184. The Court had ordered that £90 of this amount should be paid out of the funds of the Charities. It also ordered that £110 of Councillors Parrott and Green expenses be paid out of the Charities' funds. The new Trustees appointed by the Chancellor, therefore, started the winter with no funds even to continue to pay out the usual small sums to the occupants of the Almshouses. The Council thereafter were not involved in the administration of the old Corporation's Charities which included the 12 Almshouses given to the Corporation by George Garland in 1815 on the corner of Hunger Hill and West Street with another piece of land to provide income for their maintenance. The Charities also included Henry Harbin's free school legacy, John Bennett's legacy, Christopher Jolliffe's legacy, Roger's Almshouses and the Church Street Almshouses.

By December 1836 the Council had nearly completed the first year of its existence. Throughout the year there had been a constant drain on its resources. It had kept its police and its gaol going, its Quarter

Alms Houses Church Street

Roger's Alms Houses West Street

Sessions Court and its Coroner's Court. Its income from its Harbour dues had remained fairly buoyant, thanks to its growing clay exports and its coasting traffic, but its rents could not meet even these expenses. Its extraordinary expenses of litigation and now the expenses of compensation to the ex-town clerk were expenses which could only be met from rates.

At its meeting on 10th December the Council decided that it would require at least £5,000 in 1837 to meet its expenses on top of such income as it would receive from its land ownership. In fact it decided at a further meeting to reverse its previous decision not to treat with the Bridge Company and the Turnpike Company over the sale of land required by these Companies to make the use of the bridge more reasonable, — at least so long as these Companies would pay the Corporation £500 for the small pieces of land required.

The reaction in the already depressed town to such a proposed first Poole rate of £5,000 was sufficiently hostile to make the Council have second thoughts. The Council called a further meeting on Boxing Day

Clay barges unloading at the quay

Meanwhile the Reform party had acted. The thought that this rate included the payment of the first instalment of Mr. Parr's compensation would have made the payment of any rate anathema to the reformers of Poole. They called a meeting at the London Tavern on Christmas Eve and they agreed that they would do everything conceivable to stop the Council paying any compensation to their ex-town clerk. They nominated a yeoman, Francis Turner, to appeal against any rate made. They then went on voluntarily to rate themselves at 1/6d. in the £ to establish a fighting fund to bring the whole illegality of the Council paying Mr. Parr's compensation before the Court of Chancery. Mr. Parrott was equal to the Lord of the Manor in his confidence of victory in going into his fights. Once the matter was brought properly to the attention of the Chancery Court, the ratepayers, he promised, 'would never hear more of the compensation'. The voluntary rate raised some £500 for the fighting fund — and the leading Reformers left to spend their Christmas Day happy in this thought.

When the Council met on the morning of Boxing Day the reform Councillors George Lockyer Parrott, Tom Rickman, Richard Pinney, Richard Stanworth, and William Green were all present. They had no need to tell the others what had happened on Christmas Eve for rumour ran quick in Poole. They must, though, have smiled wrily as the rather rueful Council set about trying to quieten the town's indignation and yet somehow meet its obvious commitments. The Council decided to set up a Committee to find out the best way of raising the £4,500 compensation on loan "for the purpose of relieving the Burthens imposed on the Ratepayers by a reduction in the amount of the said Borough Rate".

The Council came, also, to two further decisions on that last Council meeting of 1837:—

"The Mayor having reported to this Council that the Treasurer of the Borough is without any Funds. It is unanimously Resolved that no further expenses be incurred until Funds can be obtained to defray the same".

"Resolved that a Memorial be presented under the Hand of the Mayor and Seal of this Borough to the Ecclesiastical Commissioners praying them to take early steps to dispose of the Living of Saint James in the patronage of this Corporation".

The Council at the end of the first eventful year of its existence at least felt that it might have got its financial affairs coming into some sort of order.

High Street, Poole

The Tory majority on the Council went about the business of raising the first Poole rate early in 1837. The method then, and for many years after, was to collect the rate through the Overseers of the various Parishes. The Overseers already had assessed properties in their Parish and collected the 'Poor Rate' for the alleviation of poverty and Councils had no system of their own. Therefore, Parliament had given Councils the right to demand of the Overseers that they raise further sums with their Poor Rate for the use of the Councils, or for the assessors to levy a separate 'Borough' rate. To know what different amounts should be demanded from the different Parishes the system adopted was for the Council to summon the various Overseers to a meeting, and 'examine them upon oath touching the full and fair annual value of the several Estates and Rateable property assessed to the Poor' of their particular parish. The Poole Council did this at its meetings in early January 1837, and the first results of this examination in Poole was as follows:

	Total annual value
Parish of St. James	£15,360. 7.6.
Hamworthy	939. 2.0.
The Tything of Longfleet	3,709.15.0.
The Tything of Parkstone	3,031.11.0.

The Council thereupon resolved to raise a rate of £2,500 by way of a 'Borough' rate on these figures, — thus halving its original intention to raise £5,000, and was made up of a contribution from St. James £1,667; Longfleet £402; Hamworthy £102 and Parkstone £329, i.e. a rate of slightly over 2/- in the £, and not much greater than the Reformers had agreed voluntarily to rate themselves to raise a fund to oppose the making of this rate.

The Old Rectory, Hamworthy South East front

The Council was in desperate need of funds. The Secretary of State had called for a report on their accounts of the Council and, if money could not be quickly raised, these accounts would show the Council was already in debt. The Council thereupon borrowed £1,713 from the Quay Funds and spent it on paying the constables' salaries, insurances, the overdue interest on its mortgages to James Seager, G. W. Ledgard, George Hancock and Thomas Hancock, the legal expenses of the town clerk of (£225), and repaying the Sheriff his expenses of maintaining the prisoners. There were also, payments of £77 to the Minister for "evening lectures" — provided from an endowment left by Benjamin Lester to the Corporation for the purpose; £200 for Rev. Jolliffe's salary; £81.13.6. for the four Quarter Sessions held in 1836 — and the final account of £54.19.6. owing to George Baker Billows for the provision of the new street lamps.

The Council thought that with the proceeds of their new rate; the sale of the advowson; the sale of land at the Bridge approaches, and with a new resolve to ensure the prompt receipt of their rents (then £322 in arrear), their finances would soon improve. After all, the professional valuation of the advowson of St. James alone amounted to £3,500.

They also had set up a Committee to report on any of its properties which were unlet. This Committee was told they had one parcel of unused land at Kinson of 117 acres and twelve other pieces of land in the old town, at Parkstone, Longfleet, Hamworthy and Kinson, a total area of 223 acres, all unlet and producing no income. The area at Kinson was described as being 2½ miles from Poole and that "a fine stream of water is continually running through this Lot sufficient to drive a Mill and also to irrigate a great portion of the land". A further area of 74 acres nearby was described as commanding "excellent views of the English Channel, the Isle of Purbeck and other distant places" and was "well worth the attention of the Commissioners of the High Roads and Waywardens of the neighbouring Parishes on account of the good Gravel Pits on the East and West sides thereof". Other pieces of land adjoined the Poole-Christchurch Turnpike Road, and there were other smaller pieces of land at the back of the Angel Hotel and an area in Church Street where houses had recently been demolished. There was clearly hope here of some further income to the Council.

Castle Street South West side

But the stormclouds from the Reformers were gathering. The hearing in King's Bench of the points referred from Assizes on the **Quo Warrento** against George Ledgard and Robert Major was imminent. The Council advanced £200 to the town clerk to defend this case. Then, as agreed at the Reformers' meeting, the appeal against the rate was made and, for this, the town clerk was given a further advance of £100. Then there was the "probably not unexpected" Writ from the Chancery Court "at the relation of the Hon. W. F. S. Ponsonby and others v Corporation of Poole and R. H. Parr" "praying for a declaration that the defendant Robert Henning Parr, having resigned his office of Town Clerk to the Corporation of Poole, is not entitled under the Municipal Reform Act to any compensation in respect to the Office, and that the Town Council had not, under the Act, authority to award him any Compensation in respect thereof....."

Mr. Parr was, of course, served with this Writ as well as the Corporation, and he relieved the Council of the main burden of the defence of this suit. The Writ had asked, too, for a declaration of the Court of the illegality of the recent rate made by the Council inasmuch as it included part-payment of the compensation. Mr. Parr "demurred" against the Writ. He claimed that the Act had laid down the appeal procedure as being to the Treasury as long as a third of the Council wished it and that therefore the Act had intended to cut out any interference from the Courts. He said that it was wrong to mix up actions against the payment of compensation and the making of a rate and, in any case, the Lord of the Manor and his friends had got the parties of the action wrong. The pleadings in demurrer went on for months.

Meanwhile, the Court of King's Bench decided in the Corporation's favour on the conditional verdicts of the assizes at Dorchester against George Ledgard and Robert Major. The High Court decided that the assize Judge had been wrong in his directions to the Jury as to the acceptance of evidence and King's Bench ordered a new trial. This, in effect, was for once an outright win for the Corporation as the time had passed when a decision on this case would have benefitted anyone. It was alleged in the town that it had cost "the Parrott Party" nearly £2,000 in costs. The case was never re-heard, and, some years later was struck out at the request of the Council.

The Council was also successful in its defence of Francis Turner's appeal to Quarter Sessions against the legality of the rate. The Recorder saw nothing in the "aggrieved yeoman's" appeal and dismissed it. There could of course, in the spirit of Poole then, be no sequel to this other than the inevitable appeal disputing the Recorder's decision, to the King's Bench.

With this further appeal pending, the bitter men of Poole let their animosities throw them into further clashes. In April 1837 the appointment of the Overseers of the various Parishes was made by the Bench of Magistrates. The system was for the Parish to have a Vestry meeting prior to the meeting of Magistrates to consider what names to suggest to the Bench. St. James held their Vestry meeting and put in their list of possible names to the Magistrates. At the top of the Vestry list were the names of Henry Custard and John Sydenham. The Bench considered the list at a special session of the Magistrates on 6th April, 1837, and the Mayor, Robert Slade, and the previous Mayor, Robert Slade, attended with Capt. Festing, G. L. Parrott, James Seager, Nathaniel Brice, Tom Rickman, the Rev. William Clarke and Col. Pedlar. There was also present Mr. Welch and his clerk, Samuel Scott, the Sergeant at Mace, Benjamin Inkpen, as well as James Churchill and Thomas Arnold, the town clerk, and a number of others. The list from the Vestry was produced and handed round to the Magistrates present. The Mayor said "I shall appoint Messrs. Custard and Sydenham". He then eshewed the paper prepared by Martin Kemp Welch, the Magistrate's Clerk, saying that it was not properly drawn up in that it did not describe the signatories to the formal appointment as being "of the quorum" of Magistrates and was prepared only for signature and not for formal sealing by the three signatories, as had always been done in the old Corporation. He thereupon produced his own paper drawn up in this way and sealed it. Having executed both copies he handed them to his uncle, Robert Slade, who also signed them and passed them to Capt. Festing. Mr. Parrott, meanwhile, made a remark approving the respectability of the town men who had been suggested, and other magistrates were meanwhile studying the Vestry List. No one made an objection to the appointment. Capt. Festing added the required third signature to the two copies of the appointment. Tom Rickman and Capt. Pedlar were late and were only arriving about the time that Capt. Festing was completing the documents. The papers were handed back to the Mayor who handed them on to the Sergeant at Mace who left to have the appointments formally announced.

After the two Robert Slades and Capt. Festing had left the meeting Mr. Parrott and Mr. Rickman produced a different list of proposed Overseers for St. James. The seven other Magistrates remaining were shown this new list. They persuaded themselves that the Mayor had not given them time to object to the names suggested by the Vestry. Mr. Parrott thought he had said before the Mayor had made the first appointments that he objected to the appointment of two Tory Assessors and would rather have had one Overseer appointed from each of the parties. He remembered saying at the time that he had made this suggestion "for the peace of the town" and that he "would presently propose one and one" but that the Mayor had not given him a chance to do it: in any case, it was for a majority of the Magistrates to make the appointment, not the Mayor, even if he was Chairman of the Bench. The rest of the Magistrates thereupon went through a further election of Overseers and appointed two Reformers, Messrs. Busson and Short, to be the Overseers of St. James and completed Mr. Welch's forms with the names of Mr. Busson and Mr. Short.

S.S. Gannett — An early steam propelled vessel

However, the Parish documents were handed over to Messrs. Custard and Sydenham and it was on them that Council demanded the collection of their first rate. Messrs. Custard and Sydenham dutifully complied and demanded the required Borough rate of their assessed Parishioners of St. James.

When the demands had been delivered Councillor G. L. Parrott, J.P., called a meeting of a number of the ratepayers and told them what had happened at the Magistrates' meeting and gave it as his opinion that Messrs. Custard and Sydenham were not the Overseers of St. James at all and had no right to make a demand for rates and that such demands could be ignored.

Rates have been left unpaid for less good cause than that the Chairman of the Bench considered they were not payable. It was hardly surprising therefore that Messrs. Custard and Sydenham received little response to their demand for the payment of rates. It was, too, in the temper of the old Corporators to flinch from a challenge. The Mayor, as Chief Magistrate, promptly agreed to the issue of seventeen summonses on the leading Reformers for non-payment of the rates.

The first summonses to be heard were those against the two Reform Councillors and fellow-Magistrates, James Seager and Tom Rickman. The presiding Magistrate at the hearing of these was George Parrott. He dismissed them summarily to the cheers of the Reformers in court for the occasion. It was, therefore, not surprising that when the summons against Councillor G. L. Parrott, J.P. was heard by the presiding justice, Tom Rickman, that it suffered a similar fate!

However, by a mischance, miscalculation, or perhaps by overconfidence of the reformers who might have thought the other 14 summonses would be dropped, the Mayor and the other Robert Slade, were on the Bench to hear them. They accepted the rate demands issued by Custard and Sydenham were valid and made orders on all fourteen defaulting ratepayers. Distress warrants were issued on them all and were promptly carried out on the surprised ratepayers who were all prominent Reformers and included "the old consistent reformer" Thomas Naish also Thomas Whicker, both future Councillors.

TO THE
INDEPENDENT
Burgesses
~~AND~~
INHABITANTS
OF
POOLE.

The Friends of your late Representatives having industriously circulated a report that ~~no~~ Opposition will be offered to their return on Monday next, you are earnestly requested not to pledge your Votes and Interest, as a Candidate of ~~liberal~~ principles will certainly offer himself, and probably within a few hours, it being determined that the ~~Independence~~ of the Borough shall not be destroyed without a Struggle.

25th April, 1831.

MOORE AND SYDENHAM, PRINTERS, POOLE.

Party Strife at least provided business for the printers such as Tory printer Sydenham printing a Reform handbill

Not unnaturally an appeal was promptly made against this decision and the distress. Counsel was brought down from London to take the appeal at Quarter Sessions. The Justices gave the unfortunate Assessors, the defendants, no legal help in the hearing of the Appeal. Mr. Bingham, the counsel for the appellants, roundly denounced the Mayor, his law and his decision, and the appellants were given the verdict against Messrs. Custard and Sydenham and the Parish was left to pay the costs, including compensation to some of the ratepayers for accidental damage to furniture in its seizure by the bailiffs. Thomas Naish, for instance, was compensated for damage to his table which was scratched by Mr. Whicker's cheese which, having been distrained, was placed upon Mr. Naish's table.

The two Overseers Henry Custard and John Sydenham were now in a ridiculous position where the Council had resolved to sue them for the prescribed penalties for not enforcing the rate, yet they were adjudged guilty by the Recorder and mulct in damages by ratepayers for doing just that. To make matters worse in Poole, the costs and damages of these cases were payable from the only other fund the assessors had to pay them from, namely the fund for the relief of the poor. The Overseers took the course recommended to them by counsel as the only way out of their predicament: they applied to the High Court for a Writ of Mandamus to order the Poole Magistrates to enforce the rate. The case was heard quickly by the King's Bench Court, but the Overseers did badly, they lost their case. The Court refused to make the order asked for, and left them and the Poor rate to pay the costs of this further action.

This left the Council again on the financial rocks, for the Assessor's funds themselves now exhausted: they were almost in a worse position than the Council, for they were left paying for such urgent relief to the poor as their own pockets could manage in the hope of later recovery.

By this time the Mayor, as Chairman of the Bench, was finding his position among his Reform colleagues and their Clerk, Martin Kemp Welch, quite untenable. He reported to the Council which tried to help as the following minute of the Council shows:

"The Mayor having complained to this Council that the Clerk to the Magistrates has refused to act under his directions and having acted contrary thereto and the Town Clerk and Clerk of the Peace, conceiving himself incompetent to act in such capacity under the provisions of the Municipal Act. **Resolved** that the Mayor be allowed a Salary of Thirty Pounds per annum in order to enable him to appoint a Clerk or legal adviser with reference thereto".

It was, too, about this time, that the Council was served by Francis Edwards, the dismissed Collector of Quay Dues, with a demand that the Council should issue him with a Bond to secure an annuity of £42.9.10d. which had been awarded him by the Treasury on his appeal to them against the Council's refusal to pay him compensation. The Council at first felt bound by the Treasury's decision but decided to ask for Counsel's advice on whether the compensation was payable and, if so, if it could be paid out of Quay Funds.

There was then on 22nd June 1837, an interlude in the Council's struggles with a quickly convened meeting to receive the formal notice of the death of William IV and a request from "the Privy Council to Her Majesty Queen Victoria..... to cause her Royal Majesty to be proclaimed in the usual places in this Borough". There were thirteen members present at the meeting, all Conservatives. They resolved that a public procession of the Council was to take place at noon on the following day to proclaim Queen Victoria's accession to the throne, and they allotted £50 to cover the expenses. They asked the Rev. Peter Jolliffe to preach an appropriate sermon on the day of the funeral of William IV at a service which, they decided, the Council would attend.

Even these proceedings could not be let to pass without the Reformers' objection. The quickly-convened meeting of the Council on 22nd June had not been called with the proper three days' notice: the spending of the £50 was therefore illegal the Reformers claimed. If only the other troubles of the Council could have been so easily dealt with! They called a further meeting of the Council with the full three days' notice and solemnly approved their previous resolution.

They then made an attempt at reconciliation in regard to the collection of rates. The Council resolved that "impressed with a deep sense of the importance of endeavouring to remove the pressent embarrassment in which the Parochial Concerns of the Parish of St. James, Poole, was involved in consequence of the late

Queen Victoria 1819—1901

appeal against the Poor Rate, do recommend the Magistrates, Overseers and all other Parties concerned that the same Line of Conduct be adopted with regard to the Poor Rate as has been adopted in respect of the Registrations, namely, that all the Four Overseers appointed in March last be requested to act in the collection of the Poor Rate".

They were whistling in the wind if they thought the two Reform Assessors were going to help Messrs. Custard and Sydenham collect rates which might be partly used to pay Mr. Parr's compensation. There was no response to this suggestion.

The Council had by then heard from the Ecclesiastic Commissioners as to the tenders received for the purchase of the advowson of St. James. The best offer was £2,865 but the Council had no doubts in promptly rejecting this offer: they should get at least the amount of £3,500 which their professional valuer had told them it was worth. They decided to re-advertise the sale. But nothing went right for them. The best offer on the second advertisement was £15 less than the first, but by November they were in desperate need of some money. They could wait no longer. They accepted the offer of £2,850.

At this time, too, the Council had received a 'Rule' from the High Court demanding to know of them why a High Court order should not be issued ordering them to pay Francis Edward's compensation. The Council by now had had counsel's advice to the effect that their first decision not to pay Mr. Edwards any compensation was correct. They therefore instructed the town clerk to oppose this application in the High Court — and they had yet another High Court case on their hands.

In the November elections the three Conservatives were returned for the North-West Ward and perhaps, surprisingly, the Poole electors reacted against three of the leading Reformers then up for re-election; George Lockyer Parrott, Tom Rickman and Richard Stanworth, and returned none of them, replacing them with three Conservatives, William Adey, Samuel Clark and William Thompson, all of whom got 133 votes. The Council took no chances with this election. They carefully preserved every duplicate vote and stuck them in a volume which is still preserved in the Municipal records! The Conservatives then seemed to have received a clear mandate. Perhaps Poole's major troubles were over, especially as in that same month, the Master of the Rolls heard Robert Parr's Demurrers to the action, brought by the Lord of the Manor Mr. Ponsonby, for a declaration of the Court that Mr. Parr was entitled to no compensation. The Master of the Rolls decided that the Information supporting Mr. Ponsonby's Writ did not contain "any statement of fact which can be relied on as forming a foundation for the charge of fraud". "The facts stated", the judge said, "do not support the vague and general allegations of fraud which this Information contains". He therefore allowed Mr. Parr's demurrers on the ground that no case has been made for the Interference of the Court of Equity.

Perhaps now that Mr. Parr's costs of this action fell to be paid by Mr. Ponsonby and his fellow relators and were more than the £500 raised by the Reform Party, this major litigation would now cease. Poole needed some such relief for its affairs were getting in a most serious state. In September, for instance, the Sheriff had reported to the Council that the prisoners in the Poole gaol were "completely without maintenance" and the only response which the Council could make was to pass a further resolution to enforce their unpaid rate. They were at least encouraged in believing this might be effective for the King's Bench decision upheld the Recorder's decision on the appeal by Francis

Turner against the Recorder's decision that the rate of previous March was good.

But the Council's hopes were confounded. The position grew worse. The Magistrates reported in December 1837, on the "inadequate state of the gaol for the reception of prisoners". Prisoners in those days were often badly housed, and it says much for the terrible condition of Poole's gaol that the Council did not question the report. It resolved that "the present state of the Finances of the Borough, rendering it impracticable to effect such alterations as are now required; will take immediate steps to make the necessary contact with the County Justices so that the Borough Justices may be entitled to commit Prisoners to the County Gaol". This resolution was only 19 months after the date of its memorial to the Home Secretary in which the Council explained how expensive it would be to convey prisoners to and from Dorchester "29 miles away" and "that the Gaol of the said Town and County contains two Court Yards and a Day Room 11ft by 9. Four rooms above Stairs: Two Sleeping Cells 9' by 5'10" and 8'10" high with a House of Correction and a Tread Mill. The Court Yards are well supplied with Water and the Gaol is in good condition".

Whatever hopes for peace which the Council might have entertained after the Master of the Rolls' decision, were also soon shattered. Within a month or so, Mr. Ponsonby, 'the Paymaster General' of the Reformers as he was sometimes referred to, lodged an appeal against the Master of the Rolls' decision on Mr. Parr's Demurrers. Whatever this news did to the Council, it seemed to have little effect on Mr. Parr's nerves: he promptly issued a Writ of Summons asking the High Court to order the Council to pay him the first instalment of his Compensation.

Worse was to follow to ensure there was yet another depressing year-end for the Council. The fourteen ratepayers against whom the Mayor and his uncle had issued distress for the payment of their rates each took out separate Writs against the two Robert Slades, the Mayor and the ex-Mayor, alleging trespass and damages in causing illegal distress summonses to be issued against the fourteen Reformers following the improper and illegal appointment of Messrs. Custard and Sydenham by the Slades without consulting the other Magistrates.

At a Meeting of the Creditors of Messrs. SLADE, BIDDLE, and Co., and MAJOR, SEAGER, and Co., of POOLE, held at their Counting-House, in Poole, the 10th day of February, 1838,

IT was resolved and unanimously agreed to, That it will be highly desirable, and greatly for the interest of the Creditors of SLADE, BIDDLE, and Co., and MAJOR, SEAGER, and Co., to avoid a Bankruptcy.

It was also resolved and unanimously agreed to, That a Letter of Licence shall be forthwith granted to SLADE, BIDDLE, and Co., and MAJOR, SEAGER, and Co., for a twelvemonth, on their executing a proper Deed of Inspection, placing and vesting their Estate and affairs in the hands of, and under the general management and controul of Inspectors, for the general benefit of their Creditors. And it was further resolved, That such Deed of Inspection and Letter of Licence should forthwith be prepared by Mr. ISAAC FRYER, for execution; and that Mr. JOHN FRYER, Mr. GEORGE KEMP, and Mr. WILLIAM HARRISON be appointed Inspectors accordingly.

It was further resolved, That Mr. ISAAC FRYER shall immediately prepare a proper Power or Powers of Attorney from SLADE, BIDDLE, and Co., and MAJOR, SEAGER, and Co., and the Inspectors, to some proper person or persons in Newfoundland, for the purpose of taking possession of, and securing the whole of the Property, Estate, and Effects belonging to SLADE, BIDDLE, and Co., and MAJOR, SEAGER, and Co., in Newfoundland or elsewhere, for the general benefit of the Creditors.

ROBERT BURT.
J. B. BLOOMFIELD and Co.
H. G. KNIGHT and Co.
WM. ARNOLD.
WM. HARRISON.
ROBERT SLADE, SEN.
MARK SEAGER.
ROLLES BIDDLE.
G. B. BILLOWS and Co.
T. D. HODGES.

FRYER, ANDREWS, and Co.
GEORGE KEMP.
WILLS and STANWORTH.
F. T. and G. ROGERS.
WILLIAM BALSTON and SON.
ROBERT KNIGHT.
JOHN SYDENHAM.
JOSEPH NOTTING.
ALDRIDGE and CRABB.
JOSEPH ROBBINS.
GEORGE PENNEY.
R. and J. TURTLE.

Prominent merchants were already facing difficulties due to fall off in trade and political strife

Should the Slades lose one of these actions they would automatically lose all the other thirteen and they would have to pay the costs of all fourteen actions. What made their position so ominously bad was that the Overseers had lost both cases on similar facts, one before the Recorder and later, on the appeal, before the King's Bench.

The fact that each one of the fourteen men took out a separate summons meant that it was a concerted attack on the standing of the two Slades and, through them, on the Corporation. Moreover the costs of all fourteen actions could very well be of serious financial consequence, even to the Slades. They took the matter most seriously. We can have little doubt that Mr. Parr's services were employed and that it was he who briefed Sergeant Bompass as Counsel for the Slades at the hearing of the first two cases which were down for trial at the Lent Assizes at Dorchester in April, 1838.

The majority of the Council had, naturally, no wish to oppose Mr. Parr's Writ of Summons for the payment of his first instalment which was the next Court process to arrive at the Guildhall. They agreed that the Council would not oppose it as long as Mr. Parr agreed to a three-months' stay of execution and thus give them chance to collect some money to meet it. In February the judgement against the Council to pay the first of the four instalments of Mr. Parr's compensation, plus interest and costs, i.e. £1,350, was issued by the High Court subject to an agreed stay of execution for three months.

The Dorchester Assizes at which the summonses against the two Robert Slades was held in April. Sergeant Bompass on behalf of the Slades had a fine trial. Mr. Erle, on behalf of the prosecutors, must have been horrified at the poor showing the Magistrates of Poole and their supporters put up against Sergeant Bompass's thunderings. Whatever the Slades had suffered at the hands of the London Counsel in the case for the fourteen ratepayers at the Poole Quarter Sessions earlier, was nothing to what Magistrates George Lockyer Parrott, Tom Rickman, Nathaniel Brice and the Rev. Mr. Clarke suffered at the Dorchester Assize before a Jury and Lord Denman, the presiding judge. Even the supporting evidence from Mr. Martin Kemp Welch, Mr. Williamson and especially Mr. Samuel Scott, the clerk of Messrs. John Durant and Martin Kemp Welch, was made to look extremely mendacious. Lord Denman remarked to the Jury that if they did not accept Mr. Scott's evidence, "why, Mr. Scott must be perjured".

But the Jury did not accept Mr. Scott's evidence or the rest of the great mass of evidence submitted on the part of the accusers: they dismissed the first case, that brought on behalf of George Penney, and the Judge showed his feelings in the case by awarding treble costs against Mr. Penney.

The second case down for hearing at Dorchester the following day was that brought by the Irish landlord of the Crown Inn in Market Street, Mr. Michael Carroll. Mr. Parrott was credited by the Tories of persuading Mr. Carroll to go on with his prosecution, despite the result of George Penney's case as, with further evidence to be brought from Poole next day and a new Jury, he could not fail. At any rate the next trial of the Slades proceeded the following day at the instance of Michael Carroll and, so confident was Mr. Carroll of the outcome after the first day's hearing, that he had laid on a grand supper at the Crown the following night to celebrate the assured verdict of the new Dorchester jury.

High Street, Poole

'Piplers' Poole Quay

But the result of the second prosecution the next day was the same as the first. The jury dismissed Mr. Carroll's suit, and the Judge again awarded treble costs against the Landlord of the Crown, and Michael Carroll and his friends can hardly have enjoyed his celebratory dinner that night — assuming they attended at all.

Not, however, that that was the end of the matter. "Mr. Justice Parrott", as his Tory enemies now called him, was given the credit of persuading the two aggrieved parties to these proceedings to apply to the Queen's Bench to order a re-trial, and yet another case was left hanging over the heads of the Poole Tory Councillors.

Not surprisingly the Council could not find the money to pay Mr. Parr's judgment debt of £1,350. They had received some of the rates from their last rate but, with the necessary services to maintain and with the running costs of their litigation they were never left with anything like enough money to pay Mr. Parr his instalment of compensation. The best they could do, in

206

August was to pay him £45 of the interest on the first instalment and £29.11.1d., his taxed costs of obtaining the unopposed judgment.

Meanwhile the Reform party were themselves getting concerned at the state of the poor in Poole who were also being deprived of rates by the Reformers efforts to stop at all costs the Council getting enough funds to pay Mr. Parr. Mr. Parrott petitioned Parliament to make an order separating the two funds completely, but even his Whig supporters in Parliament could not persuade the Government to take any action.

Soon afterwards the appeal of Messrs. Penney and Carroll came to be heard in the High Court. Mr. Penney alleged that the decision was against the weight of evidence. Mr. Carroll alleged the decision had been come to by a mistake of law. The Court heard the arguments and were quite unimpressed. The appeals were dismissed and the appellants punished by the award of treble costs against them yet again.

Benjamin Inkpen delivered the Sheriff's warrant on George Penney for the payment of these costs a little while later. With the Sheriff's poundage of £20 they came to £598.13.3. Michael Carroll, the Crown's landlord, had his Sheriff's execution a day or so later. He was slightly luckier: his warrant for costs was for only £571.19.3.

The other 12 accusers of the two Slades were allowed to withdraw their summonses on payment of treble the Slades' legal costs, then not aggravated by any trial. They had, in addition, their own legal costs to pay.

There then followed proceedings to quash the appointment of Messrs. Bussom and Short by the Assessors. This was finally done but the Parish had to pay its own expenses of the application and a further £216 was subtracted from the Poor fund and another year of little or no receipt of Poor rates had passed.

The Board of Guardians wrote to the Council explaining their position and suggesting that the poor were suffering because of the conflict over the raising of rates for the borough's purposes and it might help the poor to keep the two rates separate. The Council considered the proposal but passed the following:

"Resolved unanimously that the Council are convinced that the present distressed state of the Poor and the Invalid state of the Finances in this Borough are mainly attributable to those who attend the Board of Guardians solely for the party and political purposes, who have openly resisted the payment of thier Rates and, from the Bench, have incited the Public to the same improper and illegal Resistance, and to the Extraordinary Conduct of the Parties involving the Council in a most expensive and groundless Chancery suit and that therefore the severing of the Borough from the Poor Rate would only tend to insolve the Town more deeply than it is at present, and that a copy of these resolutions be sent to the Clerk of the Guardians".

It was now an appropriate time for the Conservatives to bring forward their old arguments about the constitution of the Poole Bench. Passions in Poole had got into such a state that the Bench and the Church as well as the Council and the Law were all used indiscriminately to defeat the enemy, all of it without regard to the welfare of the town, its poor, its church or, least of all, the Council. The Conservatives petitioned the Secretary of State on the quality and balance of the Bench.

Parish of St. James, POOLE.

Notice is hereby Given, that a MEETING of the Inhabitants will be holden at the Vestry, on FRIDAY the Fifteenth of June, instant, at 10 o'clock in the Forenoon, at the toll of the Bell, to determine on the mode of appointing an ORGANIST, MR. JOSEPH GOSS having signified his intention of resigning at Midsummer next.

WILLIAM HILL, } Church-
THOMAS G. HANCOCK,} wardens.

June 9, 1838.

By the above judicious Notice of the Churchwardens, posted yesterday on the Church Doors, the Inhabitants must see the propriety of giving to each Candidate for the situation, Fair Play, by testing their merit before competent Judges, and every honest straightforward Ratepayer should attend the Vestry, and carry out such well meant intentions so as to secure to the Parish, the most competent and efficient Organist.

A RATE-PAYER.

Controversy extending to Parish affairs

Mr. Robert Parr in the cases of Penney v Slades and Carroll v Slades had prepared Sergeant Bompass's brief with the greatest diligence. He had found out more about the Reform Magistrates of Poole than they almost knew themselves. Sergeant Bompass had flayed them with this research to destroy their characters: it had been most necessary that this should be done, it must be admitted, to give the Defendants a chance of winning in the face of the testimony of so many magistrates against the Slades. After the Dismissal of the appeal of Messrs. Penney and Carroll by the High Court, anonymous notices appeared round Poole giving the gist of Sergeant Bompass's accusations. Then, to make sure full use of the research was made, a pamphlet was sold entitled "An epitome of the Biography of the Magistrates of the Borough of Poole, appointed by Lord John Russell in opposition to the recommendations of the Council". The pamphlet was "dedicated, as a mater of course, to his Lordship" and "was to be had of all respectable booksellers price 1/-".

From the style, the literary illusions and the inherent patriotism, it was probably true to attribute it to George Ledgard, the Tory stalwart. He starts off by addressing Lord John Russell. "My Lord", he says, "Certainly nothing could give you more pleasure than having in your library a correct Biography of persons whom your Lordship has elevated to honour, that your posterity might know the description of tools you employed in repairing the Constitution of Old England. I do not condemn or accuse the Magistrates of the reports mentioned in the following pages; but as they are current and general in the neighbourhood, your Lordship, with the facilities you possess of referring to the Records of the Courts of Justice, Court of Admiralty, the offices of Customs and Excise, can ascertain the truth or falsehood of them; and, if false, disabuse the public mind thereof; it true, apply your Lordship's purge in the most stringent form..... (signed) John Bull, Jnr.".

The writer then deals with the local focus of all the Tory venom — George Lockyer Parrott, J.P.

George L. Parrott, said the pamphlet, was the son of William Parrott a most desperate pirate who lived at Purewell near Christchurch. With a dozen depraved characters he became the terror of the neighbourhood. He landed his smuggled goods quite openly, the revenue officers being frightened to intervene.

THE TORIES.

Who took one Member from our Town,
And stripped us of our old renown;
Who still attempts the trick to crown?
                    The Tories.

Who made a mess of the Franchise,
By corruption, fraud, and lies,
With Poor Rates blest poor tenants' eyes?
                    The Tories.

Who still maintain each State abuse,
With Principles play fast and loose,
Who keep the eggs, but kill the goose?
                    The Tories.

Who kept us out of our Birthright
For twenty years, by main and might,
And still the notion does affright?
                    The Tories.

Who placed Three Millions on our backs,
And Twopence more for Income Tax;
Who stick to office—tight as wax?
                    The Tories.

Whose War Expense—in Peace profound,
Is Sixteen Shillings in the Pound;
And not a ship that's safe or sound?
                    The Tories.

Who burked Reform and stopped Free Trade,
And who set on the Hyde Park raid?
The Corn Laws by themselves were made;
                    The Tories.

Who ruined Poole, and brought her low,
By law, for Thirty years or so;
Who still keeps up this "little go"?
                    Our Tories.

Who cheat the Town of Harbour Dues,
Who let a Bridge out for our use,
And kindly load us with abuse?
                    Our Tories.

Who hate the Ballot, love the Screw,
Forsake their youth, and hang out "blue,"
Forgetting what they used to do?
                    Our Tories.

Who level homes, who drive the Poor
As Paupers to the Workhouse door;
Who raised our Rates? Yes, to be sure,
                    Our Tories.

Who take our money—elsewhere spent;
Who bring this Boy to represent
Our SILENCE in next Parliament?
                    Our Tories.

Who now inspire the Longfleet Swell,
To send with Judas down to hell,
All who would ring the Irish knell?
                    Our Tories.

Meek, gentle saint! to preach and pray
This gospel new—"Who go one way,
The Irish Church and Christ betray"!
                    Our Tories.

Who did dismiss the Rifle Band,
Because for WARING they did stand?
Thus TYRANNY stalks through the land,
                    Our Tories.

In fine—who seek the Empire's fall,
Would mortgage Church and State, and all
And hold, at last, their Country's Pall,
                    THE TORIES.

Contemporary handbill

The people of the neighbourhood had, in 1784, applied to the Government for help in seizing the gang and the Government sent a sloop, the Orestes, to Christchurch. The Orestes in a hurry to catch the gang, who had just run two large lug-sail vessels filled with smuggled tea and spirits on to the shore, ground itself on a sandbank at Havenhouse. As the Gazette reported, the ships in the customs service were then "most violently and forcibly resisted by William Parrott and a large body of smugglers armed with fire-arms and other offensive weapons..... who fired upon the officers, and killed Mr. William Allen, the master of the said sloop of war, the Orestes, and also dangerously wounded the boat's crew....." Knowing that retribution would follow if they stayed in Christchurch the gang split up. One of the gang was later caught and hanged at Winchester. Parrott was outlawed and a reward of £250 was put on his head, but he escaped to Holland.

It was while Mr. Parrott, Snr., lived in Holland and continued his smuggling that George Lockyer Parrott was born. The French became in possession of Holland in the Napoleonic Wars and the two Parrotts, father and son, became employed as pilots to shipping in the Scheld with which they have become acquainted through their smuggling activities. In 1804 the Dutch and French fleet was moored in Scheld and George Parrott was sent over to England by his father to inform the Government of the position of the French and Dutch fleets and an offer to conduct British ships into the Scheld to attack the enemy ships in exchange for a free pardon. It was said in the pamphlet that eventually the Admiralty paid the Parrotts' demand and fitted out a fleet which "Capt. Harvey", alias G. L. Parrott, piloted the Walcherin expedition into the Scheld to attack the enemies' ships. "The unhappy fate of this expedition is well known to all"; says the pamphlet, "and what could be expected from such a diabolical origin, and with a man of such a character for its pilot? Heaven recoiled at the foulness of the dead and overwhelmed British valour with misfortunes".

Mr. Parrott thus settled in England with a Master's half-pay. After a while he was made master of a merchant ship and later became clerk in a Newfoundland Merchant's office. He turned to the Reform Party and "was appointed leader and spokesman, by acclamation, by the political cobblers and dissenters of Poole, and was used as a utensil by the aristocratic Whigs, to push them into power and place....."

Tom Rickman, J.P., was second in line. He "made his debut in the world by engaging in very extensive speculations in corn, on the anticipated profits of which, he furnished a house at Spitsbury most handsomely and lived in great style. However, his speculations turning out failures, he soon found himself greatly embarrassed, and overwhelmed with debts; consequently his second effort was to emancipate himself from his debts and unfortunate speculations. To accomplish this, he hit upon a most extraordinary strategem; he stripped himself stark naked, and in this state ran about his house among the females and jumped into a tub of water (if this was his original intention, he did well to take off his clothes). He then went into the madhouse at Laverstock and remained there until his friends had settled, in different ways, with his different creditors".

In September 1826 he was fined by the Magistrates of Poole for having a "small Bushel" and, later that year, fined for defrauding the revenue on the malt. In 1832 the pamphlet accused Tom Rickman of stealing part of a consignment of corn he had sold to a London merchant and of committing perjury at Dorchester in the trial of Carroll v Slades.

The Rev. William Clarke was let off relatively lightly. He had, it was said, admitted at the trial of Carroll v Slades to being the author of "very many scurrilous, false and malicious libels". But, said the pamphlet, he had resigned his Commission and was about to leave the country for Australia and, "having made the apology, that he only accepted the appointment to keep Francis Timewell Rogers out, whom he knew had been convicted of defrauding the revenue and other worse delinquincies, we will let him pass".

Nathaniel Brice was a Lieutenant in the Navy, bringing home despatches from the Mediterranean when he "suffers himself and vessel to be captured by a row boat which his officers and men wished to fight". Brice resigned the commission rather than face court martial. Sir John Bickerton, being a candidate for Parliament in Poole about this time, and Brice's father being a burgess and having a vote, an arrangement was made with Sir Richard, then Lord of the Admiralty, to have Nathaniel Brice replaced in the Navy List on the understanding he would never rise in rank or again be employed — for which arrangement "Sir Richard obtained Brice's vote and interest".

The pamphlet writer was most scathing, too, about the private life and morals of Lieut. Nathaniel Brice.

Next on the list was George Penney, J.P., who, it was said, had done as much as any man to disturb the peace of Poole — and yet professed to be a Quaker, a man of peace. He took the Chair at a Church meeting after turning out the Churchwardens despite being "a swear-not-at-all Quaker and was one of the first to refuse to pay poor rate; prosecuted the Mayor for trespass and even lost that case at Dorchester with Mr. Greathead of Uddens, a liberal-Whig as foreman of the jury". He was only a general agent, "obliged to anyone to give him a job and, as such, under the control of others". Moreover, he was an extreme radical.

As may be easily understood the result of the cases of Penney v Slades and Carroll v Slades and the subsequent proceedings, did nothing to abate the hatred which existed between Mr. Ponsonby, Messrs. Parrott, Lankester, Rickman, Naish, Penney and others on the one side and the Slades, the Ledgards, and the Hancocks and others on the other side,

View of Poole from Constitution Hill

and the drama of thrust and counter thrust went on. George Kemp, the ex-leader of the Whigs in Poole, the Deacon of the Congregational Church for so many years, was perhaps the one man who could have brought about peace in the town, did his best. He pleaded with the contestants to have regard to the welfare of the town rather than continue with the internecine fights which was reducing the value of property and the commerce of the town to bankruptcy. But even his words fell on deaf ears.

The hearing of the Mandamus in Queen's Bench by which Francis Edwards tried to enforce the Council's compliance with the Treasury's award of compensation by way of an annuity failed. The Council's law costs were left to be paid by the Council but so were Mr. Edward's not inconsiderable costs left to him or, as the Tories asserted, to "Mr. Parrott's Paymaster-General", for the town's turmoil was basically caused, most people thought then, by the hatreds born at the time of the Bridge controversy between some of the old Corporators and Mr. Parr on the one hand and the Lord of the Manor and his Reform friends on the other.

As in previous years, 1838 ended in a flurry of legal actions. As in the case in all long wars, battles were won and lost. It was now the Reformer's turn to win a notable legal battle. They won their appeal against the 'Master of the Rolls' decision of the previous November allowing Mr. Parr's Demurrers against their original Writ demanding the payment of his compensation to be declared legal. The Lord Chancellor decided that the Chancery Court had jurisdiction and, though he agreed with Mr. Parr as to his objection as to parties to the suit, he gave leave to Mr. Ponsonby and his co-suitors to amend their Writ and start again. Each party were left to pay their own costs in this case.

This decision in no way put Mr. Parr off his course. Immediately after his second instalment of compensation was due at the end of November he issued a Writ for the High Court's judgment ordering it to be paid. He also applied to the High Court for a Writ of Elegit for the Court to take charge of the means of satisfying the judgment debt he had obtained for the first instalment. He also appealed against the Lord Chancellor's judgment on his Demurrers.

It therefore seemed to the Reform Party that Mr. Parr was now approaching the position of getting the payment of at least his first instalment. This had to be stopped at all costs while they got the Court of Chancery's decision that the payment of his compensation was illegal. They therefore made an application to the High Court for an injunction ordering the Council not to make any payment on account of Mr. Parr's compensation pending the judgment in the Chancery Case brought by Mr. Ponsonby — or, as he became in 1838, Lord de Mauley.

Curiously enough, too, for the legal battles in the year had seemed to go mainly for the Conservatives, the Reform candidates did well in the November elections and the Reform Leader, Mr. George Parrott, was elected back on to the Council.

The Council had now at last collected most of its previous year's rate and, in January 1839, made an estimate of its likely requirements for the year which included provision for Mr. Parr's second instalment despite the fact it had paid only some of the interest and costs on the first. The estimate included £1,000 for law expenses, presumably to meet some of the very extensive legal costs of its town clerk, Thomas Arnold, whose accounts had never gone further than the Finance Committee promising to bring them to the Council's attention.

Meanwhile Mr. Parr's application to the High Court for a Writ of Eligit had been granted. Under the orders following this Writ a Sheriff's jury had been empanelled to inquire into the means of the Council to meet the judgment. As a result of this examination Mr. Parr was awarded all the 'personal' property of the Corporation and was put into possession, or in receipt of the rents, of all land and buildings of the Corporation which were not mortgaged so long as the Jury assessed a lettable value on the property.

Therefore early in 1839 the Council had what one might have thought must be the final indignity of officers of the High Court seizing all the property of the Corporation. They seized everything moveable of the Corporation, even the new furniture which the Council had installed in the Guildhall in 1836 which they had so prized as to ban the use of the Guildhall for any other purpose than Council meetings.

But some of the Tory Councillors were losing heart at the continued bickering and fights of the Council. The Council paid Mr. Parr £300 of his last Writ, but some had no stomach for further squabbles. D. O. Lander, a Mayor of the old Corporation, the Collector of Customs, was reported to have finally left Poole early in the New Year, and Alderman Robert Slade, Snr. resigned, for his business was failing.

The obdurate Mr. Parr pressed on. He obtained a Writ of Mandamus from the High Court ordering the Council to enforce the rate it had made so that it could pay Mr. Parr's second instalment, but the Council could manage to pay only £350 of their debt to him. The Council was coming to the end of its tether. Mr. Parrott and his advisers had thought up something else to confound them: it was illegal under the Municipal Corporations Act to make a rate for anything but prospective expenditure. He obtained Counsel's opinion saying that it was illegal for a Council to make a rate to pay for retrospective expenditure: and, of course, Mr. Parr's compensation was clearly a retrospective expenditure. As the Reform Assessors of Longfleet obediently pointed out, it was also clearly illegal for the Council to rate householders in Longfleet for

POOLE
SUNDAY SCHOOL JUBILEE.

This being the Fiftieth year since the Establishment of the Church Sunday Schools, for Poole, Parkstone, Longfleet, and Hamworthy, the Jubilee was commemorated by an appropriate Festival, on Friday, September 27th, 1839, for the arrangements of which a Committee had been appointed. The Teachers and Children assembled at their respective School Rooms, and walked from thence to the Market Place, near the Guild-hall, where a Procession to the Parish Church of Saint James, was formed in the following order:—

THE TOWN CRYER, IN COSTUME, WITH GILT ROD
BARTER'S BRASS BAND.
THE CHURCHWARDENS OF THE DIFFERENT PARISHES
THE BIBLE AND CROWN,
(BORNE ON A VELVET CUSHION, BY FOUR BOYS, SUPPORTED ON EACH SIDE BY A SERGEANT AT ...)
THE CLERGYMEN IN THEIR ROBES.
THE COMMITTEE.
THE CHILDREN OF THE SUNDAY SCHOOLS.
THREE ABREAST, ACCOMPANIED BY THEIR RESPECTIVE TEACHERS.

In the course of the Procession a great number of handsome flags and banners were borne, bearing loyal and appropriate mottoes. On arriving at the Church, the Boys proceeded to the South, and the Girls to the North Gallery; the congregation, which was very numerous, being confined on this occasion, to the body of the edifice. The Services of the Church were read by the Rev. W. M. Dudley, after which, the Rev. P. W. Jolliffe preached an impressive and highly appropriate Sermon, from Leviticus, xxv, chap. 10, 11, verses.—"And ye shall hallow the fiftieth year; a Jubilee shall that fiftieth year be unto you." Appropriate Hymns were sung on the occasion, accompanied on the Organ by Mr. Sturmey. At the conclusion of the Sermon, the Procession formed in the same order, and went from the Church, through Thames Street, round the Custom-house on the Quay, up High Street and the Parade, down Hunger Hill and Market Street, and round the Guildhall, to the Butter Market in Hill Street, where arrangements had been made for the Children partaking of Tea. Five tables, each one hundred feet long, had been prepared, and were laid with a profusion of every material necessary for so numerous a Tea party. The tables were ornamented with boquets of flowers, and after the Children had taken their seats, the colours borne in the Procession, were displayed in various parts, and the whole Market being most tastefully decorated with dahlias and other flowers and evergreens; the scene had altogether the most pleasing appearance. The Clergy presided at the respective tables:—the Rev. P. W. Jolliffe, Incumbent of St. James, taking the centre table as President, having at the tables on his right, the Rev. J. C. Parr, and the Rev. W. M. Dudley; and at those on his left, the Rev. R. O. Wilson, and the Rev. J. Mitchell. The Ladies of the Clergymen assisting in making Tea for the Clergy at their respective tables; the Churchwardens officiating as Vice-Presidents. Before Tea, the Children, Teachers, &c., sung the Grace before meat, and after partaking of Tea and Plum Cake, to their hearts' content, they sung the Grace after meat. After all had joined in singing the National Anthem, the Children with their Teachers, &c., retired in the same good order as that with which they had assembled. The spectacle was altogether of the most interesting description, and not the least pleasing feature was, the manifest delight that beamed on the countenances of the Children. Total present 702, Children, Teachers, &c.

ACCOUNT OF EXPENCES AND RECEIPTS.

Dr.	£ s. d.	Cr.	£ s. d.
657 lbs. Cake	19 3 3	Subscription received of the Honble. C. F. A. Ponsonby, M.P.	5 0 0
10 lbs. Tea	2 16 0		
53 lbs. Sugar	1 17 6		
14 gallons Milk	0 14 0	Ditto, G. R. Philips, Esq., M.P.	5 0 0
Hire of Earthenware, &c.	1 14 6		
Men carrying ditto	0 12 6	Ditto, Inhabitants of Poole and Parkstone	22 5 6
Women cleaning ditto	1 0 0		
Erecting Tables, &c.	3 2 6	Received of Mr. Stanworth, Treasurer of Saint James' Sunday Schools	15 0 0
Table Cloths, and ornamenting Market Place	0 19 6		
Coal, Candles, and Refreshments for People employed, &c.	1 13 3		
Men and Women waiting at Table	1 2 6		
Printing Hymns, Cards, Bills, &c., &c.	6 1 6		
Sundry incidental Expences	3 0 0		
Band, Ringers, &c., &c.	3 8 6		
	£47 5 6		£47 5 6

JOHN SYDENHAM, Chairman of the Committee.

compensation for Mr. Parr for, after all, he had never been town clerk of Longfleet. He had been town clerk of the old Town, which was entirely in the Parish of St. James. The ratepayers of Longfleet had therefore, they pointed out sadly, not having had the great benefit of Mr. Parr's previous wise advice, they could, therefore, hardly be called upon to pay for its loss!

The Corporation had to raise some money: it still had not received the £2,850 for the sale of the advowson. The title to the advowson was difficult to prove and the purchaser's solicitors had no reason to expedite their orderly inquiries into the Council's title which, indeed could hardly be claimed as being without doubt, for it itself had been the subject of much litigation in the town over the centuries. Moreover Mr. Parr now claimed and the purchasers insisted that a Conveyance would not be effective without his approval under his Writ of Elegit.

The town was being ruined by the incessant squabbles. The new bridge had been opened with the new Turnpike road through Hamworthy. The Tory Councillors blamed this for part of the lost values of their properties, for the empty shops and houses in the town. They even resolved to sue the Bridge Company alleging that the Bridge had caused much of this damage to the town: certainly it had ruined the licensee of the Ferry Boat. The Hamworthy Ferry was no longer viable: the Mayor was told to sell the best Ferry boat and the winch and chain of the 'Hamworthy Passage' at the best price he could get. But the Tories were being worn down. Their businesses were suffering, houses were tenantless, money on mortgages of property was being lost, or in jeopardy with property reduced to one-fifth of its former value. Some merchants left the district altogether: others were beginning to see more scope for business in the rising town of Bournemouth nearby. Robert Slade the Elder, and Robert Major had been made bankrupt in May 1838. Two stalwarts of the old Corporation, one on each side, James Seager and George Welch Ledgard, who could between them, perhaps, have persuaded many to make peace in the town's affairs, had both died. There was perhaps just one possible hope which was rising: the character of the Council was changing. The Reformers were gaining seats at the expense of the Tories. The people of Poole were beginning to believe that only the Reformers might bring stability.

To the INHABITANTS of POOLE.

"The contest for a worthless victory of Party gives reason to fear entire ruin."

Notwithstanding the contemptuous sneer with which the writer of the handbill, signed "An Inhabitant," has noticed the published statement of Mr. Kemp, relating to a recent attempt of that Gentleman to bring to an end the troubles of this place, I can assure him that even in his own party there are many respectable individuals who are thoroughly tired of the struggle which has brought the Town to its present state of misery and desolation. I would ask the individual who governs the little oligarchy which is attempting to monopolize all authority and influence amongst us, what has been the result of those confident predictions with which he has so often favoured us respecting Mr. Parr's compensation? Have we not received assurance upon assurance that if the people would but be firm and unflinching in their opposition to Mr. Parr's claim, they would not have to pay one farthing, and but little time would be necessary to satisfy them of the truth of his statement? Now then, in what sort of position do we find ourselves after all the legal opposition which money could purchase has been made to this claim? Surely I need scarcely answer. The evidences of disappointed hopes, (of hopes that never ought to have been raised, because there never existed any good foundation for them), are, unhappily but too apparent in the extinction of Trade, the closing of Shops, the great increase of untenanted houses, and, as a consequence of all this, the anxiety depicted in the countenance of almost every inhabitant. Are we not now reduced to the necessity, an unavoidable necessity, of paying into Court all the money necessary to satisfy Mr. Parr? By the peremptory Mandamus which he has obtained, (and which we were so confidently told he could never obtain), Thousands of Pounds must be immediately forthcoming to satisfy this order of the Court: and does the infatuated man who has been the chief cause of all these ruinous proceedings still insist that there will be nothing to pay?

Let no one suspect that I am an advocate of Mr. Parr's claim, lest it should be thought that the writer has even a negative feeling on this subject, I will just state, that so alien are my notions to the grant that sooner than have made any provision at all for Town Clerks in the Municipal Reform Bill, had I been the author of it in Parliament, I would have abandoned the Bill altogether, and have left the old rotten Corporations alone, quietly to have become extinct through their own weakness and corruption.

It may here be enquired, would you quietly have yielded to the unjust award of £4500 by paying the money? No I would not, until I had at least tried to have made a better bargain for the public. It is well known, although Mr. Parr would much rather have had the principal of his compensation, still that he was open to be treated with to receive an annuity instead. Suppose even £300 a year had been given in lieu of the grant, however unpalatable such a mode of adjustment may have been to an honest man's feelings, it would nevertheless have saved incalculable distress and suffering. If Mr. Parr had been offered to be reinstated in the office of Town Clerk, there cannot be a doubt that a much more favorable bargain in the way of an annuity would have been obtainable. But no, this quiet way of managing matters did not suit the ambitious views of certain parties who foresaw in the wrangle consequent on an opposition to Mr. Parr's claim that an opportunity would be presented, of which advantage might be taken to exalt themselves at the expence of the public.

I well remember when a friend of mine once suggested that an arrangement of differences was practicable, and that the peace of the Town could be secured, "what!" exclaimed a party present, "would you sacrifice principle, would you pander to iniquity, and be for ever open to the taunt, 'You sold your honor?'" "ah!" thought I, "this is all very fine, and sounds well enough;" it was rejoined. "Will it do thus to speak, when you were foremost in hoisting a banner for the march of Mr. Tulk from the Bull's Head Inn to the Hustings, in the year 1834, with the words on it, 'We have no bribed man amongst us?'" Now, however immaculately *that* Election might have been conducted, I beg to ask what has taken place since? What was the course pursued at the last contest, when Mr. ——— was returned? Why the very same parties who railed at the proposal to treat with Mr. Parr, because such a course would occasion the sacrifice of principle, would be pandering to iniquity, and for ever subject the party to be taunted with the loss of their honor, yes, these men were the very same who distributed thousands of Mr. ———'s money to corrupt the Electors of Poole, and to gain the majority by which that Gentleman was sent to Parliament. Well then, was not this with a vengeance sacrificing principle, pandering to iniquity, and leaving the managers of the Party, (for 'tis of them we have to complain) open to the charge, "You sold your honor?" Then, where is the consistency of these men, when they tell you that only to treat with Mr. Parr would be acting the traitor to principle, yet, go with their wholesale corruption to buy the return of their Champion to Parliament.

Gentlemen, it is time that every man should think for himself, and that those especially who have *property* in the town should take some decisive steps to preserve what little remains of it from entire overthrow. The present, probably is almost the last moment in which a great effort may be made to relieve the public from their dreadful burthens. Mr. Kemp has shewn a laudable and praiseworthy desire to contribute his influence and ability in furtherance of the great object sought to be accomplished, and if a few more would put their shoulders to the wheel, the redemption of our Town from its present burthened and wretched state may be nearer than even its agitators dream of: that this happy consummation may be arrived at is the sincere wish of

January 1st, 1840.

AN OLD INHABITANT.

The Reformers themselves were feeling that power was coming to them and only the Mayor's casting vote kept them from forcing an all-out opposition to Mr. Parr's further proceedings in January, 1840. This decision had been preceded by a report from the Committee which included Richard Stanworth, John Gosse and Edward Mullett of the Reform Party. It reported that, to try to fulfil the Council's intentions, it had had an interview with Mr. Parr "of whose sincere disposition to meet the conciliatory views of the Council they assured themselves" and Mr. Parr had agreed to settle all litigation on payment of £4,000 in annual instalments from the rents of Corporation property. They then approached the solicitors to Lord de Mauley, the Lord of the Manor. George Ledgard, the Mayor, wrote to Messrs. Kinderley, Denton and Kinderley, Solicitors of Lincoln's Inn, as follows:

Poole, Dec. 14th 1839
As Chairman of the Committee appointed by the Council of this Borough for the purpose of endeavouring to suggest such arrangements as shall tend "to adjust the pecuniary difficulties of the Borough" I have been requested to forward you (as the Solicitors to the Relators in the suit of the Attorney General v the Corporation of Poole) the following resolution..... and shall feel obliged by your laying the same before the Relators and communicating to me their answer as early as possible as the Corporation have a Peremptory Mandamus from the Queen's Bench for payment of the sum of £1,668 due on the Bond given to Mr. Parr returnable on the 25th January next.
I am Gentlemen, etc.
George Ledgard
Mayor

The Solicitors reply of 19th December asked the Mayor for a "distinct proposition" to lay before the Relators, but, they added, "the resolution under consideration seems to us to call on the Relators to concur in carrying out a Measure which they have felt themselves grieved by and against which they are seeking protection from the Court of Chancery".

The Mayor set out the proposition: Mr. Parr would agree to cancel the Bond: the Relators would abandon their case in Chancery; Mr. Parr would have the receipt of Corporation rents till £4,000 had been paid to him.

The reply from the solicitors was dated five days after the Mayor's letter and was on Boxing Day, 1839:

"We are favoured with your letter of the 21st inst. inclosing a Copy of a Resolution entered into by the Committee after their interview with Mr. Parr on ours of the 19th instant and are surprized that they could seriously enter into such a Document or Instruct you to communicate it to us. Such treatment is quite trifling with the Relators and Ourselves.
We are, Sir,
Your Obedient Servants
Kinderley, Denton & Kinderley

The Committee reported to the Council this outcome of their negotiations. "They cannot, however, make this Report" they added, "without expressing their deep regret that an arrangement that would have permitted the payment of Mr. Parr's compensation out of the **Rental** of the Corporation by annual instalments whereby the Rate Payers would have become completely relieved, should have been regarded as 'trifling' by the Relators: Moreover the Committee lament that so prompt, so easy and so efficient mode of satisfying the peremptory mandamus and thereby preventing all attachments or personal inconvenience to the members of the Council should have been so unceremoniously rejected".

The Council felt it had no alternative in the face of the Peremptory Mandamus from the High Court but to make a rate including the payment of the amount of £1,668. It was received with similar reactions by the Reformers and some Assessors. It was 'bad on the face of it' as it included retrospective charges and the Assessors of Longfleet, in particular, refused to take any action whatever on it.

In May the Council wondered if the rents Mr. Parr had received to date alleviated the position. They asked him for an account. Mr. Parr responded promptly but it was no comfort to the Council. He had received £1,308.1.8d. from which he had deducted his costs of £608.11.2d. before paying the balance into Court for, by now the High Court had dismissed the Reformer's action to stop Mr. Parr receiving any of his compensation before the Chancery Case was decided. They had, however, ordered that he pay his net receipts into Court, awaiting

Number 13 Thames Street, North East front

the final outcome of the Chancery Case.

Meanwhile in the previous month the Reform Councillors had taken the Council's standing order at their word. The Order said "If the Mayor refuses to call a meeting after a requisition for that purpose signed by five members of the Council the same five members may call a Meeting by giving three days notice, such Notice to state the business to be transacted".

The prescribed number of Councillors duly called a meeting of the Council which they held at the Guildhall on the morning of 4th December, 1838. There were present Councillors Parrott, Rickman, John Gosse, John Williamson, Richard Stanworth, Robert Wills, Anthony Trew, John Lankester, Henry Mooring Aldridge, and Richard Pinney. There was also George Penney (who had been made Magistrate in James Seager's place) who they made Chairman. Then these ten Reformers solemnly dismissed Thomas Arnold, the Town Clerk, and appointed James Churchill; they reappointed the dismissed Francis Edwards as Collector of Quay Dues, after sacking John Adey, and then reappointed all the Committees entirely composed of Reformers.

The Council went on for a time apparently in ignorance of this meeting though it had, somehow, been formally entered in their Council record book. Then, a few meetings later, the Council solemnly rescinded the resolutions one by one.

In June 1840 the Council hit a new "high" for litigation. The Sheriff's Jury, which had been empanelled to enquire into the Council's assets had put an annual rental value of £50 on the Guildhall. Previous Juries empanelled following the issue of Writs of Eligit had put a nil or nominal value on the Guildhall but, with a value of £50 a year on the Guildhall, Mr. Parr decided he might as well have this £50 or the possession of the building. He also had thought up another way of pressing his claim: at his instance 22 of the members were served with a 'Rule' from the High Court to "show cause" why the Court should not issue a "Writ of attachment" on them personally for not making a proper rate to pay off their judgment debts, and this procedure really worried many members. It was this month, too, in which Mr. Arnold's bills, which he had from time to time drawn to the attention of the Finance Committee, make sure some of them were submitted to the Council. These early bills amounted to £3,746.

Most of the members of the Council were horrified at these three developments in mid-1840, but even these potentially calamatous events did not draw them together. The Finance Committee had been asked to take Counsel's opinion on enforcing the payment of their last rate. They replied that it was essential for Council to enforce payment but they could not execute the full instructions of Council "for the want of funds to supply even the fees of Counsel with the necessary statement of the Case for his opinion"!

Perhaps the Council did think that there had been a rapprochement, for Mr. Parrott was able to persuade the Council in August that the likelihood of receiving much of the rates it had levied that year was small and that the best way out of the problem was to make a single rate to swallow the other two 3/- rates which the Council had made that year and to make one which was quite separate from the Poor rate. Most surprisingly the Council took this advice from its old arch enemy and make a Borough rate for 6/- in the £ intended to take the place of the two earlier 3/- rates.

This last and despairing effort by the Tory Council to put its house into some sort of order went the way of all its other efforts. St. James Parish had in fact collected £400 from some of their ratepayers on the earlier levies and, even though the overseers of Longfleet, armed with their counsel's opinion as to retrospective expenses, had absolutely refused even to make a rate and there was doubt whether any payment of the old 3/- 'swallowed' rates could be credited as a payment towards the new, inclusive rate. The overseers of the Parishes held a meeting to consider their position to try to agree on this point and they could not agree. They decided to check the matter by bringing the matter before George Parrott, J.P. and even the Poole Reform Councillors must have been astounded to find that Mr. Parrott refused to support its legality or enforcement.

The Tories on the Council were really now utterly defeated. The Council was grossly in debt and had lost all control over its properties to Mr. Parr, and Mr. Parrott and his friends had finally assured themselves that the Tories would never successfully raise a rate to pay any compensation to Mr. Parr. The Tory Council had made various rates in their

REGATTA, POOLE.

SECOND DAY, SEPTEMBER 18, 1840.

This day was delightful. Barter's Brass Band was in attendance. The Quays were crowded. The Shore, opposite Brownsea, was lined with Carriages and Horsemen; this place commanding the best view of the Yachts passing and repassing. The weather was everything that could be anticipated or required for a Regatta. Wind N.N.E., a fine breeze.

FIRST MATCH.

FOR YACHTS NOT EXCEEDING FORTY-SIX TONS,

A SPLENDID SILVER CUP, VALUE THIRTY-FIVE GUINEAS.

The three YACHTS which entered for the First Prize, were the

Arab,	45 Tons,	T. Slade, Esq.	Blue, White, and Blue
Elizabeth,	35 Tons,	R. Wright, Esq.	Yellow and Blue, 4 blue squares
Zadora,	32 Tons,	C. Bromley, Esq.	Red and White Cross

At 16m. to 12 o'clock, by the watch used for this occasion, the gun for starting was fired. The E. was off first; they passed the Basket Boom at 5m. to 12, Z. was 1st. A. 2nd. and E. 3rd.—gibing the point at Brownsea, Z. 1st., A. 2nd. E. 3rd., all passed within ¼ a minute, and were about an equal distance from each other. At 1, from a view taken at the Sandbanks, the Yachts opened Old Harry from Swanage, A. 1st. Z. 2nd. E. 3rd. Before the A. had reached 6 miles of the offing, the Z. came up to her, and they appeared to be nearly neck and neck, the A. to windward. The A. began to draw on the Z.—again they were neck and neck ; at 13m. past 1, the Z. drew a head of the A. A. still to windward. At 22m. past 1, A. a head, but could not see between them; the E. about a mile a stern, and to leeward. At 25m. past 1, Z. shot a head, so as to be able to see between them, A. to windward. The A. appeared to have a man on the gaft, as if something was foul. Both the A. and Z. gibed at 19m. to 2, towards Bournemouth Mark Vessel, Z. a head, A. to windward; E. gibed at 15m. to 2. The Z. and A. tacked at 12m. to 2. A. to windward, E. tacked to go up along at 10m. to 2. [Here a remark was made, that if the A. was able to keep to windward until she rounded the Bourne Mark, she must win.] 8m. to 2, Z. a head, A. to windward; 4m. to 2, Z. a head, E. tacked, and appeared about 1¼ mile a stern. 5m. past 2, A. watering her sails. 25m. past 2, Z. rounded Bournemouth Mark, A. 25½m., and E. 27m. past 2. At 27m. to 3, Z. and A. both gibed at the back of the Hook, about 2m. after the A. came up with the Z., notwithstanding she appeared before her gibing to be a long way a stern. At 3m. past 3, the A. closed the Z , 12m. past 3, the A. a head. 12½m. Old Harry closed them. the A. being a head ; 22m. past 3, E. was also closed. At 1m. to 4, A. first in sight from Old Harry. A. at the Bar Buoy ¼ past 4, Z. 20m. past 4, E. at 23m. A. at the Brownsea Point and round 13m. to 5, E. 9m. to 5, Z. 7m. to 5. A. round the James Manlaws, and gun fired at 9m. past 5, E. 13½m. past 5, Z. 16m. after 5. This was the best contested Match we ever saw.

SECOND MATCH.

FOR YACHTS NOT EXCEEDING TWENTY-FIVE TONS,

FIRST PRIZE,

A SILVER SALVER, VALUE TWENTY-FIVE GUINEAS.

SECOND PRIZE,

A Silver Claret Jug, value Twenty Guineas.

The First Yacht in, won the First Prize, and the Second Yacht in, won the Second Prize.

Gulnare,	21 Tons,	J. Kemp, Esq.	White, under Red
Alarm,	18 Tons,	T. Wanhill, Esq.	Red and White Cross
Coquette,	15 Tons,	J. F. Silby, Esq.	White and Blue Cross
Mazeppa,	12¼ Tons,	C. Bromley, Esq.	Red and White Cross

At 12m. past 12, the gun was fired for starting. Brownsea clock struck 12. They gibed round the point opposite Brownsea Castle—C. 27m. to 1, A. 26½m. past, G. directly after, M. next,—all within a minute. A. rounded the Bar Buoy at 8m. to 1 ; all round in the minute. A. tacked to reach in for Bournemouth at 27m. to 3, a mile a head. At 3m. after 3, A. gibed round the Bourne Mark, G. 10m. after 3, M. 12m. after 3, C. 17m. after. A. rounded Bar Buoy 12m. to 4, G. 3m. to 4, M. 1m. to 4, C. 3m. past 4. A. rounded the point at Brownsea, ¼ past 4, G. 23m. past 4, M. 30m. past 4, C. 37m. past 4. Gun fired on the A. rounding the Station Vessel at Stakes, at 5m. to 5, G. 7m. past 5. It was evident that the C, carried too large sails for the fine breeze that was outside.

THIRD MATCH.

FOR YACHTS NOT EXCEEDING TEN TONS,

A SILVER CUP, VALUE TWELVE GUINEAS,

A TIME RACE.

Vixen,	9 Tons,	R. Wright, Esq.	Red and Blue
Othello,	5 Tons,	H. Hamilton, Esq.	Red
Sylph,	7 Tons,	C. Wheeler, Esq.	Blue and Red Vertical

At 10m. after 1, gun fired for starting. V. at the point opposite Brownsea, 28m. to 2, S. 27½m. to 2, O. 27m. to 2. In returning, V. rounded the Point, and tacked at 4 o'clock, S. 6m. past 4, O. 23m. past 4. V. rounded the Station Vessel at Stakes, 19m. to 5,—gun fired.

J. R. JUSTICAN, PRINTER, HIGH STREET, POOLE.

Some aspects of life continued normally

five years in office amounting to £22,790.11.7d. and they had collected only £7,842.12.7d. of this. They had paid Mr. Parr only some £860 of this from the sale of land at the Quay. Moreover they had paid none of their enormous litigation bills and it is surprising that Mr. Arnold had himself been able to continue to finance the enormous out-of-pocket expenses of the cases, let alone do without the payment of his legal costs.

The Council were able to use the new furniture it had bought in 1836 for the refurbishing of the Guildhall only by the good offices of the executors of George Welch Ledgard who had bought it at auction and hired it back to them for £6 a year. Even their maces and the Water Bailiff's silver oar of office and their old seals had been seized and sold. They were utterly in disarray.

The last nail in the Tory coffin was the result of its sale of the St. James' advowson. They had mortgaged the advowson to Mr. Hancock for £1,200. When the law bills for making out the council's title to the Rectory were submitted to the Council it is not difficult to imagine the sinking despair with which they were received. They came to £1,217. 12.9d! The Council appointed a Committee to look into the bills for they felt quite certain they were very excessive. However, the purchaser, Mr. J. M. Elwes was insisting on completion as he now had a right to do, and the Council agreed to complete subject to the bills being later taxed. The Council finally received only £66.16.10d. of the purchase money towards liquidating his enormous debts. It was enough to break the spirits of anyone. The Accounts were as follows:

Rectory Sale Account

Dr.						
1840 March 12	To Mr. Hancock, to pay off mortgage		£1,200. 0. 0.	1840 Feb.18	By cash of J.M. Elwes Esq.	£2,850. 0. 0.
	Ditto for interest		32.14. 3.			
	Law Charges					
	Arnold	762.17. 3.				
	Bartlett	10. 5. 8.				
	Castleman	114.11. 3.				
	Davy	10.11. 5.				
	Parr	303.12.10.	1,201.18. 5.			
	Sundries					
	Rev. P.W. Jolliffe arrears of salary	300. 0. 0.				
	Trinity College	3. 0. 0.				
	Mr. G. Glynn	9. 0. 0.				
	St. Margaret's Hospital	14.14. 0.				
	Churchwardens of Wimborne	2. 0. 0.				
	Tullock, surveying	16. 0. 0.				
	Carriage of Parcel	2. 6.				
	H.M. Aldridge	2. 6. 0.				
	Balance to Treasurer	66.19.10.	416. 7. 4.			
			£2,850. 0. 0.			£2,850. 0. 0.

There were only two further indignities to be suffered by the Council before the elections of November 1840.

The first was that the Chairman of the Magistrates, Mr. Parrott, refused to enforce the Lamp Rate, a special, small rate raised by the body set up to continue the lighting in the Poole streets converted to gas by the old Corporation six years previously. This decision led to the now usual Poole procedure of the issue of a Writ of Mandamus on the Bench directing them to enforce this rate and incurring further legal costs of the town clerk of £130. But meanwhile the town was plunged into darkness for the whole of that winter. The following winter and for some years thereafter, the Commissioners could only afford to light half the lamps. The town was made to look as miserable as it felt.

The last indignity was inflicted by Mr. Parr, on whose behalf his Tory friends on the Council had suffered so much over those five years. He served on the Mayor a Declaration of Ejectment from the Guildhall itself. The Council made itself afford yet another counsel's opinion. The advice they got was that there was probably no effective defence to such an action now that the Sheriff's Jury had placed a £50 yearly value on it: the best the Council could do was to raise various legal points to defer the decision, — but, of course, this would be a costly matter and

High Street, Poole

probably would give more satisfaction to Mr. Parr. Hopefully, though, the Council's final humiliation of being ejected from its own Guildhall could be deferred until the result of Lord de Mauley's Chancery Case was known. Some of the Tories must have wondered whether the best way out of Poole's troubles might not have been for Lord de Mauley to win his case against Mr. Parr.

It was therefore probably with feelings of relief that some of the Conservatives heard the results of the November Council elections which put the Reformers in power at last. The Poole electorate probably reasonably thought that the Conservative Council had become quite ineffective. The likely loss of the Guildhall and the blacked-out streets of Poole that winter were symbolic of the Council's utter bankruptcy: things could not be worse under the Liberals' control.

The new Council at its annual meeting on 9th November 1840 set off in great style. It elected the extreme radical George Penney as Mayor and Richard Pinney, Sheriff. It removed Richard Ledgard from his office of Treasurer of the Quays and Treasurer of the Council and appointed Martin Kemp Welch to be Treasurer of the Quays and John Fryer as Treasurer of the Borough. It then removed Thomas Arnold from his offices of town clerk, Clerk of the Peace and Registrar of the Court of Record and appointed James Churchill to these offices. It removed Stephen Adey from his office of Collector of Quay Dues and appointed its old favourite, Francis Edwards, back into his old post and ended its clean sweep by appointing Reform members to compose the Watch, Finance and Quay Committees.

It then set about putting Poole affairs in order. It agreed to sell land to the Bridge Company to allow the proper use of the new bridge to Hamworthy; it instructed a defence to be made to Mr. Parr's action to eject the Council from the Guildhall; it set up a Committee to defend Thomas Arnold's Writ for the payment of his legal costs, and made a Watch rate of 6d. in the £. It also, that month, agreed to pay George Ledgard £6 a year "as rent for the Furniture in the Guildhall so long as the same shall be used by this Council provided that such payment would not be an acknowledgment of the legality of the proceedings under which the same was seized and sold to Mr. Ledgard".

The new Council even revised and extended its byelaws — which it now had to submit to the Secretary of State for approval: it adopted a modified version of the old Corporation's byelaw about oyster dredging in the harbour. Its new byelaw prohibited the taking of any oyster from the harbour less than 2½ inches in diameter. But, as the old Corporation had warned years before, the Secretary of State would not agree that the Council now had any power to make such a byelaw.

Vegetable farmer delivering greens to the Market circa 1910

The Mayor also retook possession of the Guildhall which Mr. Parr had let for 21 years (with the meat market below and other property), to quote the information of Mr. Parr which led to the new Council's first Writ, one of Trespass and Ejectment "with force and arms etc. entered into the said Tenement with the appurtenances in which the said John Doe was so interested..... and ejected the said John Doe from his said last-mentioned Farm".

The new Council, however, had now two aggrieved ex-town clerks to contend with. Thomas Arnold had not even been paid the £100 salary for 1840 let alone the quite enormous expenses and costs of the previous five years' litigation. Judge Coleridge at the Dorset Summer Assizes had, with the consent of the parties, entered a verdict for Thomas Arnold for £500 damages, £10,622.4.0d. debt and 40/- costs subject to the consideration of an arbitrator appointed to look into the ten bills submitted by Mr. Arnold. Thomas Arnold had not pressed his claims on the Council earlier. He had spent a most hectic five years and he had known there had been no hope of being paid. He had received only £350 towards his litigation costs for the whole period, even though he had spent out £3,000 of his own money in the various cases for the Council in witnesses' and court expenses. But the new Council were convinced that he should get no more from them: if anyone should pay his bills, they said, it was not the ratepayers but his Tory friends on the Council who had started the litigation or caused it to be necessary. They decided to oppose payment of any of the bills, instructing their new town clerk, James Churchill, to do all he could to ensure this.

As for the legal bills of the Reform Party it is to be doubted whether any one will ever definitely know how these were liquidated. It was asserted by the Conservatives that Messrs. Durant and Welch, their solicitors, had themselves advanced £3,500 to carry on these various Suits.

The Reform Council, however, seemed to have at least some respect for George Ledgard. They voted him into the Chair at their meeting in December, 1840, in the absence of George Penney so that the patriotic Alderman could move a vote of congratulation to Queen Victoria on the birth of her first child, the Princess Royal. This having been done George Ledgard left the Reformers to get on with their business under the chairmanship of John Gosse. They then made a rate of £809.12.6d. which included £50 for the Town Clerk's salary; £27 for the Recorder; £20 for the Sergeant at Mace; 10/6 for the Town Crier; £15 for the Gaoler's salary; £100 for the maintenance of prisoners; £150 for Quarter Sessions and Magistrates' Orders; £160 for the eleven police and £300 for "probable expenses of Law Suits now depending". They recommended Thomas Salter, a surgeon, to the Home Secretary as Magistrate in place of Col. P. Pedlar, who had left the area, and paid James Churchill £200 to defend the action being brought against the Council by Thomas Arnold.

> **I, the undersigned, THOMAS WILLIAMS**, do hereby express my sorrow and contrition, for having, in a state of intoxication, and without any provocation, on the Fourth day of June, instant, Assaulted and Abused, MR. CHARLES SATCHELL, the Bourne Postman, whilst in the discharge of his duty; and I am very thankful to MR. SATCHELL, for accepting this Apology, instead of Prosecuting me.
>
> **THOMAS WILLIAMS.**
>
> Dated this 12th day of June, 1841.
>
> J. R. JUSTICAN, PRINTER, HIGH STREET, POOLE.

Midst the legal turmoil daily life continues

The Council then turned its attention to the demolition of its major enemy, Robert Parr. It submitted a case to Counsel setting out the old accusations of how he plotted with his Tory friends to get compensation and the history of his iniquities and those of the five Tory Councils in the previous five years. It also set out the story of the Guildhall, the meat market below and the "10 messuages, 10 shops, 10 sheds, 20 other acres of arable land and 20 other acres of other land with the appurtenances" which Mr. Parr had let to Mr. Loftus for 21 years.

The Council pleaded with its counsel to find a way of stopping Mr. Parr. "As the Guildhall, the Building of which Mr. Parr is seeking by this Action to obtain possession, is that which nearly all the public business of the Town is transacted, the present Town Council (a great majority of whom are opposed to Mr. Parr's claim for compensation) are anxious to prevent his obtaining a Judgment in the present action if it can be done by any legal means".

The Council had had great difficulty in preparing its case for submission to counsel because Thomas Arnold had seized all the Council's deeds. Mr. Arnold claimed he had a lien on the deeds for the debts which the Council owed him and for which he had got a conditional verdict at the Summer Assizes at Dorchester. He had handed over to the new town clerk only the current record books and wrote, "I am advised that I have a lien on all Deeds, Papers and Documents that shall have come into my hands as their Town Clerk, Attorney, and Solicitor, until payment be made of the Bills for business done by me. I am also advised that I have a lien on the Watch Committee Book until the amount of my bills for business done as their Solicitor be paid, but rather than obstruct public business I shall be ready to furnish copies of what shall be wanted". James Churchill and the Council could not let anything impede their defence to Mr. Parr's claim to seize the Guildhall. James Churchill accordingly made an appointment at Thomas Arnold's office to see the deeds of the Guildhall, and was accordingly personally debited by Mr. Arnold for a substantial fee for inspection of the Corporation's own documents!

The Council probably thought the fee worthwhile. They found that among the deeds was an old mortgage of 1793 of the Guildhall for £1,000 to Ann Strong and Hannah Strong and, although the Deed was endorsed 'Discharged' there was only a receipt for £440 inside the Deed and there was no formal assignment of the premises back to the old Corporation. Could that defeat Mr. Parr? Could the Council claim it didn't even have the legal ownership? The Council and James Churchill were clutching at straws.

It was a similar case with the extra £500 which the old Corporation had raised on a mortgage of the tolls of the market to finish the building of the Guildhall when the £1,500 provided by the two Members of Parliament had been spent and which mortgage, finally had to be increased by a further £260.14.0d.

The Council put the following questions to Montague B. Bere, Q.C., of Lincoln's Inn Fields:

"Your Opinion is requested — Whether any defence to the Action brought by Mr. Parr can be sustained either on the ground that the Corporation held the Guildhall merely as Trustees for the Inhabitants at Large or that the legal estate is vested in the Representatives of Ann and Hannah Strong, the Mortgagees in the Deed of 23rd January 1793 or any other ground".

"And whether supposing both or either of these grounds of objection to Mr. Parr's Claim be valid any or what steps would be necessary and could now be taken to set aside the several Inquisitions in this respect".

"And you will be pleased to advise the Council generally as to the best course to be pursued by them under the circumstances".

The reply of Mr. Bere was not encouraging. Mr. Bere was "inclined to think the Inquisition is good and that the Eject may be maintained. Still there are so many points of Law which raise a doubt that I think the Corporation would not be justified in giving up public property without taking the opinion of the Council on the subject".

Mr. Bere listed three possible defences which could be raised by the Corporation. "I am not prepared to say that any of these three objections can be sustained at the same time," he cautions, "they present so much doubt that the Corporation would not be justified in attorning till Mr. Parr has established his right and probably, before the points are decided, the Appeal might be decided".

"Various objections may be taken at **nisi prius** but the Corporation ought to apply for a special Consent Rule, qualifying the admission of possession. If the Market Place is leased the Lessee might appear to defend for that portion".

"I think the Mortgage will be presumed to have been satisfied as the Mortgage could not now recover the premises more than 20 years having elapsed since the receipt of the last Rent or Interest".

That advice had been given to the Council at the end of 1840. By the middle of 1841 the case had been heard by Judge Littledale and the Corporation's 'Rule Nisi' as to possession had been discharged with costs against the Council. Mr. Parr proceeded against the Council quite unmercifully. He served notices of eject-

Dolphin House, Market Street

ment on the Council for possession of the Quays and even the gaol and James Churchill spent much of his time drafting cases for the opinion of Counsel, either the ratepayers were now paying up on the Reformers' modest rate or they had funds from other sources. Mr. Churchill was even driven to ask advice and help from none other than Sergeant Charles C. Bompass who had done his very best to destroy the reputation of the then Mayor and their new leading member of the Council, Mr. Parrott.

The new Council soon found itself short of money even totally disregarding the claims of the two ex-town clerks. It ordered its new town clerk to do what he could to expedite the hearing of the appeal to the to the House of Lords by Mr. Parr against the Lord Chancellor's decision on the Demurrers. If they would get rid of that millstone from their necks and regain their property things might take a turn for the better. Meanwhile, to economise they reduced the size of their 12-strong police force. They were, too, still only affording to light half the street lamps.

Mr. Parr had been having legal fun with Lord de Mauley's London solicitors in his Chancery action. For some reason Mr. Parr certainly did not seem to want the Lords' decision on his appeal dealt with quickly. Lord de Mauley's solicitors replied to the new town clerk's enquiry by explaining how Mr. Parr had been making applications to the Lords not to hear the appeal merely on the papers sent from the Appeal Court but to hear case again properly "to call to their aid and assistance the Judges' in so involved a case". The Lords had fixed a second date to hear the case, but this had elicited only a further petition from Mr. Parr which had been referred to the Appeal Committee for consideration. It was clear that no early solution of the Parr problem could be hoped for, even if Lord de Mauley won the Lords' appeal the case itself still had to go back to the Chancery Court to be heard.

The new Council had further demands made on it in the shape of a demand from the Rector of Poole. He gave them notice that "for upwards of 7 years previously to the 5th day of June 1835 a certain stipend and allowance of £100 per year had been annually paid and granted to me for providing a Curate....." and that this payment was £175 in arrear. A further £100 was then payable, wrote Mr. Jolliffe, and he therefore demanded a Bond for the payment of £275. Counsel advised they had no option — and the Bond was given.

Like its predecessor the Reform Council looked round for funds other than rates and they remembered that £1,713.10.0. had been appropriated by the old Council from the Quay Funds and had not been repaid. They told the whole story to counsel and asked if he thought they could sue James Slade for this amount, as he had been Treasurer at the time. Mr. Bere, the counsel, thought they could recover the whole amount from Mr. Slade in an action for debt but, as the whole Council had passed the accounts where it was clearly shown as being used for Borough debts, he thought the action should be against the individuals authorising the misapplication. They took further opinions of a Mr. Follett, Q.C., and spent much time and money on this hope but for once desisted from issuing a Writ for they seemed mainly interested in suing James Slade and he, at least, seemed to have a good defence. This did not stop them, however, meanwhile instructing its town clerk "to write Mr. James Slade, the former Treasurer of the Borough and the Quays, informing him that the Council as Trustees of the Quay Funds are advised by Counsel that he is liable to the repayment of the sum of £1,713.10.0d. ..... misapplied, and requiring payment of the same sum and interest thereon".

It was about this time in 1841 that "a Conservative" wrote a pamphlet which he called "A few brief explanatory remarks for the assistance of Mr. Thomas Naish, 'the old consistent reformer' who had, as Treasurer of the Reform Party in Poole, appealed to the people of Poole to contribute to a testimonial to Mr. G. L. Parrott. Mr. Naish had suggested that donors would wish to contribute to the testimonial out "of respect and gratitude for his arduous, perservering and successful exertions, during the last five years, in promoting the welfare of the Borough of Poole".

Mr. George Ledgard, for the pamphlet seems to bear the hall-mark of his style listed the twenty "exertions" of Mr. Parrott to cost the ratepayers up to that time the sum of £16,780.2.4d. which had already ended with tenantless houses and property reduced to one-fifth of its former value and with upwards of £8,000 of uncollected Borough rates hanging over "its devoted head".

The pamphlet had Mr. Ledgard's best misquotations and was headed:

> Proud man!
> Drest in a little brief authority,
> Most ignorant of what he's most assured
> ..... Like an angry ape
> Plays such fantastic tricks about this Boro'
> As makes the rate-payers weep.

There was the usual riposte but the pamphlet effectively dampened any generous response to Mr. Naish's appeal, though it probably did little to reduce the heat of Poole's animosities. This was perhaps especially so after George Ledgard could not resist coming back with a reply to Mr. Parrott's riposte with "Further Detail of Facts", headed by his usual verse:

> In full-bloom dignity, see PARROTT stand,
> Law in his voice, the Boro' in his hand:
> Still to new heights his restless wishes tow'r:
> Claim leads to claim, and pow'r advances pow'r

> Unnumbered supplicants crowd preferment's gate,
> A thirst for wealth, and burning to be great;
> Delusive Fortune hears th' incessant call,
> They mount, they shine, evaporate, and fall.

So it was back to the defence against Mr. Arnold, and here the Council were in luck. In the past the actions or decisions of any body could only be legally given by a formal document under seal. However, with the pressure of the rising commerce of the country this rule had been relaxed, but when the Arbitrator appointed by the Assize Judge came to give his findings in July 1841 he had decided that although a Municipal Corporation could properly be held responsible for expenses incurred in carrying out their frequent and usual orders to take proceedings for recovery of rents, to obtain possession of corporate property, and the like, the Corporation, although it had passed resolutions instructing Thomas Arnold in their various Court cases, it had never given him their retainer to act for them under the Common Seal of the Corporation. The Arbitrator on these grounds disallowed the six large bills submitted by Mr. Arnold, including the £3,000 he had actually spent out on behalf of the Council, and awarded him judgment for only £718.9.7d. Mr. Arnold had already been paid for his five years' service the sum of £350: he was therefore left with an actual cash deficit of £1,931.10.5d. for his five years' hectic job as the first town clerk of the Borough of Poole! He, not unnaturally, felt constrained to follow the usual Poole pattern. He appealed against the Assize Judge's decision following the Arbitrator's Award.

After the 1841 November elections the election of aldermen was due to take place. The Reform/Liberal Party now had fourteen Councillors. They made sure of removing the Tory Aldermen. George Ledgard, John Adey and James Kemp lost their office of Aldermen and were replaced by George Penney, George Lockyer Parrott and John Gosse. Now not only was there not a single Tory on any Committee but no Tory was even present that year at a Council meeting. At least there was no further party disputes inside the Council.

One of the last actions of the Council in 1841 was to lay the basis for future quarrels in Poole based now on the separation of the government of the town from the management of the commercial and navigational aspects of the use of the harbour. The Council decided that it could improve the entrance to the harbour and the depths of the Quays by the use of a dredger owned by the Weymouth Corporation and it instructed its Quay Committee to contact the Weymouth Council with a view to hiring this dredger for six months.

Early in 1842 Mr. Parr's appeal to the House of Lords finally came to be heard. Lord de Mauley had revised his action by dropping the part of it against the legality of the rate made by the Corporation in order to try to pay Mr. Parr. There were two days of argument and Mr. Parr lost — it was decided that it was quite competent for the Court of Chancery to look into the whole question. It must have been ironic for Lord de Mauley to have heard the Lord Chancellor refer to the undertakings as to compensation for Corporate offices given by his brother-in-law, Lord Melbourne, in the House of Commons, but the Lord Chancellor had no doubt: the Borough Fund was held by the Council as trust property and, as such, was subject to the Court of Chancery's jurisdiction and there was, in the information laid by Lord de Mauley and others, sufficient grounds for the court to feel there might well

Vessel drying Canvas at the quay

have been fraud and the Bond given by the Council in breach of trust and illegal. Lord Campbell, Lord Cottenham and the Lord Chancellor were unanimously of this opinion. The year was opening well for Poole's first **Reform** Council. The case was now referred to the Court of Chancery to hear the substantive arguments, but from the incidental remarks of the judges the Council had good reason to feel confident.

The decision was a wonderful tonic for the Reformers. They now felt not the slightest doubt as to the outcome of Mr. Parr's case. Mr. Ponsonby and his counsel would soon put paid to Mr. Parr and his pretentions. Their own scribe — probably the Rev. Clarke, J.P. — put these thoughts into blank verse which, as usual, they had printed and published anonymously under the title "The Crisis", and subtitled "There is a tide in the affairs of men" which **ebbs** as well as **flows**". It was an attack of the character and motives of Robert Parr and his friends Robert Slade and G. W. Ledgard, glorying in the thought of the "searching trial" now awaiting them in the Chancery Court, as a result of which they were "doom'd perhaps within a Prison's wall" and ended:

"Madden'd, infuriate, at last undone,
His character, and compensation gone,
P..r now abhors the sight of friend and foe,
Neither can soothe his overwhelming woe.

Whence is the smooth-tongued L......d? P..r, oh where
Is he who ought thy punishment to share?
Patron and head of that most worthy clique,
That ne'er existed but for private pique,
False-hearted — doth he keep behind the scenes,
Thinking seclusion his base conduct screens
From dark suspicion resting on his name?
He is mistaken — let him hear the same:
Thou lofty Pigmy, still attends St. Paul's,
But learn humility within its walls;
The ground is near thee — kiss the dust in shame,
Confess thy guilt and take they share of blame,
Can rogues, and knaves be friends? I answer, no, —
P..r, L......d, S...e, they all will tell thee so,
They once professed a friendship, but 'tis fled,
And from henceforth their boasted Party's Dead".

In the same month of February, however, the Council suffered a blow to their confidence. The Tories had won the General Election in August 1841 under their new name of "Conservative" by a substantial majority. Their Secretary of State, Sir James Graham, was more sympathetic to the Poole Tories' petitions about the constitution of the Poole Bench: he appointed five new Magistrates for Poole, all of them Conservatives. The Poole Council received the news with at least apparent innocent astonishment.

"Resolved", its minutes read without preamble, "that this Council feels itself imperatively called upon to express its sense of astonishment and alarm at the determination of the Secretary of State to insert five additional names in the Commission of the Peace for this Borough, no vacancies having occurred to call for such an addition..... and no complaint having ever been raised touching either the number or efficiency of the Bench of Magistrates as now constituted".

"That this Council on the occurrence of a Vacancy would always feel it to be a matter of indifference as to the political party from which a selection to fill such vacancy might be made.....; but that this Council cannot but entertain the most serious apprehensions for the effects of such a sudden and uncalled for increase in the number of Magistrates with apparently no necessary or justifiable object, and which in public opinion is too likely to be understood as resulting only from a determination to further the views of a particular line of politics through the agency of a Bench of Magistrates....."

The Magistrates, Councillors Parrott, Penney, Salter and Gosse expressed their determination not to take part in the proceedings and did not vote.

It was also then, in June 1842, that one of the members of Parliament for Poole, Mr. G. R. Philips, gave the Borough a "handsome present of an ancient seal said to have formerly belonged to this Corporation". It is likely that the new Reformers, none of whom, other than George Parrott, had been Corporators, knew that this was part of the Council's 'personal' property seized and sold by Mr. Parr and it is doubtful whether the seal was able to be retained from Mr. Parr's High Court Writs of Elegit allowing him to seize all the personal property of the Corporation.

For Sale

BY PRIVATE CONTRACT,

THE

HOUSE,

GARDENS, & FIELD,

Late in the occupation of the Owner, situate in

MARKET STREET

IN POOLE, DORSET.

The LAND, including that on which the House is built, and comprising the Gardens and Field, Fence Walls, and other Fences, and the Trees, at 8d. per foot.

The MANSION HOUSE for £530.

To be taken altogether.

GEORGE KEMP.

Poole, August 1st, 1842.

LANKESTER, PRINTER, HIGH STREET, POOLE.

The low value of this property illustrates the depression which corporate intrigue brought on the town

The Council at its annual meeting in 1842 elected John Durant as their Mayor and they were still without money, subsisting from day to day with small rate demands which they now enforced ruthlessly. They still, however, did everything to impede Mr. Parr in his campaign to extract his compensation. They felt they had only to hang on till the substantive trial of Lord de Mauley's Chancery action had taken place so, as the old leases which Mr. Parr had taken over from them fell in, they stoutly refused to sign any new leases granted by Mr. Parr. At least they would make things as difficult as possible for him.

Then on 22nd November Judge Tindall finally gave his reserved judgment on Thomas Arnold's appeal against the judgment of the Dorset Assize. The Court of Common Pleas upheld the Arbitrator's Award despite the arguments of Sergeant Bompass who claimed that the various resolutions of the Council were sufficient to prove Mr. Arnold was duly retained to act on behalf of the Council and should therefore be paid his proper bills for the various actions in which the Corporation had been involved. But the Corporation's Counsel won the day. He argued that a municipal corporation could only properly employ an attorney by a document given under its common seal.

The Judge concurred in this argument. He said that at least in the case of two of Mr. Arnold's larger bills that "the claim of the plaintiff on these two bills was a just and equitable claim, although, from the absence of a contract under seal it could not be made the subject of an action in a court of law".

The hapless Mr. Arnold was left with judgment against the Council for £718.9.7d. the amount awarded him in respect of his 'general' business by the Arbitrator plus some costs, making £1,134. It would probably have been no comfort at all to Mr. Arnold to have known that he had made new law; that his case became the leading case on the subject to be followed and quoted for many decades thereafter in cases of contract.

It was followed, in fact, by the Poole Council within a week of the decision, for James Churchill, its new town clerk had no retainers under seal. At its meeting on 28th November James Churchill was given a retainer under seal in the cases in which the Council was then involved and it was delivered to him there and then. The cases were:

Corporation of Poole v Arnold
Corporation of Poole v The Attorney-General
Corporation of Poole v Doe on the demise of Parr
The Queen (on the prosecution of Parr) v Corporation of Poole

The following year was a dreary one of stagnation. The pleadings and other troubles of the Corporation's litigation took up much of the Council's time, but there was no relief from the financial troubles of the Council. Of the rates it had levied in August that year only £25 had been paid on 2nd October. Mr. Arnold still held the Council's Deeds and Papers: they had still no furniture in the Guildhall other than that which they hired from George Ledgard — though later in the year, on hearing that Richard Pinney had bought up the old Corporation's maces they did offer to hire them from him "at a rent not exceeding £6 per annum".

But they could not afford to pay Mr. Arnold any of his judgment debt of £1,134. With interest it now amounted to £1,255.10.7d. Mr. Arnold wrote to all members of the Council asking them to pay him. The members passed a formal Council resolution, drafted with most careful cruelty. "Resolved", it read, "that Mr. Arnold be informed in reply thereto that this Town Council will be ready to pay Mr. Arnold his claim for £1,134.9.7d. out of the Borough Fund as soon as the Council shall again be able to resume control and appropriation of the Corporate Property which is at present held by Mr. Parr under Writs of Elegit". Mr. Arnold did not even bother to proceed to judgment on his Writ. He was not well. He had suffered as much as most in the enmities of Poole. Early in 1844 he wrote a letter to the Council: he would consider "any fair proposition the Corporation might submit for an amicable adjustment" of his judgment. The Council told him that if he had any specific proposition to submit it would be considered, but Mr. Arnold died on 7th February, 1844. His death was apparently reported to the Council at its meeting on 17th February for the following resolution was passed —

"Resolved that the Mayor and the Town Clerk be requested to apply to the Executors of the late Mr. Thomas Arnold for the delivery to the present Town Clerk of the several Charters, Books and Documents belonging to this Corporation and which were in Mr. Arnold's possession and to report the result of such application to this Council at an adjourned meeting". The Executors declined to part with the documents until their debt to Mr. Arnold was discharged. The Council then had a special adjourned session of their meeting to decide to take counsel's opinion on suing the Executors and were advised to make a demand and then issue a Writ of Detinue or Trover.

Timber imports

But it was now the Tories turn to harass the Council. Messrs. Gaden and Adey had frequent scuffles with the Collector of Quay Dues. Messrs. Gaden and Adey were timber merchants and imported much timber from Quebec. There were frequent disagreements as to Quay dues, measurement of loads. The Corporation tried to bring Mr. Adey and his skippers to heel by refusing to load ballast from Ballast Quay for the returning ships and Mr. Adey and his men helped themselves and escaped the 6d. a ton charged by the Corporation for loading the ballast. The Corporation prosecuted some cases and were for ever taking counsel's opinion despite the poverty of their funds and their continual struggles to collect the most minimal Borough rates they felt courageous enough to make, for the once wealthy and proud Poole was nearly on its knees: the value of property had fallen disastrously.

But, as usual, their biggest quarrel was with the Slades and their solicitor, Mr. Parr. The old Corporation owned, not as Trustees of the Quay, but as corporate property three ship-building yards on the Hamworthy side of the Quay. In 1838 they had mortgaged the yards to George Frampton who, because the council had not kept up their payment of interest, had put them up for auction to realise his security and they had been bought by Robert Slade. The Council claimed that from time immemorial there had been two public roads crossing the yards which led from the Hamworthy Turnpike road to Ballast Quay;

'Shipwrights Arms' from Poole Quay

a footpath and a carriage road. Mr. Slade erected a high fence enclosing the yards and completely stopped up both roads. This deprived the Council of access to Ballast Quay. It also effectively stopped the crews of ships lying at Ballast Quay of their usual access to the Shipwrights Arms and the Royal Oak, both owned by the Corporation. The Royal Oak was let on a long lease, but the landlord of the Shipwrights Arms, seeing his customers now crossing to use the public houses on the Poole side of the Quay told the Council he "refused to remain except at a very reduced rent".

The executors of Thomas Arnold were not even as accommodating as Mr. Arnold himself had been. They would not produce the mortgage to Mr. Frampton and the Corporation could not check whether there had been a reservation of the public's rights of way over the roads. The two Councillors Stanworth and Wills could produce two old leases which their predecessors had had from the Council of two of the yards in which the boundaries of their yards had been described as finishing before "the road leading from the Passage Steps to Higher Ham" on the North West and the boundary of their land only coming up to the "road leading from Higher Ham to Bulwarks" on the South West side.

However, the Council was advised that, even if the mortgage had not reserved these rights of way over the roads there was good evidence of the public's rights and the Council could pull down those parts of the fences which obstructed these roads and plead justification of opening up public rights of way if Mr. Slade sued them. On the other hand, the Council could, if it preferred, indict Mr. Slade for obstructing public highways.

The Council decided to act on the first advice. They instructed the Quaymaster with four of the Ballast men employed by him and two sawyers to saw down the fences. "But" to quote the town clerk's later report, "in a few minutes a large body of men hired and employed by Mr. Slade, armed with Bludgeons appeared inside the Fence and commenced breaking the Laws. The Quaymaster and his men continued for some time their endeavours to remove the Fence, but were resisted with such violence by the parties inside, whose members rapidly increased, that they found it impossible to effect their object without a serious breach of the Peace, and therefore gave up the attempt. Mr. Slade immediately afterwards caused large iron chains to be interwoven with the Fence so as to render any attempt to remove or beat it down without the use of the most violent means utterly hopeless, and also caused large pieces of Timber to be placed across the road inside the Fence still further to obstruct the passage".

The Quaymaster reported his failure to the Council and they decided to take a third line of action suggested to them: to sue Mr. Slade for damages and they appointed another Committee to carry the resolution into effect.

The Town Clerk, James Churchill, wrote and told Mr. Parr, as attorney for Mr. Slade, what counsel had advised should be done by the Council. Mr. Parr asked Mr. Churchill to show him Counsel's Opinion. Mr. Churchill said he had no authority of the Council to do that. "Come", said Mr. Parr, "we apprehend you would be permitted to exercise a discretion which may have for its object to keep the ratepayers from expensive litigation....."

The Mayor, of all people at that time, was John Lankester. Probably for the first time since that fateful call on Mr. Parr to see the voting papers at the end of 1835, John Lankester called on Mr. Parr to ask why Mr. Parr wanted to see the opinion. Mr. Parr said that Mr. Slade was ready to produce his title deeds and to give any other information in his power so both parties could know all the facts and Mr. Parr would then agree to take the opinion of an eminent counsel: if the Mayor felt he had no discretion, perhaps he should call a meeting of the Council.

Mr. Parr wrote to the town clerk on 13th December, 1844, following the meeting with the Mayor. "This being a mere question of a right of way and being therefore a matter in which an abundance of money, if litigated, would be thrown away far beyond any supposed value of it by either and which in our experience we have so often seen exemplified we venture to suggest that the object we had in view was for both sides to thoroughly understand their respective positions..... so that..... a communication should be opened to see whether some plan could not be adopted to avoid a Law suit; and that as regards the Corporation we confess we cannot understand their position. Should that body succeed against Mr. Slade they would be liable to him on their covenant for quiet enjoyment....."

The Corporation were advised now to indict Mr. Slade for stopping up public highways and, to avoid a local trial, applied to have the case transferred to the Assizes at Dorchester.

Meanwhile, however, two weeks before John Lankester's visit to Mr. Parr, Lord Langdale, the Master of the Rolls, had at least heard and decided the case of Lord de Mauley v Poole Corporation and Robert Henning Parr. It had been a nice touch of Mr. Parr in his letter to the town clerk, then knowing Lord Langdale's decision, to have referred to "our experience" of an "abundance of money" being thrown away in litigation, for the costs of this Chancery action which had lasted seven years was enormous.

Lord Langdale in his judgment set out the facts alleged by Lord de Mauley: that Robert Parr "having voluntarily resigned the office of Town Clerk of the Borough of Poole, is not under the Municipal Corporations Act entitled to any compensation.....; that if it should appear that he did not voluntarily resign..... then..... he was entitled to compensation only in respect of the office of Town Clerk..... and that the award of the sum of £4,500 having been made to him in respect not only of the office of Town Clerk, but also of several other offices, was illegal and not binding on the Corporation, and that a Bond given to him for that sum was fraudulent and void, or else ought to stand only as a security for such, if any, sum as he should be properly entitled to....."

The judge set out the facts and questions that had to be answered, and went on "for after the best consideration which I have been able to give to the subject, and admitting the great possibility, which there is, of some improper conduct in the formation of the Burgess List, and in the management of the Election, I do not find any proof of the allegation on the part of the Case which it is important to me to notice, namely, that the adjournments, the foundation of the Burgess List and the Election of the Town Councillors, was fraudulently contrived for the purpose of procuring, or had the effect of procuring the award in Mr. Parr's favour. It is impossible to hear of such contrivances which seem to have been resorted to for the purpose of influencing the election of Town Councillors without very strong feelings of disapprobation; but whatever may be the truth as to the contrivances themselves being employed for the improper purpose of unduly influencing the Elections, in my opinion, it is not proved that they were employed by Mr. Parr for the fraudulent purposes of procuring an improper Compensation for the loss of his offices or for procuring the Bond now in question, or for preventing the reconsideration of that matter by a proper tribunal. The evidence, indeed, on the whole matter induces me to think that the consideration of Mr. Parr's claim was from time to time adjourned, not at his contrivance, but against his will; but whether this was so or not, it appears to me that these allegations of fraud as to the subject matter of this Information are not proved".

The Master of the Rolls gave a short history of the trials of Mr. Parr's Demurrers to the Writ to show that no previous decision had been come to on the substance of the action, and then went on to give his decision on these points. "Instead of proof of resignation (of Mr. Parr)", he said, "an attempt has been made to establish by argument, that the acquisition of an office, for his own purposes, in the appointment of another to the office which he held, amounts to and ought to be considered as a voluntary resignation by himself; that the omission to declare his wish to be re-appointed, is evidence of voluntary resignation ..... I feel assured that no such consequence was intended by the legislature, and I think that it is not within the meaning of the words of the Act....."

George Lockyer Parrott, Tom Rickman, Tito Durell Hodges and Francis Trimwell Rogers all were called to give evidence against Mr. Parr. "Parrott, however, is the witness most relied on in this part of the Case", said the Judge, and he said, "that the question as to the disposition of the office was much discussed, it was a question of interest, and was productive of much anxiety between the parties during the election, and the course which would be adopted with respect to the office by the Conservative party, in case such party succeeded in obtaining a majority of Town Councillors, at such election was generally understood, talked of, and known as having been arranged and agreed upon, and intended by and amongst the old members of such party; such course being to the effect, he particularly states in his evidence, and he says, that from his knowledge of the proceedings of the party, he believes that they intended to adopt that course, and the intention was a matter of general notoriety ..... Parrott says Parr was not removed from either of the offices, but he was not re-elected or re-appointed by reason of his having previously resigned, or retired therefrom, and such resignation or retirement, as the witness believes, in consequence of a previous arrangement, and with the consent of Parr....."

"I have read this Evidence with my best attention, and supposing the witness to be a competent witness, as to which there are serious doubts, the result is that there was much excitement in the Borough, and a great deal of talk..... It is plain that very little of this can be considered as legal evidence..... it was easy to infer Mr. Parr did not mean to make any attempt to procure his re-election, and it was not difficult for heated political, or party adversaries to infer some improper or corrupt arrangement..... but the short fact of the Case is simply this, that the office of Parr was filled up by the appointment of another man, without any opposition on the part of Parr. By those Acts which were done under the provisions of (the Act) I now think that Parr was removed from his office".

The Judge, however, did not think that some of the appointments held by Mr. Parr entitled him to compensation. Some had been held at times other than by the town clerk, such as Under Sheriff, which had at one time been held by Mr. Aldridge; or Solicitor to the Coroner. The offices for which Mr. Parr was entitled to compensation were Town Clerk, Solicitor to the Corporation, Clerk of the Peace, Clerk to the Justices, Solicitor to the Quay Commissioners, Solicitor to the Water Bailiff and Prothonotary to the Weekly Court of Record.

The Judge therefore referred the final settlement of the Case, to ascertain the proper amount of compensation for these offices to take into account the money already received by Mr. Parr and decided what was owing to him. The Bond given by the Corporation in 1836 was to stand as security for the sum of money which the Master of the Court should decide as being due to Mr. Parr.

The Judge refused to make any order to stop Mr. Parr taking further proceedings to recover any money from the Corporation, for regardless of his efforts, there was less than £1,000 in Court to credit against any

BOROUGH OF POOLE.

"STRIKE, BUT HEAR!"

THE circumstance of a True Bill having been found against Mr. PARROTT, and others, for Perjury, does as he states, in his handbill of the 19th March, 1844, excite a considerable degree of interest, and more especially as connected with the incidents out of which it has arisen.

No reply to it has appeared from Mr. PARR, and if he is the acute lawyer that he is reputed to be, in all probability there will be none. But the garbled statement, founded on the usual sophistry of Mr. PARROTT, as appears in his handbill, ought to be exposed, to guard other unfortunate persons, on his theory, probably some two years hence, from making such like "*unimportant mistakes.*" It is therefore from "*respectable and proper motives,*" that I purpose to analyze his statement, and shew that misrepresentation does exist, and that to a "vicious malignity" in such "short explanation." Without wishing to impugn the legal acumen of Mr. PARROTT, who it must be admitted, has had great experience, it may be as well to remark, that in cases of Perjury the onus does not at all times rest on the Prosecutor, to actually prove a corrupt motive; for parties have been convicted of Perjury, merely on two contradictory statements, and even where the corrupt motive was *only inferred:* indeed, it would be impossible at times to do so. It would be hazardous to swear *positively* to a felonious intent, even on finding a person's hand in another's pocket, it could only be inferred from the circumstance.

It however appears, on Mr. PARROTT's reasoning, that it was only necessary for him to publish the statement made in October, 1836; viz.—

"That the profits of the last five years on which Mr. PARR's average is founded, (and in which year the Bridge and Municipal Reform Bills were opposed,) shew £962," to justify him two years afterwards in swearing that the profits (for opposing the Bridge and Municipal Bills) were *actually* included in the Compensation. And further assuming the language of *insulted virtue,* he says that "no contradiction ever appeared from Mr. PARR, or any one else, on the subject;"—What was there to contradict? It does not state the charges were included, but merely calls attention to a period, as if it were said, in which year the New Poor Law Act, or the building London Bridge was opposed. Was it to follow that any uncontradicted statement, however incorrect, may be sworn to as a matter of fact? At the Council Meetings, the Schedules shewing the profits of the five years, on which Mr. PARR claimed his Compensation were read, and examined, therefore it appears altogether incredible, judging from Mr. PARROTT's accredited knowledge of accounts, that he should have contended as he did, during such investigation, through positive ignorance, against an item, which never appeared, or was even mentioned therein.

It should be remarked, that the Affidavit made by Mr. PARROTT, and five others, on which the True Bill of Indictment has been found, was used in the Court of Chancery, to restrain Mr PARR from obtaining his Compensation, and did have the effect of depriving him of his income, by an order to pay the money into Court. What were Mr. PARR's views in not earlier indicting the parties, is not the business of the writer; he has however, had the benefit of a *cross examination;*—in this, he extracted from Mr. PARROTT, that he had sworn that, which was altogether untrue, and that he founded his *knowledge* of the profits of the Municipal Bill *being included in the Compensation,* from the evidence of Mr. PARR before the House of Commons, of his *intention* to do so. It is but charitable to suggest, that as Mr. PARROTT, by his own admission, has made a so-called "*unimportant mistake,*" affecting the character of Mr. PARR by swearing to a falsehood in one thing, where he ought to have been well informed, he may also do so as regards Mr. PARR's motives, of which he must be entirely ignorant. But is this *mistake* either *unimportant,* or *accidental?*—Is it an error of date or figures; or even, as to particular persons, immaterial to the points at issue?—Or is it a case of pure invention?—Is it not a deliberate statement, on which a superstructure has been built, charging, by implication, a cool and preconcerted fraud?—And is there not dovetailed into it a variety of things, which, without this basement never could occur.

It appears from a handbill of Mr. PARROTT's dated the 14th October, 1836, that he then considered that Mr. PARR "*had been examined upon his claims, and that sufficient progress had been made to have enabled the Council to determine thereon at an early hour;*" so that I must, as he requires, acquit him of any charge of *carelessness,* particularly as it appears from his own statement that "he made repeated applications for the schedules connected with Mr. PARR's claims," but without being able to see them. The fair inference must be, from his own expression that "there was no reason whatever why he should hesitate in concluding as he did, that the profits of the charges for opposing the Municipal Corporation Bill formed a part of his claim for Compensation," he must have made his Affidavit upon *mere conclusions,* and *not from actual knowledge.* To substantiate a charge of Perjury, it is held "not to be material whether the fact that is sworn be in itself true or false; for howsoever the thing sworn may happen to prove agreeable to the truth, yet if it were not known to be so by him who swears to it, his offence is altogether as great as if it had been false; inasmuch, as he wilfully swears that he knows a thing to be true, which, at the same time, he knows nothing of; and impudently endeavours to induce others, to proceed upon the credit of a deposition, which any stranger might make as well as he."

Much has been said by Mr. PARROTT, as to the mode in which he met this formidable affair, and he has certainly not been sparing in his invectives, because Mr. PARR did not choose, prepared or unprepared, to proceed at once to Trial. It is well known, that in a *prima facie* proceeding, those witnesses only attend, who are needful to warrant the Grand Jury in finding the Bill, and not necessarily all those to make out the case on a Trial.

Having disposed at some length of the principal points affecting that part of the alleged Perjury, commented on in Mr. PARROTT's bill, I will now, for the guidance of my readers, as to the facts connected with this affair, draw their attention to the relative positions and circumstances in which Mr. PARR and Mr. PARROTT are, and have been placed:—Mr. PARR was Town Clerk, and held also other offices, at the passing of the Municipal Reform Act, averaging about £700 per annum; through the working of this Act he lost those offices, and it is well known that he does not hold them now, (save the Clerk to the Taxes, about £9 per annum.)—Mr. PARROTT has uniformly objected to Mr. PARR receiving any Compensation at all for the loss of these offices, although the Act provided for it, and although he himself was instrumental, if not the leading person, in removing him from the Magistrates' Clerkship, to serve, as is the fact, party purposes, without any stated reason, or cause of complaint. He has, also, openly and publicly avowed, that not a penny of such Compensation should ever go into Mr. PARR's pocket. In his attempts to accomplish this, he has acknowledged, in his cross-examination, to have joined with others of his party in a systematic subscription, to the amount of SEVERAL HUNDRED POUNDS, backed by the Trustees of the Canford Estate. This fearful odds against a single individual, one would suppose was of itself sufficient, without the aid of such a comprehensive Affidavit; to say nothing of the annoyances arising from the groundless charges contained therein.—Mr. PARROTT says *he* had forgotten the Affidavit, the case must have been quite different with Mr. PARR.

The Affidavit states that Mr. PARR's claim was *ostensibly* made up for a period of five years, from the 1st January, 1830, to the 1st January, 1835, but *really* included Mr. PARR's charges for this Municipal Bill, which were not in being or incurred until July, 1835, six months afterwards. Assuming that this fraud had been committed, the Compensation was thereby increased £700, and the Inhabitants plundered to that extent. With reference to Mr. PARR's evidence before the House of Commons,—I have carefully perused the printed Report, and I defy even the expedient understanding of Mr. PARROTT to gather from such examination, that Mr. PARR intended to include such Bill of profits in his Claim.

When the circumstance of the Affidavit became known in the Town, some months since,—What was the conduct of Mr. PARROTT? Did he publicly or privately offer any explanation, as asserted in his handbill? No;—on the contrary, he publicly and *voluntarily in the Town Hall,* turned the whole affair into ridicule, and treated his making a false Affidavit a matter more of self-congratulation and bravado, as furthering his views, than in expressions of honorable contrition. He now, indulges throughout his explanation in coarse invectives; and, with the same breath, coolly asks the public—as if *he* were the only party injured—"to suspend any *unfavorable prejudgment* against *him,* until the proceedings are brought to a proper termination."

The public will, I have no doubt, judge impartially whether Mr. PARR had or not "the smallest shadow of foundation for the vicious charge he had made against Mr. Parrott and his friends." All I ask, is a cool and dispassionate consideration, reminding them that there are two sides to a question; and that

> "Tis magnanimity to keep,
> When most provok'd, our reason calm and clear,
> And execute her will from a strong sense
> Of what is right, without the vulgar aid
> Of heat and passion."

POOLE, April 1st, 1844.

VERAX.

J. R. JUSTICAN, PRINTER, 103, HIGH STREET, POOLE.

finding. The Judge could not resist a last remark in the case. "I should be very glad to see this business settled", he exclaimed as he rose to leave, "it is the most foolish dispute that ever I have seen!"

Within five weeks of this decision the Council resolved to prosecute Robert Slade for obstructing the highways at Hamworthy. In February, though, on receiving a letter from Mr. Parr they had second thoughts. They were able to swallow their history at a gulp: their resolution read that although they could not accede to Mr. Slade's solicitors proposition, "yet being anxious at all times to avoid any unnecessary litigation and expense" they authorised their town clerk to see if a settlement could be reached.

In March they were back to their belligerant best. The Town Clerk was directed to impress on their London agents the importance of Mr. Parr paying in everything he received from public property held by him and seeing that the Master saw to it that every receipt was accounted for. They also appointed Counsel to prosecute Mr. Slade. They also instructed the Town Clerk to try to get the Special Case in Parr's case for Ejectment from the remainder of their properties settled quickly. They thereupon decided to sue the licensee of the Markets and Fairs. They had suddenly found from the returns of receipt made by Mr. Parr that he had received no rent from Mr. Whitt. They had let these rights to Mr. Whitt for £206 a year and they had accepted as guarantors the old Corporator and Tory Joseph Bloomfield with Joseph Morcom they first sued Whitt who, defended by Mr. Parr, got the case referred to Assizes. A new trial was granted..... finally Mr. Whitt had gone bankrupt and the Council turned on the guarantors. Joseph Barter Bloomfield had then gone bankrupt and the case of Morcom went its now usual 'Poole' way of complication and delay: Morcom was soon suing the Corporation in the Chancery Court while the Corporation was suing him on his guarantee in Queen's Bench!

It was at this juncture that a Memorial was presented to the Council, signed by a considerable number of ratepayers. The Memorial was quite short and to the point. It was this:

"We, the undersigned owners and occupiers of Property situated in the Borough of Poole, have for some time past deeply lamented the unhappy differences which have existed so long among us, which have been productive of an enormous legal expenditure, that has already depreciated the value of Property, and is declared by Farms and Tradesmen to be quite ruinous of them".

"We are desirous of seeing a termination put to these Legal Expenses, being assured a better feeling would thereby soon prevail among all classes of Society, and by a Reduction of Rates a greater stimulus would result to every branch of Trade".

"We, therefore, most respectfully but earnestly entreat the Mayor and Council of the Borough to devote their best attention to this subject, and consider whether it would not be ultimately more advantageous to the unanimity and prosperity of the Borough, to compromise all present Law Proceedings, rather than by a continuance of them add difficulties and distress to a period most unusually severe".

The Council received this memorial in May 1847, John Durant, the Reform solicitor, was Mayor. There were 15 members present, including three Conservatives. The Memorial had made not the slightest impression on them. Of the signatories, the Council decided, only 30 were property owners out of 463 in the town and "though the Council would not disregard any application coming from however small a proportion of owners..... provided it seemed founded on just and reasonable grounds, and suggested some practical remedy for any evils....." this Memorial did not. It obviously originated, the Council decided, with a party in the Borough who had had misgoverned Poole for five years and "to excite an unfounded idea in (the Ratepayers') minds that they owe their burthens to the love of litigation in the majority of the present council, and to gain for their party the Votes of those Burgesses who may be operated upon by their misrepresentations".

The Reform Party then set out their old list of the Conservatives iniquities from their opposition of the Bridge Bill to the present time and ended by even blaming the Tories for their action against Whitt, the licensee of the Markets. The Reformers went to great pains finally to ask "Now what course can the Council, in justice to the Ratepayers, pursue, but to continue the proceedings?"

In fact, it was not until December that year, before the Council finally confessed failure in its action. It had lamely to cancel its Bond. Both sides paid their costs (less £60 paid by Morcom for his Chancery Writ) and the Council's costs to Mr. Kemp Welch, who they had appointed their attorney for this case (no doubt under seal!) was much greater than the lost rent for which they had been suing Mr. Whitt.

Again from the end of 1844 when Lord Langdale had decided the case of Lord de Mauley v Mr. Parr, it took a further three years' of wrangling and procrastination — one can only presume on the part of Lord de Mauley — for a final settlement to be ordered by the Master.

In these intervening years, the Council did little but live from hand to mouth with its modest demands for rates. The one thing, however, that gave hope for some peace in Poole at this almost-too-late date was that at the election for Aldermen in November 1847 the 12 Reform/Liberal Councillors' votes were divided between four candidates, for Francis Trimwell Rogers put up for Alderman as well as the retiring Aldermen Parrott, Penney and Gosse and, although all twelve voted for Penney and Gosse, four did not vote for the re-election of their old leader, George Parrott and, as a consequence, John Adey was elected as the third Alderman.

Something had obviously gone wrong in the Liberal party for, at its following meeting, the Council "proceeded to the election of two Aldermen of this Borough, in consequence of George Penney and John Gosse, Esquires, who were re-elected Aldermen of the said Borough on the 9th day of November instant, not having made the required Declaration required by law within five days after notice of their re-election — And the following Aldermen and Councillors delivered Voting Papers to the Mayor, who openly read the same and declared the vote to be as follows:—"

George Penney	12
John Gosse	11
George Ledgard	9
Francis T. Rogers	7

The two new Aldermen thereupon took their declarations, though the only apparent effect on Mr. Parrott, apart from his loss of face and standing, was that he thereupon attended future meetings of the Council as "Councillor".

The new railway crosses the High Street

The only notable event of those years again revolved round the irrepressible Mr. Parr and his Merchant clients. The merchants had seen the hope of increased trade from the proposal that Poole would soon have a railway to serve it — but they would need to be able to use larger ships. They decided to adopt a plan proposed by a Mr. Revely which had been discussed in the town for some time. This plan was to build a pier or piers at the entrance of the Harbour, embanked on one side and stretching out into the sea about 1½ miles, with two sets of sluices. The Merchants had taken the opinion of Mr. Joseph Gibbs, an eminent engineer at the time, who had confirmed the plan's practicability and estimated its cost at £150,000. Mr. Parr had then in 1846 drafted a bill (the Poole Harbour Bill) to present to Parliament under which the promoters were to be given powers to construct and charge for the use of their works, designed to give a sufficient depth of water at all times of the tide for shipping to come into and out of the port. Mr. Parr was doing for his clients what Mr. Welch had done for the Lord of the Manor with his Poole Bridge Bill.

The Council, having been sent a copy of the deposited Bill resolved to "dissent in the most positive and unqualified manner from such proposed undertaking".

Mr. Mawe wrote to them from New Bridge Street, London — for to make sure everyone knew of their opposition the Council published their objection in the Gazette and all local papers — pleading with them to consider the advantages which would accrue to the port of Poole when the proposed railway came to Poole if shipping had unrestricted use. "Your neighbouring Port of Southampton", he said, "has increased its exports since the construction of the South Western Railway from £200,000 to upwards of £3,000,000....." but, he ended, "While the Bar and Harbour of Poole remain as they are, it is quite impossible for ships of competent burthen to enter the Port with safety especially at Neap tide".

The Council were utterly unimpressed. They were furious at this "ex-party" attempt "to obtain Parliamentary Authority for making a visionary experiment upon this excellent Harbour". It was "evidently absurd to pretend that 1½ miles of Pier, carried out on a Quicksand, in face of the Ocean, together with more than the same length of embankment, and two sets of sluices, could be erected upon anything like adequate principles for anything like such a sum (as £150,000)".

The Council composed their letter carefully and ordered it to be printed and generally circulated and authorised its Quay Committee to take any steps to defeat it.

Meanwhile Mr. Parr had been receiving and paying into Court all the rents of the Corporation as he had been doing since 1837 — less, that is, his very considerable legal costs. But, suddenly, about this time the Master of Chancery sent them a draft of his proposed settlement of the terms of the **de Mauley v Parr** case and the Council were apalled at the suggested terms. They sent their Town Clerk posthaste to the

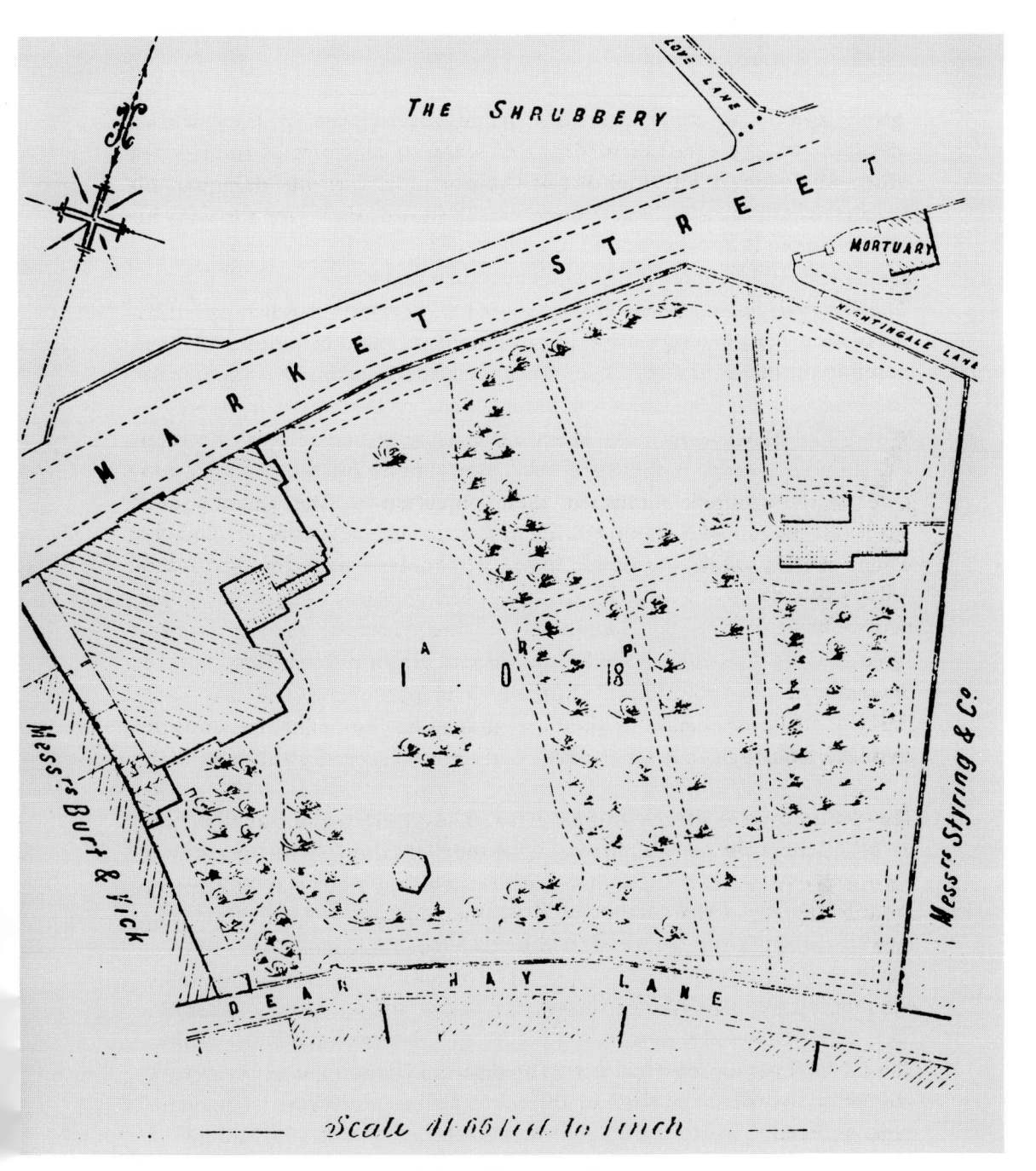

Sir Peter Thompson's House

Sir Peter Thompson's house in Market Street, later known as "Poole Mansion",
was built for him in 1746 by John Bastard of Blandford, the well known Dorset builder.
On Sir Peter's death in 1770 the house passed to his heir, who in 1781 sold its
contents and let the house. It was subsequently bought in 1788 by George Kemp,
who was Deacon of Skinner Street Congregational Church for many years.
Sir John Guest of Canford Manor, later Lord Wimborne, bought the house in 1890 and in
1897 presented it to the trustees of Cornelia Hospital, so named after his wife. When
the hospital moved to new buildings in Longfleet Road, on the site of Poole General Hospital,
the house passed into the possession of the Corporation who used it as their municipal
offices until 1932, when the new municipal building at Park Gates East was opened.
After serving as a clinic for Poole's health services, it is now occupied by Poole Technical College.

Master's Office to argue against the proposed judgment.

When Mr. Churchill returned, the Council at last set up a Committee to see Mr. Parr to try to settle all matters in dispute — for the Council and its advisers had been able to stall Mr. Parr's Writs to obtain possession of the Guildhall itself, the Gaol and the Quays.

Mr. Parr agreed the terms of the settlement of the Master on the Bond and the Lord de Mauley Case — but he wanted, in addition, payment for his costs for the still outstanding Writs of Ejectment if he was to withdraw them.

Lord de Mauley's solicitors too were now pressing the Council to pay his costs or, at least some of them. The arguments went to and fro from August 1847 to April 1848, when Mr. Parr wrote to James Churchill:

Dear Sir,

Att-Gen and Poole

In reply to your letter of the 1st inst, I beg to state that I am willing as arranged with Mr. Longbourne to limit my claim for the costs to which I am entitled to in this Chancery Suit as against all parties thereto to £1,300 and that I will call on the Relators for £650 only part thereof and the Corporation for £650 only being the residue thereof on the agent to the Corporation consenting to the Master's Report going out finding the sum of £4,500 to have been due to me on the day named in the decree and also consenting before the Master of the Rolls to the payment to me of £650 last mentioned out of the money in Court to discharge such latter portion of the costs, as I have no remedy against a Co-defendant which proves that this unnecessary difficulty should never have been started, and I consider I have very serious reasons of complaint at the obstacles so often thrown in my way without any authority that I can discover from the Corporation.

Dear Sir,
Yours truly,
Robt. H. Parr

It took the Council till after the following November elections and Committees formed of both parties' representatives to get nearer a final settlement. By December 1848 the Council agreed to leave Mr. Parr's cases for Ejectment out of the reckoning. The Council agreed it owed Mr. Parr £4,660.3.2½d. plus interest at 5% from 29th November, 1848. The Council would pay off their debt to Mr. Parr from the Corporation rents, and if necessary, make them up to at least £400 a year plus £233 interest in the first year. It agreed that it would pay £650 costs from the rents in Court.

The Council then set about trying to settle their debt to Mr. Arnold's Executors. They withdrew the action they had started against them for Detinue of their Charters and documents and applied to the Treasury for permission to borrow £5,000.

Lord de Mauley had now sold out the Canford Estates to the Hon. J. J. Guest and had left Poole finally. He had spent a good portion of his fortune in the various Poole litigations. With his sponsor and "Paymaster-General" gone and his own party deserting his leadership even George Lockyer Parrott was losing heart. He had run the Magistrates Court for over ten years. He had been by far its most regularly sitting Justice but after the Court on 27th June, 1850, when he dealt with three most minor cases, he attended no more.

Neither was Mr. Parrott at the Council meeting on 17th March 1851, which ended the squabbling over Mr. Parr's claim for £1,600 costs in his Ejectment actions. The Economic Assurance Co. would not complete the Mortgage unless Mr. Parr joined in to free the Corporation property from his High Court judgment and Mr. Parr would not join in without his £1,600 costs. But Mr. Parr suddenly relented. He wrote:

"In order to restore peace, and I hope, prosperity to the Town I am ready to take a sum of £200 in discharge of the £1,600 costs of the Mandamus and the Ejectment Suits of the Town Hall and the Gaol and all other matters by me and my firm against the Corporation and, upon receipt thereof, to execute the necessary Release of all claims save the money to be received from the Mortgage by the Corporation and as hereinafter mentioned, such Release to be at the expense of the Corporation it being perfectly understood that the Mortgage to the Economic

8 PAGES, WITH ILLUSTRATIONS, FOR ONE PENNY!

WEDNESDAY NEXT, FEBRUARY 1st, 1854,

WILL BE PUBLISHED, THE SECOND NUMBER OF

The Poole Monthly Entertainer:

GENERAL ADVERTISER,

AND MISCELLANY OF LOCAL, AMUSING, AND USEFUL INFORMATION.

CONTAINING:

THE QUEEN'S SPEECH

ON THE OPENING OF THE NEXT SESSION OF PARLIAMENT, ON THE 31st INSTANT.

of the Times!!! Advice to Young Men. A Case of Imagination. A Strange ...tive. Causes and Effects of Improvidence. Poetry, "The Hearts we Love." ...ep at Poole in 1754. Astronomical, Agricultural, Horticultural and Botanical Notices. South-Western Railway Time Table, for February. Hints to Mistresses. Dindar Agha, the Eastern Detective. Biography of Marshal Ney, with the following Engravings: the Retreat from Moscow, Execution of Marshal Ney, in 1815, and Erection of Statue to the Marshal, at Paris, in 1853. Adventure at the Diggins. Nooks and Corners in England, with Illustration. Births, Marriages and Deaths. Life with the Esquimaux. Simple Experiments. Wonders of the Railway. A Gossip with Housewives. Cookery for the Poor. Useful Receipts. Gleanings and Gatherings. Facts from the Census Tables. The Price of a Pipe of Tobacco---Destruction of Harper, Brothers', Printing Offices, in America. Wit and Humour, &c. &c.

TO ADVERTISERS.

ADVERTISEMENTS are inserted in the POOLE ENTERTAINER on the following terms.

Four lines and under, - - - One Shilling.
Every additional line - - - One Penny.
Contracts by the Year at a Reduced Charge.

Servant's Advertisements, Half Price.

POOLE: PRINTED & PUBLISHED BY J. R. JUSTICAN, BOOKSELLER, &c., 10...

by the Corporation be immediately carried out incident thereto borne by the Corporation and thereupon I agree to enter satisfaction on all Judgment Rolls at my Suit against the Corporation".

The Conservatives had now resumed power in the Council. The Sheriff of 1835, Richard Ledgard, was Mayor as, indeed, he was for the next five years. They settled on these terms and, as Mr. Parr had mentioned, they had agreed to borrow £5,000 from the Economic Assurance Co. Then, in May 1851, when all set to complete the mortgage, the Economic Assurance Company refused to complete the loan on finding that the Corporation held none of the documents of title to any of the properties they professed to own!

Thomas Arnold, an executor of his father, was approached. He would agree to execute a Release of the Corporation's debt to his father and give up possession of the Corporation's deeds on payment of the High Court's judgment, plus interest, plus his own costs of £300. Mr. Parr offered to pay £75 of these costs. The Committee recommended the Council to accept these offers, but the added amounts now meant that £5,000 would be insufficient to cover all these debts. The Council resolved to borrow £1,200 from the Quay accounts and they instructed their Treasurer, Martin Kemp Welch to pay over this money on their promise to repay it in 1869. Mr. Welch remembered when, only a few years earlier the Council had been avid to sue its previous Treasurer, for doing just that. He refused to pay over the £1,200. There was a meeting of the special Committee set up by the Council at which Mr. Welch was present. The minute of the meeting said that there was "much discussion with reference to the advance from the Quay Fund, but no resolution was passed". The Committee resumed its discussions the next day and, to quote their minutes, "A suggestion was made that the Mayor should call upon Mr. Welch to resign the office of Treasurer" but again, there was no resolution. The Committee met again a week later without Mr. Welch and a resolution was at last arrived at: the Town Clerk was to communicate with Mr. Welch and offer him a Bond of Indemnity under the Corporate Seal against any claim that might be made against him.....

A further clash of the Members with their Officers was avoided by Richard Ledgard and William Pearce offering to lend the Corporation £700. The Council was only too relieved to accept the offer, and a final settlement of the two cases was worked out. The whole of the Corporation's property was mortgaged to the Economic Assurance Company for the sum of £5,000 which was to be repaid with instalments off principal of £300 a year plus 5% interest and, after five years, the repayments would increase to £400 a year. It was agreed that the debt owing to Mr. Parr on the Chancery judgment less the net rents he had received was £3,463 after drawing out the balance then in Court plus his solicitors' costs of £200; the amount owing to Mr. Arnold's executors was £1,513.15.8d. plus costs of £300. The Town Clerk's own bill for his work in the Mortgage of just over £204 would have to wait as the funds would not stretch this far.

But, some time before this final settlement was reached, James Churchill, the town clerk, had "in consequence of the very uncertain state of my health" resigned. This was at the end of 1849 and Henry William Dickinson, a solicitor then practising in Weston's Lane, and Clerk to the County Court, was appointed in Mr. Churchill's place. Mr. Dickinson was, under the terms of the Mortgage to the Assurance Company, also appointed "Receiver of the Rents of the Corporation". It was a post which took Mr. Dickinson over until 1865 when, at last, the rents, with odd supplements from the rates in the early years, finally paid off the mortgage. By that time the Corporation had received no rent from its properties for nearly thirty years, — and must have lost over £20,000 of income in this way.

The Corporation was solving its problems too late. The affairs of the town had gone from bad to worse. The railway, which had come to Southampton in 1840 had, under the promotion of the Wimborne solicitor, Charles Castleman, had extended on its tortuous route from Southampton through Redbridge, Lyndhurst, Brockenhurst, Ringwood, Wimborne and Wareham and became known as Castleman's Corkscrew. Poole was served from this line by a branch swinging back from a junction called Hamworthy Junction, to the station called Poole, then to the side of the new Turnpike Road (now Blandford Road) built from the recently completed Poole Bridge to lead to Upton. The line was completed in 1847 and, with its use, the extensive trade in small goods carried into and out of Poole Harbour in coastal vessels had completely collapsed in 1852. In 1847 there had been 64 ships engaged in this trade in Poole: there were none five years later.

Another barometer of Poole's standing and trade was its Market. After Mr. Whitt's bankruptcy the Corporation had let these rights to Joseph Knight at an annual fee of £200. Mr. Wright's letter to the Council in April, 1852, tells its own story:

"…..the proceeds of the Markets ….. for the past year from all sources amounts to £181.10.0d., less cleaning etc. £7.2.0d.; nett £172.8.0d."

"This leaves me in arrears on the rent for the past year £27.12.0d. and leaves me nothing for collecting the tolls. I beg to give you the following names showing beyond doubt the actual decrease of the last year".

"Ridout less per week	1s. 6d.	Keynes less per week	2s. 0d.
Porter　" 　" 　"	1s. 6d.	Lambert " 　" 　"	6d.
Horder 　" 　" 　"	2s. 0d.	Cosser 　" 　" 　"	6d.
Weekes 　" 　" 　"	1s. 0d.	Taylor 　" 　" 　"	3d.
King 　" 　" 　"	9d.	Hillier 　" 　" 　"	6d.

Amounting to 10/6d. weekly".

"In addition to what I have shewn I beg to state the following causes to account for the general falling off of the income. The Fish Shambles was scarcely ever known to have been so little frequented as in the last year and generally what fish have been caught have been taken away to other Towns and villages and not brought to the Market. This fact can be fully proved by Mrs. Matthews and others who are always at the Shambles when fish are brought. Potatoes are fetching better prices in Southampton and other Towns and the Jersey potatoes being brought to Poole has stopped another good source of income, sometimes to the amount of 2/-, 3/- and 4/- per week for months following. The Cart Hawking with potatoes have always been considered the best part of the hawking. Many of the dairymen finding a better market by sending their goods to Southampton and London have left Poole altogether. The vegetables brought to Poole are for the most part taken direct to small shops and by that means avoid paying market or hawking tolls. Councy Butchers also finding any place better than Poole Market on account of the larger number of butchers' shops established here have ceased to attend so that the Meat Market, as may be constantly seen, averages about four persons and no more, producing a revenue of 3/- per week only. I would respectfully ask the Committee to recommend the Council to allow me the unpaid balance of last year of £57....."

Joseph Knight had two Reformers as his guarantors, John Williamson and William Waterman. The Council, at the Guildhall in the middle of the Market, must have been well aware of the state of trade. The Council agreed to write off the unpaid rent and to cancel the Bond of the guarantors. They took over the management of the Market themselves, but they must have known that the income of the Market was now lost to them along with their rents.

Gradually the Council got themselves into some sort of order, even if the town continued on its downward path. A year or so later it bought back the Guildhall furniture from George Ledgard for £46.1.3d. At the same time, Martin Kemp Welch sold them back the large Maces and the silver oar for £82.1.6d. It was not for another 80 years that it recovered its old seals and its small William and Mary maces. Mr. J. Hayter Slade left them these in his Will when he died in December, 1931.
Mr. Slade left them the two Ancient Maces bearing the Arms of the United Kingdom and the initials 'N.R.'; a silver seal bearing the representation of an ancient ship; a silver seal bearing the representation of a Tudor

The Poole Exhibition of Industry and Art held at the Guildhall 1854

Rose; a seal with ivory handle bearing the Borough Arms of a dolphin and three shells and a brass seal bearing the Borough Arms of a dolphin and three shells.

The gift was made subject to the Corporation paying any death duties on the gift but the Estate Duty office remitted any duty for, as the town clerk had written in his application, "the articles in question are of little or no value except for their antiquity". As he said in his letter to Mr. Slade's solicitors, though, "the Council are glad that the opportunity has arisen to recover the possession of these articles". It had, in fact, taken nearly a hundred years.

Towards the end of 1851, the members of the Council suddenly seemed to remember their solemn old leader, George Lockyer Parrott. They passed a simple, hardly benedictory resolution in regard to him. It was this:

"This Council, having been informed that George Lockyer Parrott, Esq., a member of this Council, and one of the Representatives of the South-East Wards of the Borough has been absent for more than six months at one and the same time from this Borough, he having ceased to reside in the said Borough since 25th March last and that he had thereby disqualified himself from holding the said Office of Councillor under the provisions of the 5 & 6 Wm.IV c.76, s.52 **RESOLVED** therefore that the office so held by the said George Lockyer Parrott, Esquire, as a Councillor of the said Borough and as one of the Representatives of the said South-East Ward is void, and the same is hereby declared void accordingly".

Those who signed this minute were mostly Mr. Parrott's old colleagues: Thomas Naish, George Penney, G. Penney (of Longfleet), Tito D. Hodges, John Wills Martin. The only others present were the Mayor, Richard Ledgard, John Adey and Henry Harris.

George Lockyer Parrott and the Lord of the Manor had left Poole. For at least the time being there was little left in Poole to fight over.

George Ledgard, now like many of the Poole businessmen, busy in his Bournemouth affairs, must have smiled wrily when he heard of this resolution. Whether or not George Ledgard was the author of the Tory pamphlet of ten years before, he would have remembered the final prophetic paragraph. It ended, referring to George Lockyer Parrott:

"I can fancy hearing him soliloquising —

....................farewell!
I have touched the highest point of all my greatness
And, from that full meridian of my glory,
I haste now to my setting. I shall fall,
Like a bright exhalation in the evening,
And no man see me more
Aye, and hear him pronounce with emphasis —
Othello's occupation's gone".

Dramatis Personae

The events described in this volume, leading up to and centred around Local Government Reform in the 1830's involved a large number of Poole inhabitants. However, the main protagonists were most often connected with the caucus of leading merchant families such as the Garlands', Slades', Thompsons', and Jolliffes'; in order to avoid confusion some of the main characters are listed here together with brief biographical details, where known.

ALDRIDGE Henry Mooring
There was an Aldridge Merchant and Shipowner of Poole and Christchurch in the Newfoundland trade from early Poole days. In the late 18th century, John Aldridge (b.1761) was a notary public and Vestry Clerk to St. James and was schoolmaster at the Thames Street School which, in 1834 was transferred to the 'National School' in Perry Gardens with the Corporation's help subject to the Corporation's right to place there 22 boys.

Henry Mooring Aldridge was articled to Robert Henning Parr. Left to practice with Messrs. Sharp and Aldridge at 166 High Street and later to Market Place. A Corporator from 1830. Reform Councillor 1839. Sheriff 1842/43. Clerk of Peace 1849. Coroner and Clerk to Burial Board etc. Opened office in Commercial Road, Bournemouth.

ARNOLD Thomas
Tory. Solicitor practicing from The Parade, Poole. Corporator since 1830. Town Clerk of Poole, 1836–41. Died 1844.

BALLARD Michael
John Master's first friend was his business partner. He was elected to Poole Corporation in December 1747 and was then described as "a merchant".

CARROLL Michael
Reformer. The Irish landlord of The Crown, Market Place. (1803–1857)

CHURCHILL James
Reform Party. Solicitor practicing in King Street. Corporator 1830–6. Town Clerk of Poole 1841–9.

EDWARDS Francis
Reform Party. Elected Collector of Quay and Harbour Dues, 1833. Dismissed 1836. Reappointed 1841. Resigned 1854 at the age of 84 and was awarded a pension of £1.1.0d. a week, considered to be "a sufficiency to maintain a measure of that respectability which, by the blessing of God, I have been hitherto enabled to maintain by a course of honest Industry".

FOOT John (1761–1833)
Whig. Solicitor practicing in West Street. Town Clerk of Poole c.1786–1833.

GARLAND George (1753–1825)
The last "father figure" of the Garland family in Poole. A Whig and leading Merchant in Poole who married Benjamin Lester's daughter, Amy. He was a leading member of the old Corporation of Poole. A magistrate for many years. Mayor 1788 and 1810. In 1822, he gave the Corporation the 12 Alms Houses he had built in Market Street. He was M.P. for Poole 1801–1806 when he had equal votes with Sir Richard Bickerton and withdrew 'for the peace of the town'. He built 'Stone Cottage' (now a Nursing Home). The Dorset County Chronicle reported his death in 1825 – "George Garland proceeding from Stone to Wimborne in a four-wheeled gig crashed into a post on the side of the road. The coachman was thrown out and injured. Mr. Garland was thrown under the gig when it came into contact with another post and received very severe injuries. His feet and lower part of one leg was so badly injured and crushed that an amputation was necessary. He died on the 28th December. He was M.P. for Poole and a J.P., led a very exemplary life and was a great benefactor". George Garland had 8 sons and 2 daughters, one of whom, Amy, married another old Poole Merchant's son, Christopher Spurrier.

GARLAND John Bingley (1792–1875)
A son of George Garland. Lived in Newfoundland for a long time where he was in the House of Assembly and its first Speaker in 1855. He gave to St. James Church and later to the Corporation, Poole Cemetery

where he is buried. He also built the Chapel there where there are tablets to his parents and from his children to him and his first wife, Deborah Vallis, who died in France in 1839 and his second wife who died in London in 1886. He had three daughters, two of whom married clergymen and all of whom left the district. Mayor 1824 and 1830. Only two other brothers **Joseph Gulston Garland** (a Rear Admiral) lived locally at Stone House only for a few years after the death of **Francis Penton Garland** there in 1849. Of the others, two died in Paris; one at Leghorn and one at Marseilles.

HYDE Thomas

He belonged to a family which was then developing clay pits around Arne and shipping pipe clay from Poole to Portsmouth, Arundel, London and Yarmouth. The family retained this business in the 18th century and also traded in goods brought to Poole from Newfoundland.

JEFFERY John (1751–1822)

M.P. for Poole 1796–1810. Mayor 1798. The son of an Exeter Quaker who married into the very wealthy White family of New Street, he came to have a large share in the Newfoundland trade and property in Pennsylvania. He built a country house at Lytchett Minster called "Sans Souci". This is now used as a Secondary School while the grounds form a caravan park. He left the area in 1810 when he became Consul-General in Lisbon and died there in 1822, on 12th May.

JOLLIFF Peter (1659–1730)

Peter Jolliff was also honoured by King George I who appointed him military commander of the town when he came to the throne in 1714. His youngest son, William served as M.P. for Poole in the early 18th century. A modern memorial in St. James Church to one of Peter Jolliff's descendants in the present century commemorates his brave service during the Second World War. "Eagle House" in West Street, the house of the Jolliff family built about 1730, is now being refurbished by another of his descendants who has returned to live there.

JUSTICAN James Rickman

Chief Clerk to Robert H. Parr, C.1830–1838. Started stationery and printing office, High Street. His son was later a leading Actuary in London.

KEMP Martin

A Poole Merchant who married Mary Welch of Lymington, 1755. One son, Martin, changed his name to Welch at the request of his grandfather, George Welch, a London Banker and became Martin Kemp Welch. His son was also Martin Kemp Welch. Martin Kemp died while his sons George and James were still minors and the business was continued by John Green and John Holding, a London banker. Martin Kemp was Deacon of Poole Congregational Church, 1760–1772. He died in 1772.

KEMP George

Took over his father's Newfoundland Merchanting business and was shortly joined by his brother, James. The business prospered enormously. They took over the Poole firm of Pike and Green in Carboneerand became the largest firm in Newfoundland and supplied many of the dealers in St. Johns and wine to London on their return from the Continent. They had the largest fleet of ships in Poole in 1815 but, in 1824, they sold out their whole business to Fryer, Gosse and Pack of Poole but they lost much of their timely sale by investment in Poole properties. George Kemp became leader of the Whig Party in Poole but was supplanted in 1835 by G. L. Parrott. He lived at the Poole Mansion and was Deacon of the Congregational Church, Poole for 64 years before he died, aged 89. He married twice and had one son and two daughters. His son George, married Elizabeth Miller of Poole and emigrated to America where he died (in Michegan) in 1865 aged 75. His descendant, a retired engineer living in Florida still retains an interest in Poole and its Congregational Church.

KEMP James

Unlike his brother George, James was a Tory. He took an active interest in Poole Council and owned much property in Poole with his brother.

KNAPP William (1698–1768)

It is interesting to note that a descendant of William Knapp, Daniel Thomas Blandford, like his famous ancestor, was the Parish Clerk of Poole from 1915 to 1924. His brother served as Parish Clerk of Lytchett Minster from 1894 to 1925.

LEDGARD George Welch

A leading Corporator with old Corporation. Mayor 1820, 1821, 1822, 1826, and 1831. Merchant in firm of Ledgard and Gosse and family business of ropemakers in firm of Ledgard and Son. Founded the 'Poole Town and County Bank' in High Street first under firm name of Ledgard, Welch and Co., later as "G. W. Ledgard and Sons". An enthusiastic Royalist and patriot who, typically, gave to St. James Church on its completion in 1821 a sculpture of the royal arms of England for erection in front of the gallery. Made Alderman by first Poole Council, 1835. Died 1838.

The Bank suffered in the security of its loans and mortgage advances depreciating in value. In 1824, for instance, on the bankruptcy of Joseph Barter the Bank had £10,000 secured advance but when the property was put up for sale by auction there were no bids at all and the Bank and Christopher Jolliff were the major creditors. Later the property was eventually sold at low prices. Seven houses in Chapel Lane, for instance, fetched only £350.

LEDGARD George
Tory. Son of G. W. Ledgard. Corporator. Took over the management of the Bank on his father's death. The Bank also had a branch at Ringwood. Elected Councillor 1836 and Alderman and Mayor, 1840, but not re-elected 1841. Transferred much of his interests to Bournemouth's developments and established a Company there to build a pier. In 1860, however, had to suspend payments at his banks and went bankrupt, though the loss to his creditors was not great. Lived in later years in Bournemouth. His son, F. T. Durell Ledgard, M.A. (1837–99) was barrister and Q.C. in London.

LEDGARD Richard
Tory. Corporator from 1830–6. Son of G. W. Ledgard. Sheriff 1835. With his brother George ran the family Banking business. Lived at 'Ledgard House', Parkstone. Councillor. Mayor 1849–54. Died 1860, intestate.

LESTER family
One of the great Poole merchanting families. John Lester was Mayor 1716; Francis 1720; John 1744; Benjamin 1779 1781-3; John 1789-95; John 1801. In 1799 Benjamin gave the St. James' organ to the Church and left £400 to Corporation to pay the organist (whom the Corporation chose) £20 a year. Sir John Lester in his Will, 1805, left £2,566 3% Consuls to Corporation on Trust to pay Rector the income for conduct-

ing services and giving sermons each Sunday. Sir John was only son of Benjamin Lester (1724–1802) and died without issue. Benjamin Lester's fortune left to his daughter's child Benjamin Lester Garland so long as he took the surname of Lester.

LESTER Benjamin (1724–1802)
M.P. for Poole 1790–1796. Mayor 1781–1783. The son of Francis Lester who served as Mayor in 1720. Benjamin Lester was one of three brothers who played a leading role in Poole affairs. His considerable fortune came from the Newfoundland trade and he himself spent several years in Newfoundland. By the 1790's he owned no fewer than 30 ships. He built the "Mansion House" in Thames Street and owned other houses at Stanley Green, then a rural area, and Lytchett Minster. In 1744 he presented an organ to St. James Church and in his will left £400 to provide the salary of £20 p.a. for the organist. His portrait was presented to the Corporation in 1971 by Miss E. M. Lester-Garland, a descendant of George Garland, who married Benjamin Lester's daughter Amy in 1779.

LESTER-LESTER Benjamin (born Garland) (1779–1838)
M.P. for Poole 1809–1835, Mayor 1815. The eldest son of George Garland, Benjamin Lester Garland changed his name to Lester in 1805 in accordance with the will of his grandfather Benjamin Lester and "out of grateful and affectionate respect for him". A popular M.P. for Poole amongst his constituents, he was returned again and again at elections until he retired from Parliament in 1835. He supported parliamentary reform and other liberal measures. Between 1835 and 1838 he travelled widely until he died in Paris in 1838. His portrait was presented to the Corporation in 1971 by Miss E. M. Lester-Garland.

LINTHORNE Richard Roope
Corporator from 1818. Landlord of the London Tavern. Reform Party.

MASTERS John (1688–1755)
Mayor 1748 and 1752. He was born in Newfoundland where his father, a "planter" survived capture by a French raiding party only to be murdered by an Indian in 1644. John Masters went to school in Wimborne, while his mother kept an ale house in Poole High Street. Entering the Newfoundland trade as an apprentice he became a prosperous merchant and in 1746 moved to Poole from Greenwich to begin

his political career. Despite the power he obtained in Poole, he never achieved his ambition to sit in Parliament. He died in London in 1755 and was buried in Poole.

de MAULEY, 1st Baron (1787–1855)
Mr. W. F. S. Ponsonby, Lord of the Manor of Great Canford revived his title, in abeyance from 1415 to assume title in 1838. Elected Corporator, 1826. Whig MP for Poole Nov. 1826–June 1831.

MAUGER Joshua (1725–1788)
M.P. for Poole 1768–1780. He was the nephew of a Jersey sea-captain who had settled in Poole and carried on trade with Norway. Joshua Mauger made his fortune in trade with Nova Scotia, where he became a very powerful man. He returned from there to launch himself into Poole politics. He owned a wine business in the town and became the Worshipful Master of the newly established Lodge of Freemasons in Poole in 1768 and 1769. Re-elected to Parliament in 1774, he was defeated in the 1780 General Election. He became an elder brother of Trinity House and died at his house near Lymington in October, 1788.

PARR Thomas (1768–1824)
A 'master extraordinary' in the Court of Chancery and a leading mason in Dorset where for 22 years he was Deputy Provincial Grand Master. An authority on old documents and who's aid the Corporation enlisted in 1791 in High Court case against them by the Church Vestry in Corporation's disputed power of election of Rector and in the 1820's in the disputed fisheries case of Tilsted and Sir Charles Chad.

PARR Robert Henning (b. 1801)
Solicitor. Tory. Corporator from 1830–6. Agent for Tory Candidate Chas. Tulk in 1835 (January) General Election. Took over his father's law practice at 27 Fish Street with his brother Richard Parr. Last Town Clerk of old Corporation 1833–6. Later lived at Castle Eve Villa, Parkstone. His firm continued after his death or retirement about 1854 by Richard and Thomas Parr for some years.

PARR John Edward
Another son of Thomas Parr
A barrister from 1832–74.

PARR the Rev. James, M.A.
Curate at Hamworthy Church at its opening in 1833. Vicar of St. Peters', Parkstone 1834—52.

PARR the Rev. John, M.A.
Vicar of St. Peter's 1858—72.

PARROTT George Lockyer
Born in Holland, C.1783. Came to England 1804 and piloted the Walcheron Expedition of British fleet to attack French and Dutch fleets in the Scheld. Corporator 1830—6. Elected the Leader of the Reform Party by acclamation at London Tavern meeting, June 1835, and continued Leader til about 1850. Had three sons. One obtained Government post; two received presentations to the 'Blue Coat School' worth £600 each. Elected Councillor 1836; Alderman 1844. Leading Magistrate 1836—50. Left Poole 1851. Died Pimlico, 1855.

PEARCE William (1810—1889)
Born Hereford. Came to Poole, 1839. Ironmonger in High Street. Owned Poole Foundry. Sponsored Poole Literary Institute and Mechanics' Institute. Chief Proprietor of Poole Waterworks. Mayor 1847, 1857 and 1868. J.P. 1858. Gave spire of Longfleet Church. Lived at 'Springfields', Parkstone. Tory.

PINNEY Richard
Reform Party. Corporator from 1830—6. Lived in Church Street. Mayor 1841.

PENNEY George
Leading Reformer. Previously leading Corporator. Agent to Fayle & Co., Clay Merchants. Magistrate 1836. Elected Councillor 1840 and Alderman 1840. First Reform Mayor of Poole Council.

PRICE Henry (1702—1750)
Poole's poet was born in London and came to live in Poole with his father, Henry Price (Senior), a brewer who became a burgess of Poole Corporation. His service in the Royal Navy took him to the Baltic and the West Indies. In 1741 he published a book of his poetry which has now become a very rare volume. He married in 1733 but none of his four children appear to have followed their father's occupation as a poet.

RICKMAN Tom
Cornfactor. Leading reformer. Corporator 1830—6. Elected Councillor 1836. Alderman 1844. Magistrate 1836. Joined in his firm by Christopher Hill about 1854, then 'Rickman and Hill'.

SEAGER James
Corporator 1816. Leading Corporator and Magistrate immediately before Municipal Reform. Treasurer of Quays until dismissed by new Council 1836. Merchant and with Major, Seager & Co., ropemakers and marine store dealers on the Quay. Gave the clock in front of the gallery of St. James when built in 1821. Mayor 1816, 1817 and was a Magistrate 1817—1836. Unsuccessful in 1835 Council Election as Reform candidate but made Magistrate again 1836. Died 1838.

SEAGER Mark White
Merchant and Ship Owner. Tory. Leading Corporator but did not contest Council Election — was in Newfoundland at the time. Retired 1836 to live in Palermo, Italy.

The SLADES
There were too many Slades of Poole in the early 19th century to try to cover them all, or, for that matter, always to keep the many 'Robert Slades' distinguished.

The first Robert Slade to be Mayor of Poole was in 1832. He was only in office from September 1832 to March 1833. "The Corporate Body went in procession and attended the funeral of our late highly respected and worthy Mayor, Robert Slade Esq.,", the Corporation's minute read, "who was seized of an apoplectic fit at the last monthly meeting of this Corporation which terminated his existence on the 17th instant in the 65th year of his age".

His business was run thereafter by Robert, Thomas and James Slade under the title of "The Executors of Robert Slade".

On the death of Mayor Robert Slade, this left only three Robert Slades. His son and executor who lived in Market Street; Robert Slade, the son of David, who lived in Barber's Piles, and Robert Slade, Snr. who lived in West Street.

Robert 'the younger' the son of David Slade was made Mayor for the remainder of the Corporation's life and the year following Robert Slade, the son of the first Mayor, and cousin to his predecessor, was made Mayor in 1837.

The Slade family had four merchant companies in the 1830's: Harrison, Slade & Co. (the "millionaire firm of Newfoundland") on the Quay; Slade & Cox on the Quay; the Executors of Robert Slade on the Quay and Robert Slade, Snr., 81 West Street.

In 1824 Robert and John Slade had 11 ships registered in Poole trading with Newfoundland and Canada; Harrison, Slade & Co., 9; Thomas Slade, 11; Robert Slade, 8.

In 1845 when St. James was lighted with gas, John Slade bought the discarded brass chandeliers and wall sconces which he took and presented to St. Peter's Church, Twillingate, Newfoundland where they remained at least till 1936.

SPURRIER Christopher (1783—1876)
M.P. for Bridport 1820—1826. He belonged to a family which had built up a major interest in the Newfoundland trade and took a large part in Poole's life in the 18th century. He had a reputation for gambling and extravagant living. About 1816 he had Upton House built for him. Disappointed in not becoming M.P. for Poole, he successfully contested Bridport in 1820. After the sale of Upton House and the bankruptcy of his family's firm in 1830 he apparently lived abroad for much of his time. He married George Garland's daughter Amy in 1814 and lived to a ripe old age, dying at Chelmsford in 1876.

SPURRIER William (1734—1809)
Mayor 1784, 1786—7 and 1802. He was the son of a former Mayor of Poole and the father of Christopher Spurrier, the builder of Upton House. His family had a powerful position in the Newfoundland trade with "plantations" at Burin and Oderin, where like other Poole merchants in Newfoundland, they built some of their ships. In Poole the family owned properties in the High Street and coal and timber wharves on "the West Shore", off the modern West Quay Road.

STANWORTH Richard
Reform Party. Shipbuilder with partner, Robert Willis. Lived at Barbers Piles. Corporator from 1830 on nomination by partner. Councillor 1836. Assessor 1843.

STEELE Isaac (1806–1866)
Tory. Corporator. Elected Councillor, 1835. Not returned 1839. Elected 1862. Grandfather was Samuel Rolles, Merchant, of "Beech Hurst" High Street (built 1798). Also inherited fortune of another Poole Merchant, his uncle, Samuel White. Generous benefactor of St. James.

STYRING Frederick (1819–1897)
Born in Lincolnshire. Came to live at Race Farm, Lytchett Matravers in 1845. Bought Messrs. King's Brewery, founded 1795 and moved to Thames Street and later to the Poole Mansion. Elected Liberal Councillor, 1850. Sheriff 1876. Mayor 1864, 1866, 1868, 1875 and 1887. Established the 'Town and County of Poole Building Society'. Sold Brewery to George Pope. Married Henrietta Slade. Left Poole to live at the Yarells, Lytchett Minster 1888 where in 1897 he died as the result of an accident.

THOMPSON Sir Peter (1698–1770)
M.P. for St. Albans 1747–1754. Sir Peter was the third son of Captain Thomas Thompson of Poole. He was knighted by George II in 1745 when, as High Sheriff of Surrey, he presented a loyal address to the King at the time of the Jacobite rising. He survived his long widowed sister, who had also lived in his elegant house, by five days, and they were buried together in the churchyard of St. James.

THOMPSON William (1794–1864)
Tory. Clay Merchant in Hamworthy. Lived at Lake House (now Officers Mess, Royal Marines, Poole). He had a warehouse on Hamworthy side of Quay. Bottom of Poll in first Council election in Poole for S-E Ward, 1835. His son

THOMPSON William (1822–1879)
Married Robert Slade's daughter, Sarah. Owned steam yacht with which he dredged Weymouth Harbours. Lived at The Tarells, Lytchett Minster — called after a friend's name. Moved to Weymouth where he later died.

WEBB Sir John
The second baronet was the grandson of the Sir John Webb who had bought the Manor of Canford and Poole from Charles I. The family came from Odstock, Wiltshire, and owned a number of other estates, including land at Parley and Christchurch. Because of their loyal service to the King during the Civil Wars and their steadfast support for the Roman Catholic faith, the family was favoured by James. II.
Sir John did try to hold effective manorial courts in Poole between 1683 and 1688 but the inhabitants were able to prevent him from regaining any real control over the town's government.

WELCH Martin Kemp
Corporator 1830—6. Solicitor. Went into partnership with Reform Solicitor John Durant and practiced in Hill Street and High Street. Solicitor for the Poole Bridge Bill, 1833 and later Secretary to the Company. Clerk of the Peace, 1836. Solicitors to the Reform Party in Poole and for Lord de Mauley. Later on the Poole Council and Mayor in 1873/4. Interests spread to Bournemouth. Lived for a time at the Poole Mansion and later at "Woodlands" Parkstone. Later joined by William Wheeler Aldridge and had offices at Market Street.

Index

Page numbers in brackets indicate illustrations.

Absolem 88
Adey, John 129, 144, 223, 229, 239, 245, 258
Adey, Wm. 46, 57, 58, 85, 86, 87, 129, 144
Admiralty Jurisdiction 122, 132
A.-G. V. Ledgard 168
"Age" Stagecoach 61
Air Balloon 21, 60
Aldermen 162, 239
Aldridge 57, 58, 252, 269
Alehouses 23
Allen 6, 211
Almshouses 32, 184, (185)
Angel Tavern 59, 61, 148, 190
Antelope 5, 49, 60, 61, 148, 180
Arnold, Thos. 57, 104, 129, 147, 158, 159, 160, 163, 164, 169, 170, 215, 223, 229, 231, 232, 233,, 238, 244, 245, 246, 261, 263, 269
Arrowsmith, Edward 107
Ashley, Lord 99, 113, 116, 137, 155, 167, 176
Assessors 197
Attachment 223

Bailiff 122
Baiter 31
Bakers 58
Ballard 33, 269
Ballast Quay 182, 246, 248
Bankers 58
Barter 58, 91, 94, 129, 132
Bawdy House, 23
Bay Hog Lane 57
Beechurst 67
Beehive Hotel 148
Bell & Crown 180

Bennett's Legacy 184
Bere, Q.C. 233, 237
Berry 159, 164
Bessborough, Earl of 109
Best 8
Bickerton 213
Billows (of Billows Son & Turpin) 132, 190
Bingham 197
Bird 6
Bishops Waltham 20
Bloomfield 61, 144, 254
Boat Repairers 58
Boatbuilders 58
Bompass, Sergt. 204, 236, 244
Brewers 58
Bribery 35, 164
Brices 53, 172, 183, 193, 213
Bridge 77, 78, 80, (82), 147, (170), 218, 229, 255
Brinklow 6
Brown, John, 143
Buckler (Widow) 20
Bugden 61
Bulls Head 60, 180
Bulwarks 248
Burgesses 84, 87, 124, 125, (126), 135, 146
Busson 194, 207
Butler 35
Byelaws 71, 84, 88, 230
Byng 81, 99, 102, 141, 164, 172, 176

Campbell, Lord 137, 241
Canal 24, 47
Canford 108, 109, (110)
Canford Award 108
Carriers 60

281

Carroll   205, 206, 269
Castle St.   (191)
Castleman's Corkscrew   264
Chancery   239, 241, 254
Charters   106, 121, 261
Chimney Sweep   26
Cholera   119, (120)
Church St.   (185), 190
Churchill, Col.   14
Churchill, James   92, 96, 104, 119, 135, 151, 223, 229, 231, 233, 236, 244, 249, 260, 264, 270
Churchill, John   27
Clark, John   108
Clarke, Rev. Wm.   193, 213, 241
Clarke, Samuel   92, 144, 172
Clay Cellars   68, 137
Clay Trade   68
"Coach & Horses"   60
Coaches   61
Cole   152, 159
Coleridge, Judge   231
Collector of Quay Dues   229, 246
Colpis   20
Common Seal   238, 244
Congregational Church   164, 214, 259
Conservative Association   140, 176, 181, 229, 237, 242
Constables   123, 124
Constitutional Hill   (130), (214)
Conway   57
Conway, Wm.   142
Corkscrew Alley   119
Corn Meters   124
Cornelia Hospital   259
Cornmerchants   58
Coroners   123
Corporation Act   85, 89
Corporators   79, 84, 88, 92, 104, 119, 135, 138, 176
Cottingham, Lord   241
Courts   125
Cox   144
"Crown"   36, 60, 205, 206
Custard   193, 195, 197, 200
Customs House   (118)

Damer   115
Denham, Lord   166
Devonshire, Duchess of   109
Dickinson   264
Diggs   38
Dissenters   85, 87
Dogcarts   61
Dolphin   21, 60
Dolphin House   235
Dorchester Assizes   174, 192, 204, 231, 233, 238, 244, 250
Dorset County Chronicle   96
Dorset   16
Doughty   49, 57
Duke of Newcastle   10
Durant   57, 151, 159, 183, 244, 255
Durant & Welch   231
Durnfords Lane   26

Easter   24
Eastnor, Lord   176
Easton   78
Economic Assurance Co.   261, 264
Edwards   169, 198, 201, 214, 223, 229, 270
"Eight Bells"   60, 180
Ejectment   228, 254, 261
Elections   33, 34, 35, 36, 84, 85, 113, (114), 115, 139, 145, 161, 165, 167
Eligit (Writ of)   216, 242, 245
Elwes   227
Enclosure   107
Exhibition of Industry & Art   (267)

Fairs   24, 57
Ferry   29, 30, 77, 213
Festing   57, 172, 193, 194
Fish Shambles   29, 30, 266
Fish St.   19, 23, 57, 116, (117), (145)
Fisher   27
Follett, Q.C.   237
Foot   57, 147, 182, 270
Fox   115
Frampton   23, 247, 248
Freemen   125, 134
Fricker   183

Fryer   229
Fryer Andrews & Co.   58
Fryer Gosse & Pack   58
Furnell   91

Gaden   116, 172, 246
Gambier   129
Gaol   19, 30, 202
Gaoler   231
Garland   6, 7, 32, 36, 58, 68
Garland, F. P.   57
Garland, George   45, 57, 184, 270
Garland, Joseph Gulston   49, 65, 92, 94, 113
Gaslights   99, 102
Gavin   144
"George"   9, 148
Gibbs   257
Gleed   20, 35
Globe   21, 180
Gosse   9, 220, 239, 242, 256
Gowns   163
Graham, Sir James   242
Greathead   213
Green   58, 142, 154, 183, 187
Grey, Lord   94
Guest   259, 261
Guildhall   19, 27, 30, (160), 216, 223, 226, 228, (230), 232, 245, 260, 266

Hairby   140, 158
Hall   63
Hamilton   184
Hamworthy   95
Hamworthy Rectory   189
Hancock, Geo.   57, 103, 129, 144, 158, 172, 190, 226
Harbin's Legacy   184
Harbour   73, 245, 257, 258
Harbour Office   (118), 119
Harris   268
Harrison Slade & Co.   65
Harrison, John   94
Harvey, Capt.   211
Henning, Robert   104
High Sheriff   115

High St.   57, (102), 119, (143), (154), (168), (180), (188), (205), (228), (257)
Highways   98
Hiley   57
Hill St.   27, 143
Hillier   25
Hodge   151, 268
Hodges, Tito   135, 142, 154, 183, 251
Holes Bay   81
Holland   144
Hooper, John   119
Hopkins   135, 183
Horse Races   24
House of Lords   239
Hunger Hill   32
Hutchins   12, 105
Hyde   4, 53, 271
105 High St.   58
147 High St.   58
162 High St. (Antelope)   60
40 High St.   57
65 High St.   57
69 High St.   57
72 High St.   143
82 High St.   58
84 High St. (London Tavern)   60
87 High St.   (71)
90 High St.   143
92 High St.   58

"Independent" Coach   61
"Industry"   20
Inkpen   153, 162, 207
Inns & Hotels   60
Irving   150

James I   3, 5
Jeffery   36, 37, 39
Jeffreys   6, 271
Jennings   34
Jersey, Lady   112
Jolliffe   6, 7, 8, 38, 53
Jolliffe's Legacy   184
Jolliffe, Peter   9, 68, 94, 271
Jolliffe, Revd.   55, 57, 81, 183, 190, 197, 236

283

Jolliffe, Wm.   57, 70, 85, 86, 87, 91, 94, 96, 135, 142
"Jolly Sailor"   21, 60
"Joseph & Mary"   15
Juries   125
Justican   151, 152, 153, 155, 158, 159, 271
Justices   122

Kemp (Martin)   *see* Welch
Kemp, Geo.   57, 65, 81, 133, 140, 142, 164, 165, 214, 243, (259)
Kemp, James   57, 65, 239
Key Keepers   123
Kinderley, Denton & Kinderley   221
"King & Queen"   60
"King William" PH   116
King St.   19
"Kings Arms"   60
Knapp   9, 10, 35, 272
Knight   73, 91, 265, 266
Knowles   27

Lamb, William   110
Lamp Rate   228
Lander   49, 172, 216
Langdale, Lord   250, 256
Lankester   58, 148, 150, 156, 163, 169, 170, 183, 250
Laverstock   212
Ledgard, Welch & Co.   58
Ledgard, George Welch   49, 53, 89, 90, 91, 92, 96, 99, 140, 144, 148, 149, 151, 154, 165, 168, 172, 176, 181, 183, 190, 192, 207, 218, 226, 229, 231, 237, 238, 239, 241, 245, 256, 263, 266, 268, 272, 273
Ledgard, Richard   139
Leeson House   32, 65
Lester   6, 15, 53, 65, 102
Lester, Lester   32, 53, 55, 57, 81, 91, 99, 101, 113, 273, 274
Lester, Benjamin   107, 137, 190, 274
Lester, Sir John   164
Liberal Party (Reform)   239
Library   32

Lighting   79, 99, 102, 236
Linen Drapers   58
Linthorne, R. R.   60, 91, 274
"Lion & Lamb"   60
Littledale, Judge   234
Loftus   232
"London" Tavern   60, 134, 140, 148, 187
Longbourne   260
Longespee Charter   106
Longfleet   41, 95, 218
Longfleet House   116
Longford Bay   75, 76
Lord Chancellor   239, 241
"Lord Nelson"   60
Lulworth Castle   49
Lyndhurst, Lord   133, 137, 175
Lytchett Bay   75, 76, 83

Maces   138, 226, 245, 266
Magistrates   122, 174, 242 (& *see* Justices)
Mailcoach   62
Major   58, 144, 154, 165, 168, 176, 192, 218
Mandamus   197, 214, 216, 228, 261
Manlawes   26, 58, 61
Mansion House   57, 65, 66
Market House   *see* Guildhall
Market St.   25, 57, 60, 65, 119, 143, (235)
Markets   57, (230), 232, 233, 254, 265, 266
Martin   268
Master of the Rolls   251
Masters   33, 274
Matthews (Mrs.)   266
Mauger   34, 35, 275
Mauley, Lord De (Ponsonby)   215, 228, 236, 239, 244, 250, 256, 258, 260, 274
Mawe   258
Mayor   169, 198
Melbourne, Lord   105, (111), 112, 239
Members of Parliament   32, 77, 92, 99, 233

Monmouth Rebellion 4
Moore & Sydenham 58
Morcom 254, 256
Mudlands 107
Mullett 143, 220
Municipal Corporations Bill 137

Naish 143, 195, 237, 238, 268
Napoleon's Defeat-Festival 44, 45
Napoleonic Wars 13, 85
National Commercial Directory 55
"New Antelope" 60
"New Inn" 21, (83)
Newfoundland Trade 63
Nightingale Lane 26
North St. 58
Notting 143, 184

Obstruction of Quay 25
Old Town Hall 26
Orchard, Joseph 92
Osmond 29
Overseers 172, 188, 193, 197
Oysters 71, 72, 119, 230

Paddicks Lane 27
Parishes 189
Parkstone 41, 95
Parliamentary Bill 18, 107, 167, 175, 257
Parr, Rev. James 92, 276
Parr, Richard 57
Parr, Robert Henning 57, 81, 92, 94, 102, 104, 105, 116, 132, 146, 147, 154, 155, 156, 159, 169, 170, 172, 182, 183, 186, 192, 201, 202, 206, 215, 219, 220, 221, 226, 228, 232, 233, 234, 236, 239, 241, 242, 247, 249, 250, 252, 256, 260, 261, 275
Parr, Thomas (117)
Parrott 57, 83, 92, 94, 134, 135, 140, 142, 154, 162, 167, 172, 183, 184, 187, 192, 193, 194, 195, 201, 206, 207, 215, 224, 228, 236, 237, 239, 242, 251, 252, 256, 261, 267, 276

Parrs 53. 275
Passage Boat 29
Passage Steps 248
Pearce 263, 276
Pedlar, Col. 193, 231
Peel, Sir Robert 134
Penney 57, 119, 135, 164, 169, 172, 207, 213, 229, 231, 239, 242, 256, 266, 276
Perry Gardens 119
Petition 171
Phippards 6, 53
Pierce 169
Pinney 57, 146, 154, 184, 187, 229, 245, 276
Piplers (206)
Pitwines 101
Planefield House 57
Plate 138
Police 127, 231, 235
Polling 152
Ponsonby (see Mauley also) 40, 53, 55, 77, 79, 81, 82, 99, 107, 109, 110, 112, 113, 115, 116, 118, 147, 164, 167, 192, 201, 202
Ponsonby, Caroline 110
"Poole Arms" 21, 60
Poole House 65
Poole Mansion 164, (259)
Poole Town & County Bank 58
Poor House 50
Poor Rate 80, 172, 200, 208
Port 73, 74, 75
"Portmahon Castle" 21, 180
"Portsmouth Hoy" 60
Poulsom 5
Poulter 167
Powder House 31
Press Gang 14
Price (Poet) 9, 16, 17, 276
Prince of Wales 112
Printers 58
Prisoners 231
Pritchetts Alley 119
Privies 25
Public Houses 60
Putnam, E. 9

Quay   31, 32, 60, 72, 99, 119, (186), 236, 237, 239, (240), 258, 260
Quaymaster   248, 249
Queens Bench   254
Quo Warranto   84, 165, 174, 192

Radicals   152, 176
Railway   264
Rate   186, 189, 197, 231, 237
Recorder   122, 202, 231
Rector of Poole   236
Redesdale, Lord   175
Reform Bill   94, 97, 100, 130, 134
Reformers   165, 167, 174, 197, 229, 231, 238, 241, 255
Regatta   24, (225)
Rendel   72, 73, 83
Revelry   257
Richmond, Duke of   175, 182
Rickman   58, 92, 142, 153, 154, 155, 172, 184, 187, 193, 195, 201, 212, 251, 277
Roads   24, 40, 41
Robinson   5
Rogers   14, 151, 153, 154, 183, 184, 251, 256
Rogers Almshouses   184
Ropemakers   92
"Royal Oak"   21, 248
Russell, Sir John   89, 167, 172, 209

Salisbury St.   25
Salisbury (Gaol)   19, 30
Salisbury, Marquis of   175
Salter   135, 142, 165, 231, 242
Saltworks   20
Savage, Constance   19
Savannah   19
Scaplens Court   9, 41
Scott   156, 163, 170, 183, 193, 204, 205
Seager   53, 57, 119, 183, 190, 218, 277
Seager, James   94, 96, 135, 142, 164, 165, 169, 172, 193, 195
Seals   228, 238
Seldown House   57
Select Committee   170, 171

Sergeant at Mace   84, 86, 124, 193, 231
Sharp   57
Sheriff   20, 85, 97, 122, 190, 223, 228, 263
Sheriffs Meeting   79, 99
Shipbuilding   247
Ships
  "Active"   18
  "Bowden"   8
  "Comet"   49
  "Fly"   60
  "Fox"   16
  "Friendship"   8
  "Gannett" SS   194
  "Indian Queen"   19
  "Le Bon Laron"   17
  "Maria"   15
  "Meteor"   49
  "Mountaineer"   8
  "Orestes"   207
  "Robert"   63
  "Sea Adventure"   7
  "Southwell"   16, 17
  "Speaker"   16
  "Speedwell"   5
  "Sylph"   47
  "Two Brothers"   15
  "Union"   18
  "Upton"   68
"Shipwrights Arms"   21, 68, 77, 137, (247), 248
Short   194, 207
Short, Bernard   164
Simmons, Widow   23
Sims   30
Skinner   30
Skinner St.   57, 259
Slades   53, 58, 65, 79, 81, 92, 96, 97, 134, 140, 144, 152, 155, 160, 162, 172, 193, 194, 202, 204, 218, 237, 241, 246, 248, 249, 259, 266, 267, 277
"Sloop" PH   148
Smith   20, 151
South Western Railway   258
Southampton   258
Spilsbury   212

Spurrier   18, 36, 53, 58, 60, 65, 68, 69, 278
Spurrier, Thos.   94
St. James Church   32, 51, 52, 55, 76, 128, 137, 138, 183, 190, 198, 200, 208, 224, 226
Stanley Green   32, 57
Stanley, Lord   167
Stansworth   142, 154, 184, 187, 201, 220, 248, 279
Steele   57, 140, 183, 279
Stone   32, 65, 115
Strand St.   24
Streaking   212
Strong   57, 84
Strongs   233
Stuat   (112), 113
Styring   279
Sunday School Jubilee   (217)
"Swan"   21
Sydenham   70, 116, 193, 195, 197, 200

Taverns   60
Test Act   85, 89
Thames St.   29, 57, (83), 119, (222)
Theatre   24
Thompson   7, 8, 10, 26, 32, 33, 53, 136, 140, 182, 279
Thompson House (Poole Mansion)   65, 164, (259), 279
Thompson, Wm.   144, 183, 279
Thresher   20
Tilsed   8
Timber   (246)
Tindall, Judge   244
Tito   38
Tories   84, 92, (133), 134, 140, 176
Town Cellars   25
Town Clerk   57, 84, 92, 102, 105, 123, 129, 141, 147, 154, 155, 165, 166, 198, 223, 228, 229, 231, 233, 239, 248, 250, 264
Town Crier   231
Town Pump   29
Towngate Lane   26, 27

Treasurer of the Quays   229, 237
Tucker   19
Tulk   141, 150
Tulloch   57, 143
Turner, F.   187, 193, 202, 263
Turtle (Bandmaster)   36
"Two Brothers"   60

Under Sheriff   252
Upton House   49, 57, 65, 66

Vestry Meeting   193
Victoria, Queen   198, (199), 231

Wadham   35, 57, 58
Water Bailiff   123, 226
Waterman   266
Webb, Sir John   3, 39, 40, 107, 280
Welch   57, 79, 81, 142, 174, 193, 197, 204, 229, 256, 258, 263, 266, 272, 280
Weld   49
"Wellington" (Coach)   61
Wellington, Duke of   94, 132, 134
West   10
West St.   57, (185)
Western Times   116
Westons   6
Westons Lane   264
Weymouth Corporation Dredger   239
Wharncliffe, Lord   175
Wherwell   14
Whicker   195
Whigs   84, 92, 115, 134
Whitt   254, 265
Wiffin   27
William of Orange   4
Williams   115, 116, 232
Williamson   143, 184, 204, 266
Willis   26
Willis, Cheritt & Willis   1, 68
Wills   184, 248
Windmill Point   20
Wingfield   17
Wise   6
Wynford, Lord   175

Rob¹ H Bar   Geo. W. Lidgard

G. S. Parrott

John Lankester

      W. L. S. Ponsonby   Richard Lidgard

Richard Pinney   W. J. Keeffe   J. Toot

George Lidgard   George Kemp

Peter Jolliff

      H. B. Bloomfield   J. Thos Brayley

J. H. Hooper

      Thos. Adey

Sam¹ White   H. W. Aldridge

      William Parr

J. Ferris   G. W. Allen

Sam¹ Clark   Robert Mills